# My iPad® for Seniors

## FIFTH EDITION

Michael Miller

**Que®**

800 East 96th Street,
Indianapolis, Indiana 46240 USA

Real Possibilities

# My iPad® for Seniors, Fifth Edition

## Copyright © 2018 by Pearson Education, Inc.

ISBN-13: 978-0-7897-5867-5

ISBN-10: 0-7897-5867-9

Library of Congress Control Number: 2017956518

Printed in the United States of America

1  17

## Trademarks

## Warning and Disclaimer

## Special Sales

For information about buying this title in bulk quantities, or for special sales opportunities (which may include electronic versions; custom cover designs; and content particular to your business, training goals, marketing focus, or branding interests), please contact our corporate sales department at corpsales@pearsoned.com or (800) 382-3419.

For government sales inquiries, please contact governmentsales@pearsoned.com.

For questions about sales outside the U.S., please contact intlcs@pearsoned.com.

**Editor-in-Chief**
Greg Wiegand

**Senior Acquisitions Editor**
Laura Norman

**Marketing**
Stephane Nakib

**Director, AARP Books**
Jodi Lipson

**Development/ Copy Editor**
Charlotte Kughen,
The Wordsmithery LLC

**Managing Editor**
Sandra Schroeder

**Senior Project Editor**
Lori Lyons

**Indexer**
Erika Millen

**Proofreader**
Debbie Williams

**Technical Editor**
Jeri Usbay

**Editorial Assistant**
Cindy Teeters

**Cover Designer**
Chuti Prasertsith

**Compositor**
Kim Scott,
Bumpy Design

# Contents at a Glance

| Chapter 1 | Buying and Unboxing Your iPad | 3 |
|---|---|---|
| Chapter 2 | Getting Started with Your iPad | 15 |
| Chapter 3 | Personalizing the Way Your iPad Looks and Works | 53 |
| Chapter 4 | Making Your iPad More Accessible | 77 |
| Chapter 5 | Connecting to the Internet and Browsing the Web | 91 |
| Chapter 6 | Keeping Your iPad Safe and Secure | 117 |
| Chapter 7 | Controlling Your iPad—and More—with Siri | 135 |
| Chapter 8 | Installing and Using Apps | 147 |
| Chapter 9 | Sending and Receiving Email | 171 |
| Chapter 10 | Managing Your Contacts | 191 |
| Chapter 11 | Video Chatting and Texting | 203 |
| Chapter 12 | Getting Social with Facebook, Pinterest, and Other Social Networks | 223 |
| Chapter 13 | Staying Organized with Calendar and Reminders | 243 |
| Chapter 14 | Reading eBooks, Magazines, and Newspapers | 261 |
| Chapter 15 | Shooting, Editing, and Sharing Photos and Videos | 277 |
| Chapter 16 | Listening to Music | 311 |
| Chapter 17 | Watching TV Shows, Movies, and Other Videos | 325 |
| Chapter 18 | Controlling Your Smart Home | 349 |
| Chapter 19 | Traveling with Maps and Other Travel Apps | 373 |
| Chapter 20 | Keeping Fit and Healthy | 383 |
| Chapter 21 | Playing Games | 393 |
| Chapter 22 | Getting Productive | 403 |
| Chapter 23 | Managing Files on Your iPad and in the Cloud | 421 |
| Chapter 24 | Accessorizing Your iPad | 443 |
| Chapter 25 | Fixing Common Problems | 449 |
| Appendix A | Glossary | 466 |
| | Index | 471 |

# Table of Contents

**1  Buying and Unboxing Your iPad**                                  **3**

What Is an iPad?                                                        4

Choosing the Right iPad for You                                        5

    iPad mini 4                                     6

    iPad                                            8

    iPad Pro                                        9

    Which iPad Should You Buy?                      10

Unboxing Your New iPad                                                11

    What's Inside the Box                          11

Powering Up Your iPad                                                 12

    Turn It On—For the First Time                  13

**2  Getting Started with Your iPad**                                **15**

Getting to Know Your iPad                                            15

    Front                                          16

    Top                                            17

    Sides                                          17

    Bottom                                         18

    Back                                           19

Turning Your iPad On and Off                                         20

    Power On Your iPad                             20

    Lock Your iPad                                 21

    Unlock Your iPad                               21

    Power Off Your iPad                            23

    Force a Restart                                23

Using Your iPad                                                      24

    Learn Essential Multi-Touch Gestures           24

    Navigate the Home Screen                       26

View the Today Screen ........................................................................................ 28

View Notifications on the Cover Sheet ........................................................ 29

Manage Open Apps ........................................................................................... 31

Understand the Status Bar .............................................................................. 33

Performing Basic Operations .............................................................................. 34

View and Respond to Alerts ........................................................................... 35

Display the Control Center .............................................................................. 36

Adjust the Brightness ........................................................................................ 38

Activate Night Shift ........................................................................................... 38

Change the Volume Level ................................................................................ 39

Rotate the iPad ................................................................................................... 40

Activate Do Not Disturb Mode ..................................................................... 41

Enter Text with the Onscreen Keyboard .................................................... 42

Copy and Paste Text ......................................................................................... 44

Set an Alarm ......................................................................................................... 45

Set a Timer ............................................................................................................ 46

Use the Stopwatch ............................................................................................ 47

Managing Your iPad's Battery ............................................................................ 48

Recharge the Battery ........................................................................................ 48

Monitor Battery Usage ..................................................................................... 50

## 3  Personalizing the Way Your iPad Looks and Works    **53**

Personalizing the Lock and Home Screens .................................................... 54

Change the Wallpaper ...................................................................................... 54

Arrange App Icons ............................................................................................. 57

Add Icons to and Remove Icons from the Dock ...................................... 58

Organize Apps with Folders ........................................................................... 59

Customizing the Today Screen and Control Center .................................... 61

Customize the Today Screen .......................................................................... 61

Customize the Control Center ....................................................................... 63

Configuring Device Settings ............................................. 64

    Display the Settings Page ............................................. 65

    Configure Notifications ............................................. 66

    Configure the Display and Brightness ............................................. 69

    Change System Sounds ............................................. 71

    Configure Individual Apps ............................................. 72

Managing System Settings ............................................. 73

    Display and Manage General Settings ............................................. 73

**4    Making Your iPad More Accessible    77**

Making the iPad Easier to Use for the Vision Impaired ............................................. 78

    Read the Screen with VoiceOver ............................................. 78

    Magnify the Screen with Zoom ............................................. 81

    Invert Screen Colors ............................................. 82

    Make Onscreen Text Larger and Bolder ............................................. 84

Making the iPad Easier to Use for the Hearing Impaired ............................................. 85

    Use a Hearing Aid with Your iPad ............................................. 85

    Turn On Closed Captioning When Watching Videos ............................................. 86

Making the iPad Easier to Operate ............................................. 87

    Adjust the Touchscreen Display ............................................. 87

    Enable AssistiveTouch ............................................. 89

**5    Connecting to the Internet and Browsing the Web    91**

Connecting to a Wi-Fi Network ............................................. 92

    Connect to Your Home Wireless Network ............................................. 92

    Connect to a Public Wireless Hotspot ............................................. 94

    Change Networks ............................................. 96

    Connect to a Network You've Previously Connected To ............................................. 96

Using the Safari Web Browser ............................................. 97

    Launch the Safari Browser ............................................. 98

    Enter a Web Address ............................................. 98

    Use Web Links ............................................. 100

View Multiple Pages in Tabs ........................................................... 101

Bookmark Pages ............................................................................. 103

Revisit Past Pages ......................................................................... 105

Browse the Web in Private ............................................................ 106

Configure Safari Settings .............................................................. 107

Making the Web More Readable ......................................................... 108

Zoom into a Page .......................................................................... 109

Read Articles with Safari Reader .................................................. 110

Searching the Web ............................................................................... 112

Search the Web with Google ........................................................ 112

Change Your Search Engine ......................................................... 114

## 6   Keeping Your iPad Safe and Secure     117

Creating a Safer Lock Screen ............................................................. 118

Set a Simple Passcode .................................................................. 118

Use Fingerprint Recognition with Touch ID ................................ 120

Erase Data After Too Many Passcode Attempts .......................... 122

Reducing the Risk of Theft ................................................................. 123

Keep Your iPad Safe ...................................................................... 123

Enable iPad Tracking .................................................................... 124

Track a Lost or Stolen iPad .......................................................... 125

Staying Safe Online ............................................................................. 127

Protect Against Identity Theft ..................................................... 127

Keep Your Private Information Private ......................................... 129

Protect Against Online Fraud ....................................................... 129

Shop Safely ................................................................................... 132

## 7   Controlling Your iPad—and More—with Siri     135

Getting to Know Siri, Your iPad's Virtual Personal Assistant ............ 136

Configure Siri ............................................................................... 136

Summon Siri .................................................................................. 139

Using Siri to Control Your iPad and Apps .................................................. 140

Launch Apps ........................................................................................ 140

Control System Functions ................................................................... 140

Send and Receive Messages ............................................................... 140

Manage Meetings, Events, and Reminders ........................................ 141

Take and View Pictures ...................................................................... 142

Listen to Music .................................................................................. 142

Using Siri to Find Interesting and Useful Information ........................... 144

Find Information ................................................................................ 144

Solve Equations and Make Conversions ............................................ 145

Find Businesses and Get Directions ................................................... 145

**8   Installing and Using Apps                                              147**

Working with Apps ................................................................................ 148

Launch an App from the Home Screen .............................................. 148

Launch an App from the Dock ........................................................... 149

Search for an App .............................................................................. 150

Switch Between Apps ......................................................................... 151

Close an App ...................................................................................... 152

Finding New Apps in the App Store ...................................................... 153

Browse and Search the App Store ...................................................... 153

Purchase and Download Apps ............................................................ 158

Managing Installed Apps ....................................................................... 160

View and Manage Purchased Apps ..................................................... 160

Update Your Apps .............................................................................. 162

Delete an App .................................................................................... 163

Multitasking on Your iPad ..................................................................... 164

Open a Second App with Slide Over ................................................... 164

Display Two Apps at Once with Split View ......................................... 167

Drag and Drop Text and Pictures Between Apps ................................ 168

**9**  **Sending and Receiving Email**                                 **171**

 Configuring the Mail App .................................................. 171

  Add an Email Account .................................................. 172

  Get Notified of New Messages ..................................... 174

  Create a Signature ..................................................... 176

 Sending and Receiving Messages .................................... 177

  Select an Inbox ......................................................... 177

  Read a Message ........................................................ 178

  Reply to a Message .................................................... 180

  Create and Send a New Message ............................... 181

  Attach a Photo to a Message ...................................... 183

  Delete a Message ...................................................... 185

  Organize Messages in Files ......................................... 186

  Deal with Junk Email (Spam) ...................................... 188

**10**  **Managing Your Contacts**                                      **191**

 Using the Contacts App ................................................ 192

  Add a New Contact .................................................... 192

  Edit a Contact .......................................................... 194

  Delete a Contact ....................................................... 195

  Consolidate Contacts from Multiple Sources ............... 196

 Viewing and Contacting Your Contacts ........................... 198

  Display a Contact ...................................................... 198

  Search for a Contact .................................................. 198

  Change How Contacts Are Displayed .......................... 199

  Contact a Contact ..................................................... 201

**11**  **Video Chatting and Texting**                                  **203**

 Text Messaging with the Messages App .......................... 203

  Send and Receive Text Messages ............................... 204

  Send an Audio Message ............................................. 206

Send a Photo .................................................................... 207

Send a Video Message ...................................................... 211

Video Chatting and More with FaceTime .............................. 214

Start a Video Chat ............................................................ 214

Answer a Video Chat Request .......................................... 217

Make an Audio Call .......................................................... 219

## 12 Getting Social with Facebook, Pinterest, and Other Social Networks      223

Understanding Social Networking ...................................... 224

Using Facebook on Your iPad ............................................ 224

Navigate Facebook's iPad App ........................................ 225

Read and Respond to Posts ............................................ 227

Post a Status Update ...................................................... 229

Using Pinterest on Your iPad ............................................ 230

View and Save Pins ........................................................ 230

Pin from a Website ........................................................ 232

Using Twitter on Your iPad ................................................ 234

Read Tweets .................................................................... 235

Create a New Tweet ........................................................ 236

Using LinkedIn on Your iPad .............................................. 237

Navigate the LinkedIn App .............................................. 238

Create a New Post .......................................................... 239

## 13 Staying Organized with Calendar and Reminders      243

Using the Calendar App .................................................... 243

View Events .................................................................... 244

Add a New Event ............................................................ 248

Create a Recurring Event ................................................ 249

Create an Alert for an Event ............................................ 253

Invite Others to an Event ................................................ 254

Using the Reminders App ................................................ 255
   View and Manage Your Reminders .................... 256
   Add a New Reminder ........................................ 257
   Delete a Reminder ............................................ 259

**14  Reading eBooks, Magazines, and Newspapers       261**

Reading eBooks on Your iPad ................................... 261
   Find and Purchase Books with the iBooks App .......... 262
   Read a Book with the iBooks App ....................... 264
   Find and Read Books with the Kindle Book Browser ... 267
Reading News Stories with the News App ................... 271
   Personalize What News You Receive ..................... 272
   Read News Stories ........................................... 274

**15  Shooting, Editing, and Sharing Photos and Videos       277**

Shooting Digital Photos ........................................... 277
   Launch the Camera App ................................... 278
   Take a Picture ................................................. 279
   Take a Selfie ................................................... 282
   Take a Panoramic Photo ................................... 283
Viewing and Editing Your Photos .............................. 285
   View Your Photos ............................................ 286
   Organize Photos in Albums ............................... 291
   Crop and Straighten a Picture ............................ 296
   Apply Auto-Enhance ........................................ 297
   Apply a Filter .................................................. 297
   Adjust Brightness and Color .............................. 298
   Mark Up a Photo ............................................. 300
Shooting and Editing Videos ................................... 302
   Shoot a Video ................................................. 302
   Trim a Video ................................................... 305

Sharing Photos and Videos ........................................ 306

Share via Text Message ........................................ 306

Share via Email ........................................ 307

Share via Facebook ........................................ 308

## 16  Listening to Music                                        311

Listening to Streaming Music ........................................ 311

Listen to Apple Music ........................................ 312

Listen to Pandora ........................................ 314

Buying and Playing Music from the iTunes Store ........................................ 317

Purchase Music from the iTunes Store ........................................ 318

Play Your Tunes ........................................ 321

## 17  Watching TV Shows, Movies, and Other Videos              325

Watching Netflix ........................................ 326

Use the Netflix App ........................................ 326

Watching Hulu ........................................ 330

Use the Hulu App ........................................ 331

Watching Amazon Video ........................................ 336

Use the Amazon Video App ........................................ 337

Watching YouTube ........................................ 340

Use the YouTube App ........................................ 340

Buying and Renting Videos in the iTunes Store ........................................ 342

Rent or Purchase a Video ........................................ 343

Watch a Video ........................................ 346

## 18  Controlling Your Smart Home                               349

Understanding Apple HomeKit ........................................ 350

How HomeKit Works ........................................ 350

What's Compatible with HomeKit ........................................ 351

Adding Devices and Rooms ........................................ 351

  Add a New Device .............................................. 351

  Add a New Room ............................................... 354

  Assign an Accessory
    to a Room ..................................................... 355

  Create a Scene ................................................. 357

Controlling Your Smart Devices ................................. 360

  Control a Device or Scene ................................... 360

  Controlling Devices and Scenes with Siri ............... 361

Automating Multiple Devices ................................... 361

  Set Up Your iPad as a Home Hub ........................ 362

  Create a Location Automation ............................. 364

  Create a Time Automation .................................. 366

  Create a Controlled Automation .......................... 368

## 19 Traveling with Maps and Other Travel Apps     373

Traveling with the Maps App .................................... 373

  Display a Map .................................................. 374

  Generate Driving Directions ................................ 375

Exploring Other Travel-Related Apps ......................... 378

  Discover Travel Apps ......................................... 378

## 20 Keeping Fit and Healthy     383

Exploring Health and Fitness Apps ............................ 383

  Discover Exercise and Yoga Apps ........................ 384

Exploring Food and Nutrition Apps ........................... 385

  Discover Dieting Apps ........................................ 386

  Discover Cooking and Recipe Apps ...................... 387

Exploring Medical Apps .......................................... 389

  Discover Medical-Related Apps ........................... 389

**21 Playing Games**     **393**

Finding Games to Play ..... 393
    Download Games from the App Store ..... 394
Discovering Popular Games ..... 397
    Action Games ..... 397
    Adventure Games ..... 397
    Arcade Games ..... 398
    Board Games ..... 398
    Card Games ..... 398
    Casino Games ..... 398
    Family Games ..... 399
    Indie Games ..... 399
    Music Games ..... 399
    Puzzle Games ..... 399
    Racing Games ..... 399
    Role-Playing Games ..... 399
    Simulation Games ..... 400
    Sports Games ..... 400
    Strategy Games ..... 400
    Trivia Games ..... 400
    Word Games ..... 400

**22 Getting Productive**     **403**

Using Your iPad's Built-In Productivity Apps ..... 403
    Pages ..... 404
    Numbers ..... 407
    Keynote ..... 413
Discovering More Productivity Apps ..... 417
    Evernote ..... 417
    Google Docs, Sheets, and Slides ..... 418
    Microsoft Excel, PowerPoint, and Word ..... 418

**23**  **Managing Files on Your iPad and in the Cloud**    **421**

   Managing Your iPad Storage ........................................................... 421

      Examine Available Storage ...................................................... 422

      Manage Available Storage Space ............................................ 423

   Managing iCloud Files with the Files App .................................. 426

      Configure iCloud on Your iPad ............................................... 427

      View and Open Files with the Files App ................................ 431

      Create a New Folder ................................................................ 434

      Add Other Cloud Storage Services to the Files App ............ 435

   Using AirDrop and AirPlay to Share Content with Other Devices    438

      Share Files with AirDrop ......................................................... 438

      Stream Media with AirPlay ..................................................... 439

   Backing Up Your iPad to iCloud .................................................. 440

      Back Up to iCloud .................................................................... 441

**24**  **Accessorizing Your iPad**    **443**

   Protecting Your iPad with Cases and Covers ............................. 443

      Smart Covers ............................................................................ 444

      Other Covers and Cases ......................................................... 444

   Adding Functionality with Keyboards and Styli ......................... 444

      Apple's Smart Keyboard .......................................................... 444

      Other Wireless Keyboards ...................................................... 445

      Apple Pencil .............................................................................. 445

      Other Styli ................................................................................ 445

   Extending Your iPad with Bluetooth Devices ............................ 446

      Wireless Headphones and Earphones ................................... 446

      Wireless Speakers ................................................................... 447

**25**  **Fixing Common Problems**    **449**

   Troubleshooting iPad Problems .................................................. 449

      Your iPad Is Frozen ................................................................. 450

Your iPad Won't Turn On ........................................................ 451

Your iPad Won't Turn Off ...................................................... 452

An Individual App Freezes or Doesn't Work Right ................. 453

Your iPad Runs Slowly ........................................................... 455

Your iPad's Wi-Fi Connection Doesn't Work ......................... 456

Your iPad Charges Slowly or Not at All ................................. 457

Your iPad Doesn't Rotate ...................................................... 458

Your iPad Keeps Asking for Your iCloud Password ................ 459

You Forgot Your iPad Passcode ............................................ 459

Updating and Resetting Your iPad ........................................ 461

Update to the Latest Version of iOS ..................................... 461

Factory Reset Your Device to "Like New" Condition ............. 462

Reset Your iPad ..................................................................... 463

Restore from an iCloud Backup ............................................ 465

Restore from iTunes Backup ................................................. 465

**A**  **Glossary**                                                                        **466**

**Index**                                                                                **471**

# About the Author

**Michael Miller** is a popular and prolific writer of more than 200 non-fiction books, known for his ability to explain complex topics to everyday readers. He writes about a variety of topics, including technology, business, and music. His best-selling books for Que include *My Facebook for Seniors, My Social Media for Seniors, My Internet for Seniors, My Smart Home for Seniors, My Samsung Galaxy S7 for Seniors, My Windows 10 Computer for Seniors, Easy Computer Basics,* and *Computer Basics: Absolute Beginner's Guide.* Worldwide, his books have sold more than 1.5 million copies.

Find out more at the author's website: www.millerwriter.com

Follow the author on Twitter: molehillgroup

# Dedication

*To my musician friends and family here in Minnesota, who make it fun to play.*

# Acknowledgments

Thanks to all the folks at Que who helped turned this manuscript into a book, including Laura Norman, Greg Wiegand, Charlotte Kughen, Lori Lyons, Kim Scott, and technical editor Jeri Usbay. Thanks also to the kind folks at AARP for adding even more to the project.

# About AARP

AARP is a nonprofit, nonpartisan organization, with a membership of nearly 38 million, that helps people turn their goals and dreams into *real possibilities*™, strengthens communities, and fights for the issues that matter most to families such as healthcare, employment and income security, retirement planning, affordable utilities, and protection from financial abuse. Learn more at aarp.org.

---

### Note

Most of the individuals pictured throughout this book are of the author himself, as well as friends and relatives (used with permission), and sometimes pets. Some names and personal information are fictitious.

# We Want to Hear from You!

As the reader of this book, you are our most important critic and commentator. We value your opinion and want to know what we're doing right, what we could do better, what areas you'd like to see us publish in, and any other words of wisdom you're willing to pass our way.

We welcome your comments. You can email or write to let us know what you did or didn't like about this book—as well as what we can do to make our books better.

*Please note that we cannot help you with technical problems related to the topic of this book.*

When you write, please be sure to include this book's title and author as well as your name and email address. We will carefully review your comments and share them with the author and editors who worked on the book.

Email:   feedback@quepublishing.com

Mail:    Que Publishing
         ATTN: Reader Feedback
         800 East 96th Street
         Indianapolis, IN 46240 USA

# Reader Services

Register your copy of *My iPad for Seniors* at quepublishing.com for convenient access to downloads, updates, and corrections as they become available. To start the registration process, go to quepublishing.com/register and log in or create an account*. Enter the product ISBN, 9780789758675, and click Submit. Once the process is complete, you will find any available bonus content under Registered Products.

*Be sure to check the box that you would like to hear from us in order to receive exclusive discounts on future editions of this product.

→ What Is an iPad?

→ Choosing the Right iPad for You

→ Unboxing Your New iPad

→ Powering Up Your iPad

# Buying and Unboxing Your iPad

Apple's iPad is the most popular tablet today, as it has been for a number of years. In fact, Apple pretty much defined the tablet market when it released the very first iPad in 2010. Today you can use the latest iPads to browse and search the web, keep in touch with people through Facebook and other social media, send and receive email and instant messages, participate in video chats, watch movies and TV shows, listen to music, take and edit photographs and video, play games, control smart home devices, and even do word processing, create spreadsheets, and manage other productive activities. There are lots of reasons why iPads are popular among users of all ages.

This chapter examines the various models of iPads available and what they offer, and then it explains the "out-of-box experience"—what to expect when you unbox and first turn on your new iPad. (If you've had a previous version of an iPad, you can probably skip over parts of this chapter.)

# What Is an iPad?

Before we start talking about different models of iPads, we need to discuss the iPad itself. What, exactly, is an iPad—and what can you do with it?

Put simply, the iPad is a *tablet computer*—that is, a small computer in the shape of a handheld tablet. Instead of a keyboard and separate display screen, you have a touch-sensitive display. Not only do you view whatever is on the screen, you can also touch or tap or otherwise poke and prod the screen with your fingertips to make things happen. Instead of tapping the keys on a physical keyboard, you tap the virtual keys and buttons on the display, and the tablet reacts.

The iPad itself is relatively small and thin. Like most tablet computers, Apple's various iPad models weigh less than two pounds, with newer ones being markedly lighter and thinner than older models. The displays come in all sizes for your viewing pleasure, from around 8 inches diagonal (for the so-called "mini" model) to around 10 inches (for the standard models) to almost 13 inches (for the largest "pro" unit).

The iPad was not the first tablet computer, but it was the one that defined the market. When Apple released the original iPad in 2010, it established a new product category. That original iPad sold like proverbial hotcakes, and millions of people discovered that they needed something that really hadn't existed before. People thronged to Apple Stores everywhere to get this newfangled device that promised to redefine their everyday lives.

It didn't take long for other companies to get on the tablet bandwagon and Apple soon had plenty of competition, primarily from tablets running the rival Android operating system. (Apple's operating system is called iOS, and I discuss it a little later in this chapter.) Even though many of these competing tablets were significantly lower priced, the iPad remained the gold standard and the singular best seller.

What can an iPad (or any tablet computer, for that matter) do? Like a computer, it can run productivity programs that let you write letters, crunch numbers, give presentations, and edit photos and videos. You can use a tablet to communicate with others, via email, text messaging, and video chats. You can use a tablet to access the Internet and do whatever it is you want to do online, from surfing and shopping to keeping in touch via Facebook and Twitter. You can even use a tablet for fun stuff, like watching movies and playing games. Like I said, it's like a computer but crammed into a very small package.

Most of what you do on an iPad is done via *apps*. An app (short for "application") is nothing more than a software program running on the tablet. You tap to open an app and then use that app to do some specific task. There are apps for just about every task imaginable, from editing photos to writing music to tracking your weight and heart rate.

Now, you may read all of this and note that just about everything an iPad can do, you can also do on your smartphone. This is true. In many ways, an iPad is just a larger iPhone, but without the phone functionality. Or maybe an iPhone is just a smaller iPad with calling capability. However you approach it, the two types of devices are very similar in what they can do.

The big difference between smartphones and tablets is the size of the screen. Even the largest smartphones have relatively small screens. The larger tablet displays—even on the mini models—simply make it easier to view and do certain things. Watching a movie or reading an ebook or online newspaper is more enjoyable on a larger tablet than on a smaller phone, and it's a lot easier to edit photos, create newsletters, and even play virtual musical instruments on a tablet than on a smartphone.

For many people, an iPad or similar tablet is a viable replacement for a notebook or desktop computer, especially if you don't do a lot of heavy-duty technical stuff. Or you may view a tablet as a useful supplement to your smartphone, one that's just easier and more comfortable to use for many tasks.

In any instance, tablet computers have proven quite popular over the past few years, and the most popular of them are all Apple's various iPads.

# Choosing the Right iPad for You

Apple has offered various models of iPads since its introductory model, with new types and sizes being released on an annual basis.

All of Apple's iPads share a number of common features. They all have touch-screens, so you can control what you see with a tap or drag of your finger. They all have built-in speakers for listening, as well as a headphone jack to which you can connect your own earphones or headphones. They all have two cameras, one on the rear for shooting normal photos and videos and one on the front for shooting selfies or doing video chats. They all have built-in storage, to store those photos you take, as well as other data and apps. All will last about 10 hours on a battery charge, depending on your usage. And they all have built-in Wi-Fi so you can wirelessly connect to the Internet.

Beyond that, the models differ mostly in terms of screen size and resolution, storage capacity, processing speed, and a few extra features, such as cellular connectivity (so you can connect your iPad to your mobile phone network). Naturally, the bigger models with more speed, storage, and features cost more than the smaller, less fully featured ones.

So which model you choose depends on a number of factors—how big a screen you want, how much storage capacity you need, what you want to do with the iPad, and how much money you want to spend. Let's look at what's available.

## iPad mini 4

The smallest and most affordable iPad in Apple's line up is the iPad mini 4. The mini is smaller than the original iPad, with a 7.9-inch screen (compared to the traditional iPad's 9.7-inch screen). This makes the mini both smaller (just 8 inches high × 5.3 inches wide) and lighter (.65 pound) than the traditional iPad, which a lot of people prefer; you don't need to use both hands to hold it.

Of course, the smaller display also makes it a little more difficult to read what's on the screen. The text on some web pages gets a tad small for some readers, who might be more comfortable with the larger screen on the traditional iPad. That said, the screen on the current iPad mini 4 has the same resolution as the regular-sized model (measured in terms of pixels, or individual screen elements), which actually provides a sharper picture.

## Retina Display

All of Apple's latest iPad models feature what it calls the Retina display. The Retina display has more pixels per square inch, which makes text and images appear extremely crisp onscreen. The screens on the current iPad and iPad mini 4 both offer 2048 × 1536 pixel resolution, which translates to 326 pixels per inch (ppi) on the mini and 264 ppi on the larger iPad. In general, the higher the resolution (the more pixels per inch), the sharper the display.

Price-wise, you don't save much by going with the smaller screen. There's only one iPad mini 4 model, priced at $399 for 128GB of storage. (The larger iPad actually offers lower-priced models with less storage.)

## Cellular Connectivity

All iPads come with Wi-Fi built-in, so you can connect to the Internet from your home Wi-Fi network or any public Wi-Fi hotspot. Select models are also available that add cellular connectivity, so you can connect the iPad to your mobile phone's data network when Wi-Fi is not available. Cellular connectivity adds about $130 to the price of a comparable Wi-Fi-only model; because of this price differential, the non-cellular iPads are Apple's best sellers.

# iPad

Apple's flagship tablet (as of mid-2017) is simply called the iPad. This is the main-line model, with the larger 9.7-inch screen and several storage options.

One of the benefits of the current iPad over the model it replaces is the price. This newest model is priced $70 less than the previous model, and offers more onboard storage. This price reduction has spurred an increase in iPad sales, which is a good thing; people like lower prices.

The current iPad, available in 32GB and 128GB versions, is priced at just $329 and $429, respectively.

## Older Models

Apple has sold a lot of different iPad models over the years, and sometimes the naming conventions get a little confusing. For example, the current iPad (introduced summer of 2017) replaces the former iPad Air 2, which itself replaced the first iPad Air. The iPad Air, introduced in 2013, replaced the original iPad, which by then was in its fourth generation. So today's iPad shares the same name with the original iPad, even though they're seven years apart in technology.

# iPad Pro

Apple's top-of-the-line iPad is the iPad Pro. This is a fully featured model, available in two screen sizes, that is optimized for business productivity. Apple sells a special stylus (dubbed the Apple Pencil) and Smart Keyboard that turn the Pro into a viable replacement for a traditional desktop or laptop PC.

Because of the enhanced productivity (and slightly larger screens), the iPad Pro models aren't cheap. The 10.5-inch iPad Pro (slightly larger than the 9.7-inch iPad) starts at $649 for 64GB of storage, and goes up to $949 for a 512GB model. The larger 12.9-inch model, which is better suited for office use, starts at $799 and goes up to $1099. Both Pro models have a faster processor than you'll find in the main iPad and offer slightly higher resolution (but similar ppi, thanks to the larger screens).

>>>Go Further

## iOS—THE iPAD OPERATING SYSTEM

All iPad models are powered by a special operating system designed just for mobile devices, dubbed iOS. The same operating system is on Apple's iPhones.

The current version of the operating system is iOS 11. This latest version has many major and minor improvements to the older iOS 10, including redesigned screens and notifications, a new Control Center, and changes to some of Apple's most popular apps.

All current iPads come with iOS 11 preinstalled; if you have an older model, you can easily upgrade to iOS 11 by tapping Settings on your iPad, tapping General, and then tapping Software Update. You can also upgrade through the iTunes software when you connect your iPad to your computer.

This book covers iPads running iOS 11. If your iPad is running an older version of iOS, you can either upgrade your device or purchase a previous version of this book.

## Which iPad Should You Buy?

As noted previously, which iPad is best for you depends on how you intend to use it, along with what size screen you want and how much you want to spend.

In general, the most popular model with both home and casual users is the new full-screen iPad. At just $329 for the base model, you just can't beat the price.

Now, some home and casual users prefer the iPad mini 4 simply because of the size. Given that it's actually priced higher than the larger base model iPad, it's quickly becoming a niche model, however.

If you want to do serious work on your tablet, or are using your tablet in your business, then you should consider the iPad Pro models. Know, however, that you'll spend more (a lot more) for the slightly larger screens and enhanced functionality. Nice as they are, the iPad Pros are just too pricey for most home and casual users.

Whichever iPad you choose, they all run the iOS 11 operating system, and all run pretty much the same apps you can find in Apple's App Store. It really is a matter of size and storage capacity; choose the one that best fits your needs.

# Unboxing Your New iPad

Whichever model iPad you choose, it comes in a stylish white box with minimal text and graphics. (Apple is all about the style!) What's inside that box? Let's take a peek!

## What's Inside the Box

All iPad models come in similar packaging. Open the box and you see the iPad itself. Take out the iPad and remove the plastic protector sheets.

Underneath the iPad are a white cable and power adapter, which you use to both charge your iPad and connect it to a computer. One end of the cable has a small Lightning connector that plugs into the bottom of the iPad; the other end of the cable has a USB connector that you can connect to a computer's USB port or to the USB port on the power adapter. The power adapter, of course, plugs right into any wall outlet.

### Charging Your iPad

Your new iPad's battery probably has a slight charge out of the box, so you can use it right away. However, you'll soon want to recharge the battery to get maximum use out of your new device. Learn how in Chapter 2, "Getting Started with Your iPad."

# Powering Up Your iPad

Now is the moment of truth—time to power up your iPad for the very first time! It takes about five to ten minutes to get everything set up, but it's as simple as following the instructions you see onscreen.

During the course of the initial setup, you're asked to supply some or all of the following information:

- Your language and country or region. This determines how specific information, such as date and time, appears on your device.

- The name and password for your home wireless network or nearby Wi-Fi hotspot, for your iPad to connect to the Internet.

- Whether or not you want to enable Location Services. (You probably do; it's how you use Maps and other apps that need to know your current location.)

- Your fingerprint, to enable Touch ID fingerprint log in. You also might be asked to create a six-digit numeric passcode or longer alphanumeric password for your device.

### Passwords and PINs

Learn more about protecting your iPad with passwords, PINs, and Touch ID in Chapter 6, "Keeping Your iPad Safe and Secure."

- If you have another Apple device handy (and it's also running the new iOS 11 operating system), you're prompted to use the new Automatic Setup features to wirelessly transfer settings from the other device to your iPad. Just hold the two devices close together until they're properly "paired," and then let Automatic Setup do all the work for you.

- If you have an Apple ID for another Apple device (another iPad, iPhone, or Mac), you can use it to log in and transfer some system settings. You can also go this route if you have an older iPad from which you want to transfer settings and apps.

- If this is your first Apple device, you're prompted to create a new Apple ID. This is free.

## Apple ID

You don't need an Apple ID to use your iPad, although it's necessary to take advantage of many popular features and services, including iCloud online storage and the iTunes Store. You can create a new Apple ID at any time by using your web browser to go to https://appleid.apple.com.

## Turn It On—For the First Time

1. Turn on your iPad by pressing and holding the Top button (at the top of the case) until you see the Apple symbol.

2. You see the word "Hello" in many languages. Press the Home button (at the bottom front of the case) to continue, then follow the onscreen instructions to complete the initial setup.

### Start Over

When you're setting up your iPad, you can start over at any point by pressing the Home button.

→ Getting to Know Your iPad

→ Turning Your iPad On and Off

→ Using Your iPad

→ Performing Basic Operations

→ Managing Your iPad's Battery

2

# Getting Started with Your iPad

Now that you've taken your new iPad out of the box, charged it up, and performed the initial setup, it's time to start using the thing. To do so, you need to know what's what and what's where on the iPad itself— and what you need to do to operate the darned thing!

## Getting to Know Your iPad

Your iPad is a large, flat tablet with a screen on one side and a fairly plain back on the other. You can hold it either vertically (with the Home button on the bottom) or horizontally (with the Home button to the left or right side); the screen flips to accommodate how you're holding it.

There are physical buttons along the top and sides of the iPad, and on the bottom front. Let's look at these buttons now.

## Front

Looking at the iPad from the front, the first thing you see is the screen itself. This is the touchscreen (technically, Apple calls it a Multi-Touch Display), which is how you perform most of the device's operations—by literally touching the screen with your fingers. We'll go over all the touch gestures (tapping, swiping, pinching, and more) later in this chapter, but let's move to everything else you see on the front of the device.

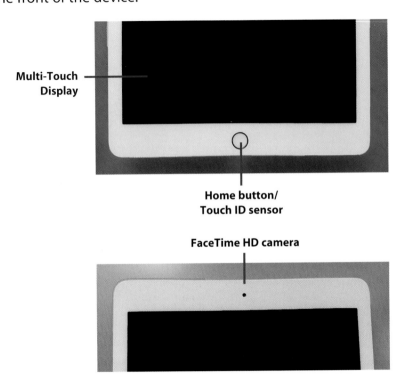

**Multi-Touch Display**

**Home button/ Touch ID sensor**

**FaceTime HD camera**

The round button just beneath the screen is the Home button. You press this button to return at any time to the iPad's Home screen. The Home button also doubles as the Touch ID sensor; if you've configured your iPad to unlock with your fingerprint, this is where you press your finger to unlock the device.

### Touch ID

Learn more about fingerprint unlocking in Chapter 6, "Keeping Your iPad Safe and Secure."

Directly above the screen is a small hole. This is the lens for the iPad's front-facing camera—the one you use to take selfies or conduct video chats. Apple calls this the FaceTime HD camera, and you probably don't want to cover it up.

## Top

There are three items along the top edge of your iPad. On the left top you find a standard 3.5mm headset jack, for connecting earphones or headphones. In the middle is a small hole for the top-mounted microphone. On the right top is a small button for turning your iPad on or off, appropriately called the Top button; press this button to wake your iPad when it's asleep, or put it to sleep if you're using it.

Microphone            Headset jack            Top button

## Sides

If you have an iPad or iPad mini 4, there's nothing on the left side of the unit. If you have an iPad Pro, however, the Smart Connector is in the very middle of the left side. The Smart Connector is used to magnetically connect so-called "smart" accessories, such as the iPad Pro Smart Keyboard. (Learn more about these accessories in Chapter 24, "Accessorizing Your iPad.")

On all iPad models, you find the up and down volume buttons on the right side of the unit. Use these controls to raise and lower the iPad's volume.

**Smart Connector**
**(iPad Pro only)**

**Volume buttons**

### Cellular Models

If your iPad offers cellular connectivity (in addition to the normal Wi-Fi wireless), it has a removable tray on the right side of the unit. This tray contains the iPad's Nano-SIM card; insert the included removal tool (or a plain old paperclip) into the small hole to eject the tray.

## Bottom

There are two (actually, three) important items along the bottom edge of your iPad.

In the very middle bottom is a small connector, dubbed the Lightning connector. You use this connector to plug in the cable that came with your iPad; the other end of the cable can connect to either your computer (via USB) or the power adapter that you plug into the wall.

There are also two speakers on the bottom of the iPad, on either side of the Lightning connector. Don't cover up these speakers or you'll adversely affect the sounds you hear.

**Speakers**

**Lightning connector**

## Back

Finally, turn your iPad over and examine the back of the unit. The most obvious thing on the back is the big Apple logo, but that really doesn't do anything.

Instead, direct your attention to the top-left corner. The big round thing you see there is the main camera. Apple calls this the iSight camera, and you use it to take pictures and videos of others.

**iSight camera**                    **Microphone**

One last thing. If you look at the top middle of the iPad, you see a small hole that contains another microphone. Don't cover up either the camera or the micro-phone, or they won't work.

# Turning Your iPad On and Off

Turning your iPad on and off is a little more complex than you might think. That's because you can completely power off your unit or just put it to sleep. When the unit is completely powered off, it takes a minute or so to power back on. When it's in sleep mode (or "locked," as Apple puts it) it can immediately come back to life, with the same apps running as when you put it to sleep.

## Power On Your iPad

When your iPad is completely powered off (as it is when you first remove it from its box), you need to power it back on.

**1** Press and hold the Top button until the Apple logo appears onscreen.

**2** After the Apple logo disappears, you're prompted to enter your passcode. Do so now to display your device's Home screen. (If you haven't set up a passcode, you won't see this prompt and instead are directly shown the Home screen.)

### Passcodes, PINs, and Touch ID

Learn more about the different ways to unlock your iPad in Chapter 6.

## Lock Your iPad

You put your iPad to sleep (but not turn it completely off) by locking the device. This is how you most often "turn off" your iPad.

( 1 )  Press the Top button.

( 2 )  The screen goes blank and the iPad is now locked.

### Inactivity Lock

By default, your iPad locks automatically if you haven't touched the screen for two minutes. You can change this auto-lock time on the Settings screen, as discussed in Chapter 3, "Personalizing the Way Your iPad Looks and Works."

## Unlock Your iPad

To reawaken a sleeping iPad all you have to do is unlock it.

( 1 )  Press either the Home or the Top button.

( 2 )  If you've configured your iPad for fingerprint operation, press the Home button (Touch ID sensor) with your finger or thumb.

**3** If you've configured your iPad for passcode operation, press the Home button again and then enter your passcode.

**4** If you have not configured your iPad with either a passcode or fingerprint, press the Home button again to unlock the device.

**5** To read any notification displayed on the Lock screen, tap that message and then use Touch ID (if enabled) to unlock your device. (Apple calls these Lock screen notifications Cover Sheet.)

**6** Swipe left on any Cover Sheet notification to bring up options to display or clear that notification.

## Power Off Your iPad

Turning off the iPad shuts down all open apps and removes all power. You have to power it back up again the next time you want to use it.

(1) Press and hold the Top button for a few seconds, until the slider appears onscreen.

(2) Drag the Slide to Power Off slider to the right. The iPad now powers down.

## Force a Restart

On rare occasions an iPad may become frozen—tapping the screen does nothing. In this instance, you need to force a restart of your device.

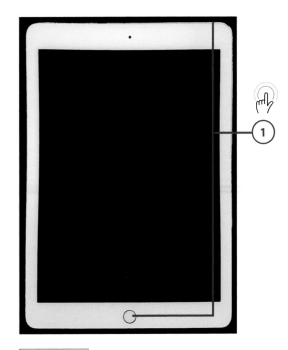

(1) Press and hold both the Top and Home buttons at the same time for at least ten seconds.

(2) When the Apple logo appears onscreen, your iPad is restarting.

## >>>*Go Further*
### SMART COVERS

Many companies (Apple included) sell so-called "smart" covers and cases for the various models of iPads. A smart cover or case not only protects your device, but interacts with your iPad to wake it up when opened and put it to sleep when closed. Learn more about smart covers and cases in Chapter 24.

# Using Your iPad

Okay, now you can turn your iPad on and off (and lock it and unlock it, too). But what do you do with it once you turn it on?

## Learn Essential Multi-Touch Gestures

You operate your iPad with your finger(s). You can perform different operations with different gestures.

Most everything you can do onscreen is based on a half dozen basic gestures. These are detailed in the following table.

**Basic Touch Gestures**

| Gesture | Looks Like | Description |
|---------|------------|-------------|
| Tap | | Touch and quickly release a point on the screen with your finger. |
| Press | | Touch your finger to the screen and hold it there. |
| Drag | | Touch and hold your finger on an item on the screen, then slowly move your finger to drag the item to a new position. Release your finger to "drop" the item to the new position. |

| Gesture | Looks Like | Description |
|---------|------------|-------------|
| Swipe | | This is like dragging, except faster. Place the tip of your finger on the screen, then quickly move it in the appropriate direction. You use swiping to scroll up or down a screen, or move the screen left or right. |
| Pinch | | Position your thumb and forefinger apart on the screen, then pinch them together. This is typically used to zoom out of a page or image. |
| Expand | | This is the opposite of pinching. Position your thumb and forefinger together on the screen and then slide them apart. This is typically used to zoom into a page or an image. |

>>>*Go Further*

## HIDDEN GESTURES

- Display the Cover Sheet (which is similar to the Lock screen, but the iPad isn't really locked) by swiping down from the top of the screen to display the Lock screen.

- Display the iPad's Today screen by swiping from left to right on any Home screen. (This screen displays headlines, alerts, and notices from various apps.)

- Display the Control Center/App Switcher by swiping up from the bottom edge of the screen. (You use the Control Center to adjust basic device settings, as well as switch between and close open apps.)

- With any app open, swipe up slightly from the bottom of the screen to display the Dock.

- Open a second app in split screen mode by displaying the Dock and then dragging the icon for that app up and to the side of the screen.

- While you're in split screen mode, tap and drag a file, photo, or selected piece of text from one app to another.

- Return to the Home screen from anywhere by pinching four or five fingers together from the top and bottom of the screen.

- Within an app, return to the top of a long page by tapping the top menu bar.

- Switch to the next or previous open app by swiping left or right with four or five fingers.

- Split the onscreen keyboard into two halves by expanding the keyboard with your thumb and forefinger. (Some people find this makes typing a little easier.) Pinch your fingers back together to rejoin the two halves into a whole keyboard.

- In a document or web page, zoom in and out by double-tapping the page.

- In a document or web page, select a word by double-tapping it.

# Navigate the Home Screen

On your iPad, the Home screen is where everything starts. When you press the Home button, you see the Home screen—or, more accurately, the first of several Home screens. All Home screens display a grid of icons that represent the apps installed on your device, along with a Dock of most-used apps at the bottom of the screen. You have as many Home screens as you need to display all your apps.

( 1 ) Press the Home button to display the first Home screen.

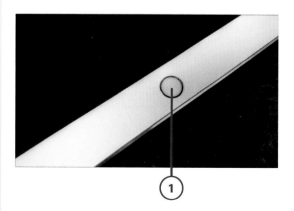

(**2**) At the bottom of the screen is the Dock, where app icons can be "docked" so that they appear on every Home page.

(**3**) The number of Home screens on your iPad is indicated by a grouping of dots above the Dock; you see as many dots as you have Home screens. The screen you're currently viewing is the solid white dot in the group.

(**4**) Swipe left or right to view the next or previous Home screen.

(**5**) Tap an icon to open the corresponding app.

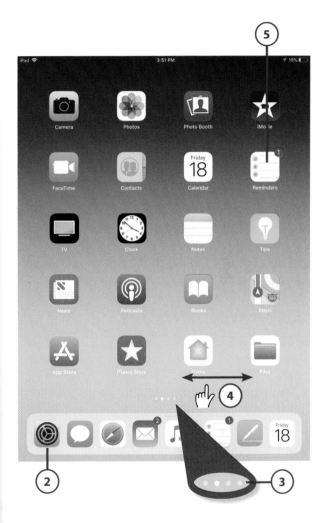

## View the Today Screen

The very first screen on your iPad actually isn't a Home screen. This screen, to the left of the main Home screen (the one you see when you press the Home button), is called the Today screen and displays a variety of "widgets." These are small panels that display specific information, such as news, weather, appointments, and the like.

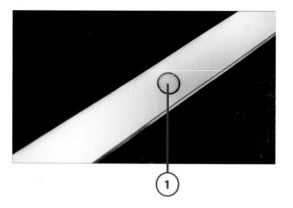

### Today from the Lock Screen

You can also display the Today screen before you unlock your iPad. Just swipe to the right from the Lock screen and you'll see all your Today notifications and widgets.

(1) Press the Home button to display the first Home screen.

(2) Swipe to the right to display the Today screen.

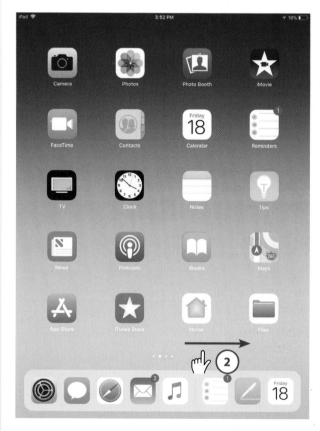

**( 3 )** You now see a single column of
widgets and notifications. Tap
any widget or notification to
view more details or to open the
corresponding app.

## Customizing the Today Screen

To add new widgets to the widgets
screen, tap the Edit button. Learn
more in Chapter 3.

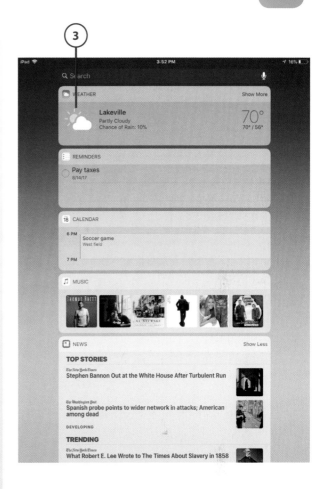

# View Notifications on
# the Cover Sheet

As you recall, the iPad's Lock screen
can display system notifications and
messages from selected apps. These
notifications are collectively called
the Cover Sheet, and you can view
them at any time without having to
unlock your device.

**( 1 )** Press the Home button to
display the first Home screen.

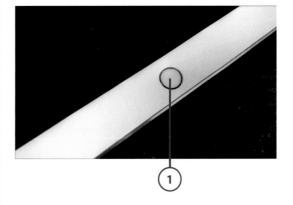

2. Swipe down from the top of the screen to display the Cover Sheet.

3. Tap any notification to open the notification and accompanying app.

4. Swipe left on any notification to bring up options to view or dismiss that item.

5. Swipe up on the Cover Sheet to return to the previously viewed screen.

# Manage Open Apps

You open apps on your iPad by tapping the app's icon on one of the Home screens, or in the Dock. You can have multiple apps open at the same time, and easily switch between them.

(1) To view all open apps, press the Home button twice. Or…

(2) Swipe up from the bottom of any screen.

( 3 ) You now see all your open apps, along with the Control Center. (The open apps are collectively called the App Switcher; the Control Center controls basic system operations.) Tap an app to go to that app.

( 4 ) Drag an app up and off the screen to close it.

# Understand the Status Bar

Running across the top of every iPad screen is a transparent status bar. This status bar displays icons for various system operations and provides information that shows you how your iPad is working.

The following table details the more common icons you'll find on the status bar, and what they mean.

**Status Bar Icons**

| Icon | Name | Description |
|------|------|-------------|
| 🔒 | Lock | The device is locked. |
| 🔋 | Battery | Shows the battery level or charging status. |
| ⏰ | Alarm | An alarm is set. |
| ✳ | Activity | There is currently app or network activity. |
| 🔄 | Orientation Lock | Screen orientation is locked. |
| 📶 | Wi-Fi | The iPad is connected to a Wi-Fi network; the more bars, the stronger the connection. |
| ✈ | Airplane Mode | Airplane Mode is engaged (Wi-Fi and Bluetooth are both turned off). |
| 🌙 | Do Not Disturb | Do Not Disturb mode is turned on. |
| ⊚ | Personal Hotspot | A cellular-equipped iPad is providing a personal hotspot for other devices. |
| ↻ | Syncing | The iPad is connected to your computer and syncing with iTunes. |

| Icon | Name | Description |
| --- | --- | --- |
| VPN | VPN | The iPad is connected to a virtual private network (VPN). |
| | Location Services | An app is using Location Services to establish the current location. |
| | Bluetooth | If the icon is blue or white, Bluetooth is turned on and the iPad is paired with a device, such as a Bluetooth headset. If the icon is gray, Bluetooth is turned on and the iPad is paired with a device, but the device is turned off or out of range. |
| | Bluetooth Battery | Shows the battery level of the connected Bluetooth device. |

### Cell Icons

If you have an iPad with cellular connectivity (Wi-Fi+Cellular), there are also icons for your cell signal and 3G/4G/LTE/EDGE/GPRS networks.

# Performing Basic Operations

Now that you know where (almost) everything is on your iPad, let's learn some of the most common operations necessary to get things done.

# View and Respond to Alerts

When your iPad or a specific app has something to tell you, you see an alert pop up onscreen. Depending on your settings and the importance of the alert, it may appear briefly at the top of the screen and then fade away, or it might remain in the center of the screen until you take some necessary action. Some alerts also appear on your iPad's Home or Search screens.

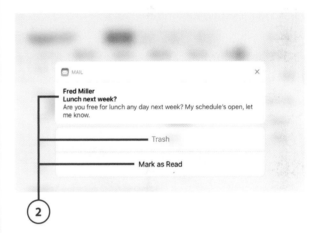

1. Most alerts appear at the top of the current screen.

2. Pull down on the alert to send it to the trash (tap Trash) or mark it as read (tap Mark as Read). Note that available options differ from app to app; for example, pulling down on a Messenger notification gives you options for Reply, Thumbs Up, Mute, and View Message.

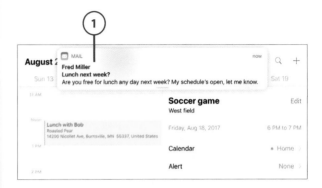

## Configure Alerts

To determine which alerts you see (and how you see them), turn to Chapter 3.

# Display the Control Center

When you want instant access to key system settings, such as screen brightness and volume, open your iPad's Control Center.

① Swipe up from the bottom of the screen to display the Control Center (along with the App Switcher).

② Tap any panel to turn on or off that control.

③ Tap and drag any slider within a panel to adjust that control.

( **4** ) Press and hold a panel (this is called a *long press*) to display additional options for a given control. For example, when you long press the Camera panel, you see additional options for taking a selfie, recording a video, and so forth.

( **5** ) Tap outside the expanded panel to return to the normal Control Center.

( **6** ) Close the Control Center by tapping on the background screen (outside the apps and controls).

# Adjust the Brightness

As noted, most of the more immediate iPad settings are accessed via the Control Center. This includes the device's screen brightness control.

( 1 ) From within the Control Center, touch and drag the Brightness slider up to increase screen brightness.

( 2 ) Touch and drag the Brightness slider down to decrease screen brightness.

## Conserve Battery Usage
Lower the screen brightness to conserve the battery.

# Activate Night Shift

The iPad's Night Shift mode subtly adjusts the screen colors so that they're warmer and easier to see at night. You can set a schedule for activating Night Shift, or simply go into Night Shift mode manually.

( 1 ) From within the Control Center, long press the Brightness panel to bring up the larger control.

( 2 ) Tap the Night Shift icon to turn on Night Shift mode. (The first time you enable this feature, you are prompted to set the Night Shift schedule.) Tap the icon again to return to normal screen colors.

# Change the Volume Level

Use the volume controls on the right side of your iPad to raise and lower the sounds you hear from the iPad's speakers.

(**1**) Press the volume up button to increase the device's volume level.

(**2**) Press the volume down button to decrease the device's volume level.

(**3**) Press and hold the volume down button to temporarily mute the sound. Press the volume up button to increase the sound again.

(**4**) You can also control the sound from the Control Center. Just open the Control Center and press and drag the Volume control up to increase the volume, or press and drag the control down to decrease the volume level.

## Rotate the iPad

As previously noted, you can use your iPad in either vertical (portrait) or horizontal (landscape) modes. The Home screen and most apps automatically rotate and adjust their displays to optimize how they work in either mode.

1. To switch from horizontal to vertical mode, simply rotate the iPad 90 degrees left or right. (Rotating left—counterclockwise—puts the volume controls on top of the iPad, and the Home button on the right.)

2. The Home screen automatically adapts to the new orientation.

## Activate Do Not Disturb Mode

There may be times when you don't want to be disturbed by alerts and notifications or by requests to video chat via FaceTime. When you don't want to be bothered by these and similar requests, activate your iPad's Do Not Disturb mode. When Do Not Disturb is activated, you won't see or hear notifications, alerts, and system sound effects. (Audio from music, movies, and TV shows is *not* muted.)

1. From within the Control Center, tap the Do Not Disturb button to mute all system alerts and notifications.

2. Tap the button again to return to normal operation.

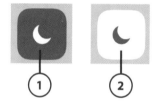

## Enter Text with the Onscreen Keyboard

Many applications let you (or even require you!) to enter text onscreen. You might be writing a note or memo, or browsing a web page that asks you to enter information into an onscreen form.

When you need to enter text onscreen, use your iPad's onscreen keyboard. In most instances, the keyboard appears automatically, on the bottom half of the screen, when you tap within a form field or document.

(1) Tap within a document or form field to display the onscreen keyboard.

(2) Tap a key on the keyboard to enter that character onscreen.

(3) Tap the Shift key to enter a capital letter. Double-tap the Shift key to engage caps lock.

(4) Tap the Number key to display numbers and special characters.

(5) Tap to enter a number or special character.

(6) Tap the ABC key to return to the normal alphanumeric keyboard.

(7) Tap the Emoji key to display and enter a range of emoji.

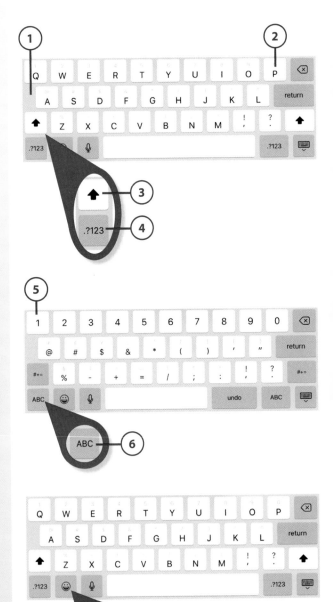

**8** Tap a tab to display different types of emoji.

**9** Tap to enter an emoji.

**10** Tap the ABC key to return to the normal alphanumeric keyboard.

**11** Tap the Keyboard key to hide the onscreen keyboard.

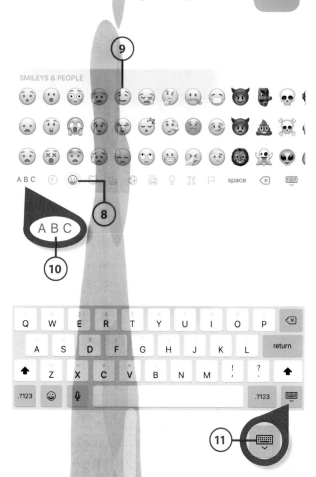

## >>>Go Further
## PREDICTIVE KEYBOARD

Your iPad uses what is called a *predictive keyboard*, in that it tries to figure out what you're typing so it can enter the word for you. You see the recommended words at the top of the keyboard; tap a word to insert it into the form or document.

The predictive keyboard lets you type without having to completely enter long words, and it can help you type faster. It also helps you avoid common spelling mistakes.

If you don't like the suggestions made by the predictive keyboard, you can turn off the predictive part of it. From the Settings screen, select General; then select Keyboard. On the Keyboards screen, tap "off" the Predictive switch.

## Copy and Paste Text

Whether you're using your iPad to write long letters or short Facebook posts, it's handy to be able to copy and paste text from one location to another.

(1) Double-tap a word to highlight that word.

(2) Tap and drag the starting and/or end points to select more or less text.

(3) Tap Cut to cut this selection (move it to another location).

(4) Tap Copy to copy this selection (duplicate it in another location).

(5) Move to where you want to paste the selected text and then press or double-tap the screen. This displays a different menu of options. (The available options differ from app to app, too.)

(6) Tap Paste.

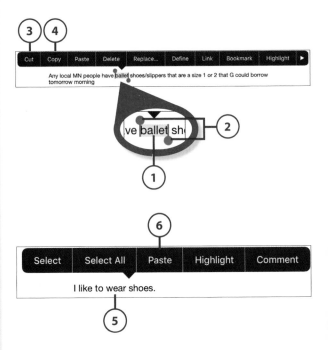

# Set an Alarm

Your iPad includes a Clock app that lets you set a timer or an alarm. It also functions as a stopwatch.

If you want to use your iPad as a (very expensive!) alarm clock, use the Clock app to set an alarm.

( 1 ) Tap the Clock icon to open the Clock app.

( 2 ) Tap the Alarm icon at the bottom of the screen.

( 3 ) Tap the + icon to create a new alarm.

( 4 ) Use the clock control to set the alarm time.

( 5 ) To have the alarm repeat on later days, tap Repeat and select which day(s) you want to use it.

( 6 ) Tap Label to create a name for this alarm.

( 7 ) Tap Sound to select the sound you want to hear when the alarm goes off.

( 8 ) Tap "off" the Snooze control if you don't want to be able to snooze through the alarm.

( 9 ) Tap Save. The alarm is created and activated.

## Turn Off an Alarm

When an alarm sounds, turn it off by pressing the iPad's Home button.

## Onscreen Switches

iOS uses a variety of onscreen switches to activate and deactivate various settings and functions. Just tap the switch to change its condition from "off" to "on," or vice versa. An "on" switch is to the right with a green background; an "off" switch is to the left with a white background.

## Set a Timer

There are times when you need to set a timer—when you're cooking in the kitchen, for example, or putting the grandkids in a timeout. You can use the Clock app for all your timer needs.

1. Tap the Clock icon to open the Clock app.

2. Tap the Timer icon.

3. Use the timer controls to set the length of the timer.

4. Tap the sound icon to set the sound you hear when the timer goes off.

5. Tap Start to start the timer.

## Turn Off the Timer

When the Timer ends, press the Home button to turn it off.

# Use the Stopwatch

Finally, the Clock app also lets you use it as a stopwatch, so that you can time any ongoing event.

**1** Tap the Clock icon to open the Clock app.

**2** Tap the Stopwatch icon.

**3** Tap Start to start the stopwatch.

④ Tap Stop to stop the stopwatch. The elapsed time is displayed onscreen.

# Managing Your iPad's Battery

Your iPad is powered by an internal battery that recharges when you connect it to the included power charger. How long the internal battery lasts before needing to be recharged depends on a lot of different factors—how you're using the device, which apps you're running, how bright you've set the screen, and so forth.

## Recharge the Battery

Use the included power adapter to charge your iPad when you're not using it—although you can continue to use the device when charging.

① Connect the Lightning connector on the cable to the Lightning port on the bottom of the iPad.

### Lightning Connector

One nice thing about Apple's Lightning connector is that it's symmetrical; you can plug the cable in right side up or upside down, it's all the same. No more twisting and turning to fit cables into connectors!

**2** Connect the USB connector on the cable to the USB port on the power adapter.

**3** Connect the power adapter to any power outlet. Your iPad should fully charge in about 5 to 7 hours—longer if you're using it while charging (which you can).

## It's Not All Good

### USB Charging

You can also charge your iPad's battery by connecting the Lightning cable to a USB port on your computer instead of to the power adapter. Recharging via computer, however, is much slower than recharging via a traditional power outlet. In addition, if you connect your iPad to a computer that is turned off or in sleep or standby mode, it might drain the iPad battery instead of charging it!

## Monitor Battery Usage

The battery icon on the right side of the status bar indicates how much charge you have left. When the charge gets too low, the status bar displays the image of a nearly empty battery, and you need to plug in and charge up your iPad before you can continue to use it.

If you want to know which apps are using the most battery power, you can do that.

① From the Dock, tap the Settings icon to open the Settings screen.

② Tap Battery in the left column.

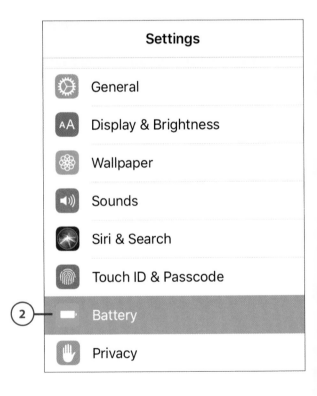

**3** The right side of the screen now displays a list of those apps and system functions that have used the most battery power, in descending order. Tap to display usage for the last 24 hours or the last 7 days.

**4** Tap any item to view how many minutes this and other items have been used.

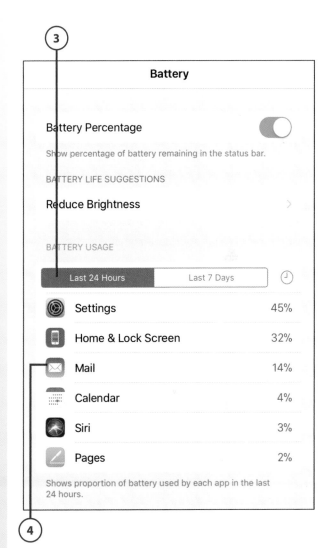

**3**

### Battery

Battery Percentage

Show percentage of battery remaining in the status bar.

BATTERY LIFE SUGGESTIONS

Reduce Brightness                                    >

BATTERY USAGE

| Last 24 Hours | Last 7 Days |
|---|---|

| ⚙ Settings | 45% |
| 📱 Home & Lock Screen | 32% |
| ✉ Mail | 14% |
| 📅 Calendar | 4% |
| Siri | 3% |
| Pages | 2% |

Shows proportion of battery used by each app in the last 24 hours.

**4**

In this chapter, you learn how to personalize various aspects of your iPad experience.

→ Personalizing the Lock and Home Screens
→ Customizing the Today Screen and Control Center
→ Configuring Device Settings
→ Managing System Settings

# Personalizing the Way Your iPad Looks and Works

Every iPad looks and acts the same right out of the box. But that doesn't mean that you can't configure your iPad to your own personal tastes.

Want a different background picture? You can do that. Want a brighter or dimmer screen? You can do that, too. Don't like the way you receive notifications onscreen, and from which apps? Then change the notification settings.

Truth is, there's a lot you can do to personalize your very own iPad. This chapter walks you through managing your screens, backgrounds, and more detailed settings. Change is coming!

# Personalizing the Lock and Home Screens

One of the most visible things that people like to change is the look of the iPad screens. You can change the background wallpaper of the Lock and Home screens, as well as the way app icons are arranged onscreen.

## Change the Wallpaper

The default wallpaper you see on your iPad's Home and Lock screens is pretty enough, but you can probably find something more to your liking. You can choose different wallpaper for the Lock and Home screens, or use the same wallpaper for both.

1. From the Dock or Home screen, tap the Settings icon to display the Settings screen.

2. Tap Wallpaper in the left column.

General

AA Display & Brightness

Wallpaper

Sounds

3. Your current wallpaper is displayed on thumbnails of your Lock (left) and Home (right) screens. Tap Choose a New Wallpaper.

WALLPAPER

Choose a New Wallpaper

**(4)** Tap Dynamic to select one of Apple's dynamic (moving) wallpapers. *Or…*

**(5)** Tap Stills to select one of Apple's supplied still photos.

**(6)** Tap one of the photo folders to use one of your own pictures as wallpaper.

**(7)** Tap to select one of the available choices.

**8** To create a slight motion effect for the background, tap to turn on Perspective Zoom.

## Perspective Zooming

When you select Perspective Zoom you enable what experts call a *parallax effect*. It essentially creates a slight motion effect on the Home or Lock screens when you tilt your iPad; the background seems to follow you as you move your device. Some people like it, some people don't. It's not really a big thing.

**9** Tap Set Lock Screen to set this picture for only your Lock screen.

**10** Tap Set Home Screen to set this picture for only your Home screen.

**11** Tap Set Both to use this picture as the background for both your Lock and Home screens.

# Arrange App Icons

Whatever size iPad you have, app icons are displayed on the Home screen in the same 4 × 5 grid. (That's 4 columns by 5 rows if held vertically, or 4 rows by 5 columns if held horizontally.) There's also the Dock that floats at the bottom of the screen, where you can permanently "dock" icons for your most-used apps.

## iOS Apps
Learn more about apps on your iPad in Chapter 8, "Installing and Using Apps."

Which icons appear where on your Home screens is totally up to you. You can easily move icons from one position to another, and even from one screen to another.

**(1)** Press and hold the icon you want to move until all the icons onscreen start to jiggle. (You also see a little X next to each icon, which means you're in editing mode.) You can tap the X to delete an app, if you want.

**(2)** Drag the icon to a new position. The other icons rearrange themselves to make room. Lift your finger when the icon is in place.

**(3)** Press the Home button to return to normal screen mode.

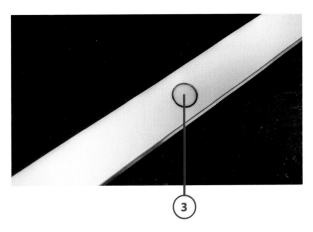

### Screen to Screen

To move an icon to a different Home screen, drag the icon to the side of the screen until the adjacent screen appears. You can then "drop" the icon to a new position on this screen. If you try to drag an icon to a screen that's already full, it pushes the last icon (on the bottom right) to the next screen.

## Add Icons to and Remove Icons from the Dock

The Dock is that area at the bottom of every screen that holds icons for your most-used apps. By default, the Dock holds five set icons—Settings, Messages, Safari (web browser), Mail, and Music—plus icons for the three most recently used apps. You can remove any of the five default app icons, or add icons for other apps. In fact, you also can populate the Dock with more than a dozen icons.

If you stock up the Dock with icons for the apps you use most, you won't have to move back to the Home screen as often. Because the Dock hovers on top of most open apps (and you can redisplay it simply by swiping up from the bottom of the screen), you can do all your app launching from the Dock rather than from the Home screen.

1. Add an icon to the Dock by dragging it from any screen down to the Dock.

2. Rearrange icons on the Dock by dragging any icon to a new position.

3. Remove an icon from the Dock by dragging it from the Dock to any Home screen.

## Organize Apps with Folders

If you have too many apps crowding too many screens, you can organize those apps into folders. Each folder can contain multiple apps; to open a folder, tap it and then tap the appropriate app inside.

(1) Create a new folder by dragging one icon on top of another. This creates the folder and displays it full screen.

(2) Tap anywhere outside the folder to close the folder and return to the desktop. The folder is displayed in position there. (You can drag the folder to move it to another position, if you like.)

(3) Add another app to this folder by dragging the app icon on top of the folder icon.

(4) Remove an app from a folder by opening the folder and then dragging the icon outside of the folder.

(5) Rename a folder by pressing and holding the folder icon to open it for editing. You can then open the folder, tap the default folder name, and use the onscreen keyboard to edit or enter a new name.

## >>>Go Further

### ORGANIZE BY TYPE

I find it useful to organize my lesser-used apps into folders. Those apps I use all the time I want to tap immediately from the Home screen; those I use less regularly I put into folders so they're not cluttering my screens.

When I use folders, I try to put similar apps together. For example, if I have a half dozen or so games, I might create a folder labeled Games to hold them all. Similarly, I might group my music, video, and photos apps into a folder labeled Lifestyle, or the Numbers, Pages, and Keynote apps into a Productivity folder.

The point is to group similar apps together in folders where I can quickly and easily find them. I've found that creating a folder labeled Misc is the best way to "lose" apps on my device!

# Customizing the Today Screen and Control Center

In addition to personalizing your iPad's Home screens, you can also customize what notifications you see on the Today screen and which controls are visible in the Control Center.

## Customize the Today Screen

When you swipe from left to right on the main Home screen, you display your iPad's Today screen. There's a search box at the top of this screen, as you might expect, but also a variety of *widgets*. These are small panels that display specific types of information—weather, news, and the like.

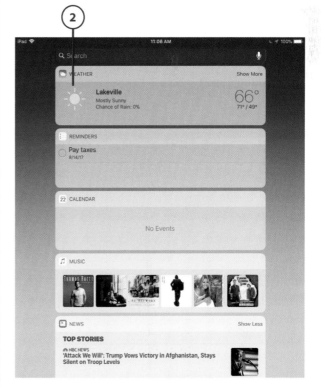

You can personalize which widgets you display on the Today screen. This makes this screen more useful for you.

1. Swipe to the right from the main Home screen to display the Today screen.

2. Your current widgets are displayed. If you have many widgets installed, you can scroll up and down through all of them. Tap a widget to display more information or open a given app.

(3) Scroll to the bottom of the Today screen and tap Edit to display the Add Widgets screen.

(4) Your current widgets are listed by their position. To move a widget to another position, press and drag it to its new position.

(5) Tap the red – button to remove a widget from the Today screen, and then tap the Remove button.

(6) Add a new widget by scrolling to the More Widgets section and tapping the green + for the widget you want to add.

(7) Tap Done to return to the Today screen.

# Customize the Control Center

When you swipe up from the bottom of any screen, you see the Control Center. (You also see thumbnails of any open apps, or what Apple calls the App Switcher.) A number of useful controls are displayed by default in the Control Center; you can further personalize the Control Center by adding additional controls.

(1) Tap the Settings icon in the Dock or on the Home screen to display the Settings screen.

(2) In the left column, tap Control Center.

(3) In the right column, tap Customize Controls.

| Notifications |
| Control Center |
| Do Not Disturb |

**Control Center**

Swipe up from the bottom of the screen to view Control Center.

Customize Controls

④ To add a new control to the
Control Center, tap the green +
next to that control's name.

⑤ To remove a control from the
Control Center, tap the red −
next to that control's name.

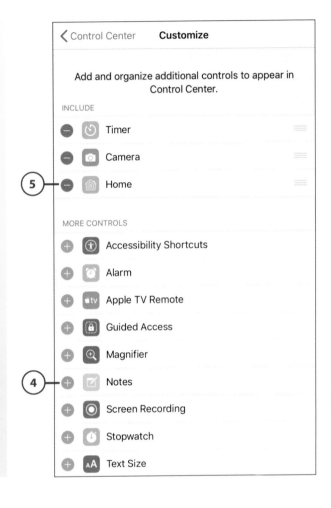

# Configuring Device Settings

There are many other settings you can configure to better personalize your iPad.
You configure all these settings from the iPad's Settings page.

## Display the Settings Page

The Settings page is organized into a series of tabs, which are accessible from the left column. Tap a tab to view the individual settings of a given type.

1. From the Dock or Home screen, tap the Settings icon to open the Settings screen.

2. Tap the tab on the left to display related settings.

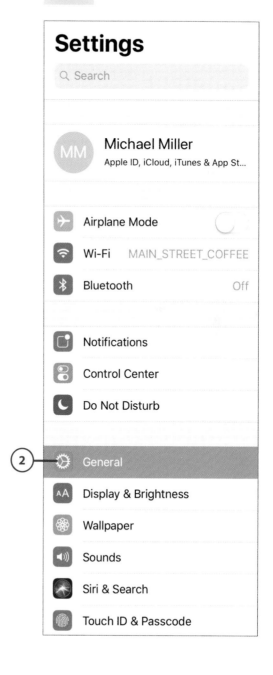

# Configure Notifications

Many apps display notifications for various types of events. The Mail app, for example, can display notifications when you receive new emails; the News app can display notifications with recent news headlines.

You can determine what types of notifications you receive on an app-by-app basis. For that matter, you can opt to turn off all notifications for specific apps, thus reducing the number of annoying notifications you have to deal with.

### Different Notifications

Different apps will have different notification options. This how-to discusses some of the more common notification options.

1. From the Settings screen, tap Notifications in the left column to display the Notifications tab.

2. Tap the app you want to configure.

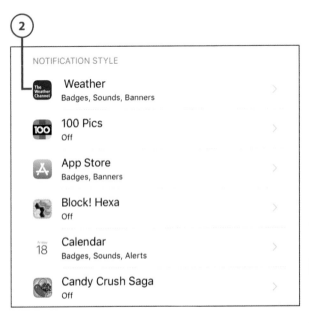

**3** Tap "on" the Allow Notifications switch to display notifications from this app. Tap "off" this control to disable all notifications from this app.

**4** Tap "on" the Sounds switch to enable notification sounds for this app. Tap "off" this control to turn off these sounds. (Not all apps have notification sounds.)

**5** Some apps display a number on top of the icon to indicate the number of notifications or actions pending. (For example, the icon for the Mail app displays a red "2" if there are two unread emails in the inbox.) Turn on this numbering by tapping "on" the Badge App Icon switch.

**6** Show notifications from this app on the Cover Sheet (and the Lock screen) by tapping "on" the Show on Lock Screen switch. Tap "off" this switch to not show notification on the Cover Sheet.

**7** Display notifications from this app in your iPad's History by tapping "on" the Show in History switch. Tap "off" this switch to not track this notification history.

**8** To display alerts as banners, tap "on" the Show as Banners switch and then select a banner style (Temporary or Persistent).

**9** To show previews from this app (not available with all apps) in the notifications, tap Show Previews and then select what type of preview: Always, When Unlocked, or Never.

# Configure the Display and Brightness

You can adjust how bright your iPad's display appears, along with several other display-related settings.

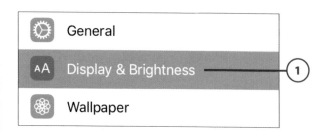

1. From the Settings screen, tap Display & Brightness in the left column.

2. Drag the Brightness slider to the left to make the screen less bright, or to the right to make it brighter. (Remember, the brighter the screen, the faster it drains your battery.)

3. To let your iPad automatically shift the display colors warmer (more reddish) after dark, tap Night Shift. You see the Night Shift panel.

4. Schedule when Night Shift is enabled by tapping "on" the Scheduled switch and making a selection.

5. Manually enable Night Shift from now to daylight tomorrow by tapping on the Manually Enable Until Tomorrow switch.

6. Adjust how warm the Night Shift colors appear by dragging the Color Temperature slider to the left (less warm) or right (warmer).

7. Tap Back to return to the Display & Brightness screen.

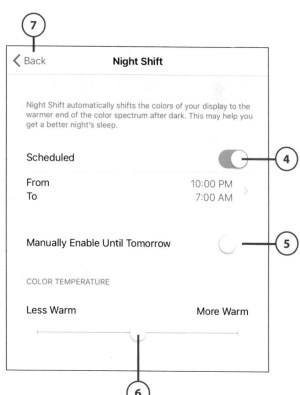

**8** Change the amount of idle time that must elapse before your iPad automatically locks by tapping Auto-Lock and making a new selection (2 minutes, 5 minutes, 10 minutes, 15 minutes, or never).

**9** If you have a Smart Cover on your iPad, you can disable it so that your device doesn't automatically unlock when the cover is opened—just tap "off" the Lock/Unlock switch.

**10** Tap Text Size to change the size of the text you see onscreen.

**11** Drag the slider to the left to make the text smaller, or to the right to make the text larger. Tap Back to return to the previous screen.

**12** To make the text for icons and other system elements bold (and thus, perhaps, easier to read), tap "on" the Bold Text switch. When reminded that applying this setting will restart your iPad, tap Continue; your iPad then restarts.

# Change System Sounds

You can select different sounds for different system actions, such as sending an email or making a Facebook post. You can also opt to hear sounds when your iPad locks or when you tap the keys of the onscreen keyboard.

**(1)** From the Settings screen, tap Sounds in the left column.

**(2)** Drag the Ringer and Alerts slider to the left to decrease the volume; drag to the right to make them louder.

**(3)** To control these system sounds with your iPad's physical volume buttons, tap "on" the Change with Buttons switch. (Otherwise, the volume buttons only control the volume of music and videos you're listening to or watching.)

**(4)** Change the sound for any specific system function by going to the Sounds section, tapping that function, and selecting a new sound.

**(5)** Tap "off" the Keyboard Clicks switch to turn off sounds when you tap your iPad's onscreen keyboard. (Some people find all these clickity clacks annoying when they type.)

**(6)** Tap "off" the Lock Sound switch to turn off sounds when you lock or unlock your iPad.

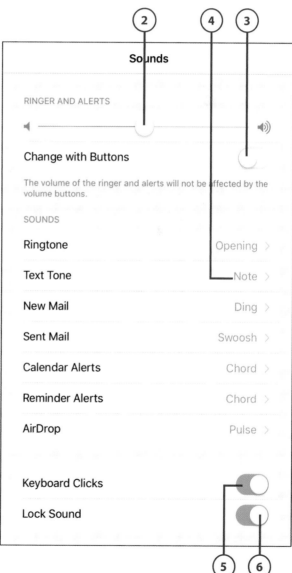

## Configure Individual Apps

Most of the apps installed on your iPad have their own individual settings you can configure. Use the Settings screen to adjust settings for any app.

( 1 ) From the Settings screen, scroll down to the list of individual apps in the left column.

( 2 ) Tap an app to display and configure its settings.

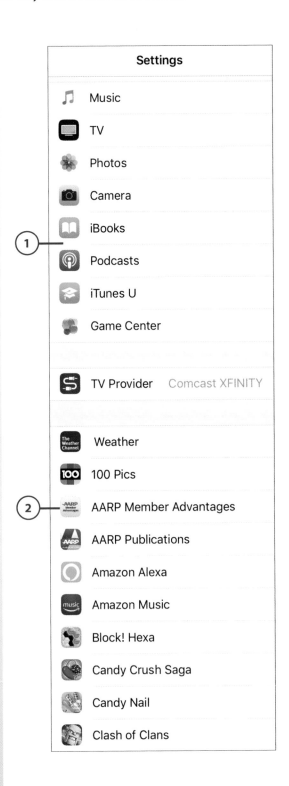

# Managing System Settings

We've covered some of the most used settings you may want to configure on your iPad. But there are more settings available, on the General tab, that let you fine-tune various system options—and show you information about your device.

## Display and Manage General Settings

The General tab on the Settings page is home to a variety of settings that affect all the apps on your iPad—as well as the iPad itself.

1. From the Settings screen, tap General in the left column to select the General tab.

2. Tap About to see information about your device—how many items of various types you have stored, total capacity, available storage space, model and serial number, and more.

3. Tap Software Update to manually force any available software update.

## Automatic Updates

Most available software updates will automatically install; manual updates are not typically needed.

4. Tap AirDrop to configure your iPad's AirDrop feature, which lets you instantly share contacts and other data with nearby Apple devices.

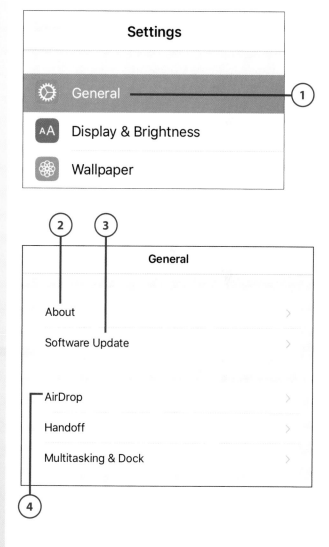

**5** Tap Handoff to deactivate the ability to start work on one device and resume that work on another device.

**6** Tap Multitasking & Dock to deactivate the abilities to use multiple apps, display a persistent overlay when playing videos, use four- and five-finger touch gestures, and show suggested and recent apps on the Dock.

**7** Tap Accessibility to configure your device for enhanced accessibility.

## Accessibility Options

To learn more about your iPad's accessibility options, see Chapter 4, "Making Your iPad More Accessible."

**8** Tap iPad Storage to view how much storage space you've used and have left.

**9** Some apps automatically refresh themselves in the background. To turn this off, tap Background App Refresh.

**10** Tap Restrictions to enable restrictions for specific apps (useful if small children are using your iPad).

**11** Tap Date & Time to set your iPad's date and time.

**12** Tap Keyboard to configure various options for the onscreen keyboard.

**13** Tap Language & Region to reset the language and region for your iPad.

**14** Tap Dictionary to select which dictionary your iPad uses when checking text you enter.

**15** Tap iTunes Wi-Fi Sync to manu-ally sync data on your iPad with your computer via Wi-Fi.

**16** Tap VPN to configure your iPad to use a virtual public network.

**17** Tap Profile to view your configu-ration profile.

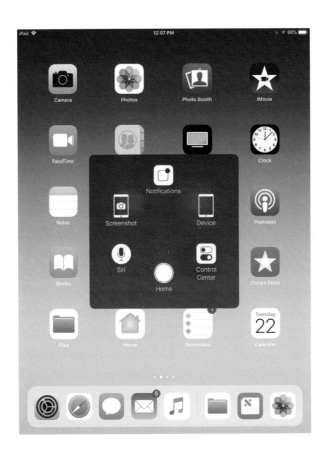

In this chapter, you explore how to configure your iPad's accessibility options—and make it easier to use.

→ Making the iPad Easier to Use for the Vision Impaired
→ Making the iPad Easier to Use for the Hearing Impaired
→ Making the iPad Easier to Operate

# 4

# Making Your iPad More Accessible

Because even the largest iPad has a relatively small screen, some of us may have trouble seeing what's onscreen, or tapping where we need to tap.

Fortunately, several settings on your iPad can make it easier to use. We'll discuss them in this chapter.

# Making the iPad Easier to Use for the Vision Impaired

Let's start with those features that can make things displayed onscreen easier to see. Many of us have some degree of vision loss, even if it's just the need for reading glasses to see fine print. Given the relatively small size of text on the iPad screen (especially on many web pages), you may want to avail yourself of these features that make onscreen text easier to read.

## Read the Screen with VoiceOver

Probably the most useful accessibility feature for those with vision difficulties is Apple's VoiceOver. VoiceOver describes out loud any screen element or text. Just touch an item or text selection and VoiceOver either reads it or tells you about it. In some instances, VoiceOver even tells you how to use a given item—"double-tap to open," for example.

When VoiceOver is activated, all you have to do is touch the screen or drag your finger over an area to hear information about what's onscreen. When you go to a new screen, VoiceOver plays a sound and then selects and reads the first item on the new screen.

Note that because VoiceOver requires you to tap the screen to "read" an item, most traditional touch gestures change when you've activated VoiceOver. Where you would normally use a single-tap, for example, you now use a double-tap.

### Other Screen-Reading Options

Although VoiceOver is the best and most full-featured screen-reading option on your iPad, other options are available. Go to the Accessibility screen and tap Speech and you can enable the Speak Selection (for reading text), Speak Screen (for reading screen elements), and Typing Feedback (for reading words while you type) options. Give them a try; they're less functional but also less intrusive than VoiceOver.

**1** To activate VoiceOver, go to the Settings screen, select the General tab, tap Accessibility, and then tap VoiceOver.

**2** From the VoiceOver screen, tap on the VoiceOver switch. (Alternatively, press and hold the Home button and tell Siri, "Turn VoiceOver on.")

**3** To "read" any onscreen item, touch it. (The item is now surrounded by a black border—the VoiceOver cursor.)

**4** To activate any operation normally done by single-tapping, instead select the item and then double-tap the screen.

**5** To activate any operation normally done by double-tapping, instead triple-tap that item.

## Turn It Off

To deactivate VoiceOver, press and hold the Home button and tell Siri, "Turn VoiceOver off."

## >>>Go Further
## VOICEOVER GESTURES

When you're using VoiceOver, how you use your iPad changes in subtle ways. Because basic tapping or touching now "reads" that onscreen item, you need to use different touch gestures to do just about anything onscreen.

The following table shows you some of the more common operations and their new VoiceOver-enabled touch gestures.

| Operation | VoiceOver Gesture |
| --- | --- |
| Select and read an item | Single-tap |
| Select the next or previous item | Swipe right or left |
| Read all elements from the top of the screen | Two-finger swipe up |
| Read all elements from the current position | Two-finger swipe down |
| Stop or resume speaking | Two-finger tap |
| Dismiss an alert or go back to a previous screen | Move two fingers back and forth quickly in a Z pattern |
| Scroll one page at a time | Three-finger swipe up or down |
| Go to the next or previous page (including on the Home page) | Three-finger swipe right or left |
| Speak additional information about the selected item | Three-finger tap |
| Select the first item on the page | Four-finger tap at the top of the screen |
| Select the last item on the page | Four-finger tap at the bottom of the screen |
| Activate the selected item | Double-tap |
| Double-tap an item | Triple-tap |

| Operation | VoiceOver Gesture |
|---|---|
| Drag an item | Double-tap and hold one second, and then drag the item |
| Initiate an action or pause an in-progress action | Two-finger double-tap |
| Change an item's label | Two-finger double-tap and then hold |
| Open the Item Chooser | Two-finger triple-tap |
| Mute or unmute VoiceOver | Three-finger double-tap |

There are also a number of settings you can configure to personalize the way VoiceOver works for you. Just go to the Settings page, select the General tab, tap Accessibility, and then tap VoiceOver.

## Braille Displays

Your iPad is fully compatible with most third-party braille displays. Use the braille display to control your iPad when VoiceOver is activated. Connect a braille display to your iPad via Bluetooth, and then go the Settings page, select the General tab, tap Accessibility, tap VoiceOver, and then tap Braille.

# Magnify the Screen with Zoom

Having VoiceOver take over your iPad's screen may be too much for those of us with only mild vision difficulties. In this instance, you might need only to zoom into an area of the screen to make it larger and more legible.

Many apps let you zoom in by either double-tapping the screen or expanding your fingers apart. (You zoom out by pinching your fingers together.) Apple also offers a dedicated Zoom feature that lets you magnify any screen.

1. To activate Zoom, go to the Settings screen, select the General tab, tap Accessibility, and then tap Zoom.

2. Tap on the Zoom switch to display the zoom box onscreen.

3. Drag the bottom of the zoom box to move it around the screen. (Not shown.)

4. Hide the zoom box by double-tapping the screen with three fingers. Double-tap with three fingers again to re-display the zoom box. (Not shown.)

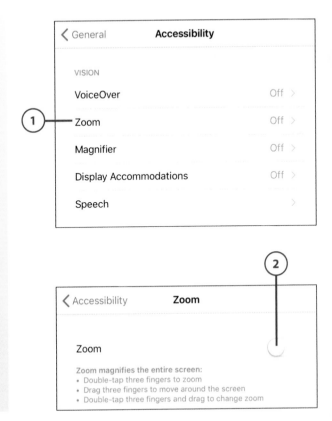

## Invert Screen Colors

If you're having trouble distinguishing elements onscreen, it may be an issue of contrast. I've found that increasing the contrast between light and dark elements can help me read even very small type onscreen.

With this in mind, Apple enables you to invert your colors onscreen. With inverted colors, black text on a white background becomes white text on a black background, and other color highlights appear against that same black background.

(1) Go to the Settings screen, select the General tab, tap Accessibility, and then tap Display Accommodations.

(2) Tap Invert Colors.

(3) Tap "on" the Smart Invert switch to reverse-display colors except for images, video, and apps that use a dark color scheme. (This is the new and preferred option.)

(4) Tap "on" the Classic Invert switch to reverse all colors in all apps.

(5) Return to your iPad's normal color scheme by returning to the Invert Colors screen and tapping "off" whichever option you've previously enabled.

## Colorblind Users

If you're fully or partially colorblind, you simply can't see some color combinations. Fortunately, you can configure your iPad with color filters, to make those otherwise hard-to-see colors pop. Just go to the Display Accommodations screen, tap Color Filters, tap "on" the Color Filters switch, and then select the filter that works best for you.

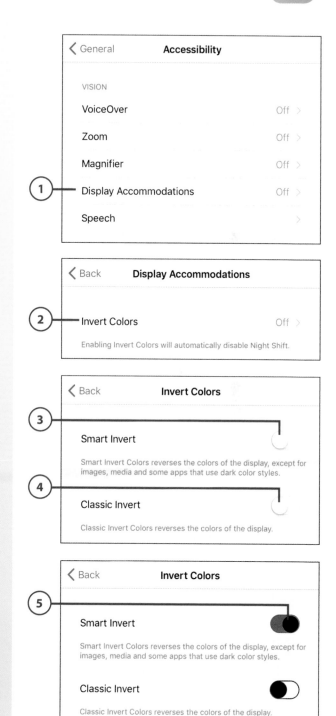

# Make Onscreen Text Larger and Bolder

Another way to make an iPad screen more readable is to increase the size of the onscreen text, or perhaps even bold that text.

**(1)** Go to the Settings screen, select the General tab, and tap Accessibility.

**(2)** Make onscreen text bold by tapping "on" the Bold Text switch. When reminded that applying this setting will restart your iPad, tap Continue; your iPad now restarts.

**(3)** Increase the size of onscreen text by tapping Larger Text.

**(4)** Tap "on" the Larger Accessibility Sizes switch.

**(5)** Drag the slider to the right to make text larger. Drag the slider back to the left to make larger text smaller.

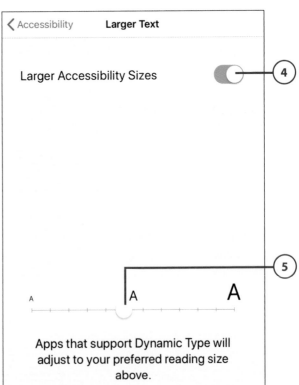

# Making the iPad Easier to Use for the Hearing Impaired

Whether you're a little hard of hearing or completely deaf, you'll be pleased to know that your iPad can accommodate various types of hearing devices, as well as compensate for hearing damage in one ear or the other.

## Use a Hearing Aid with Your iPad

Many companies make "Made for iPad" hearing aids that are officially compatible with most iPad models. When you pair these hearing aids via Bluetooth, you can use the iPad to adjust their settings, stream audio direct to the hearing aids, and more. All you have to do is configure your iPad for the type of hearing aid you have. Start by opening the battery doors on your hearing aids, and then follow these steps.

( 1 ) Make sure Bluetooth is enabled on your iPad (tap Bluetooth from the Settings screen), then go to the Settings screen, select the General tab, and tap Accessibility.

( 2 ) Scroll to the Hearing section and tap MFi Hearing Aids.

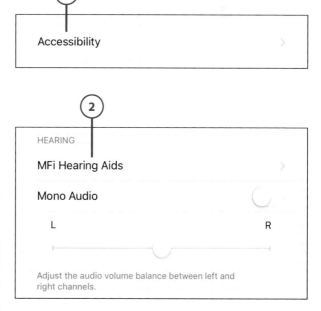

③ Close the battery doors on your hearing aids and wait for them to appear in the Devices list. When the hearing aid appears, tap its name and respond to the pairing request. You can then adjust settings specific to your hearing aids from the Hearing Devices page.

⟨ Accessibility    **MFi Hearing Aids**

DEVICES

Searching...

Pair Made for iPhone hearing aids. Other hearing aids are paired in Bluetooth settings.

## Use Mono Audio

If your hearing is weaker in one ear than the other, you might have trouble hearing sounds coming from either your left or right hearing aid. To compensate, you can mix all stereo sound to mono and have your iPad play back only mono sounds. From the Accessibility screen, go to the Hearing section and tap "on" the Mono Audio switch. You can then drag the slider to the left or right until you can best hear all sounds coming from your iPad.

# Turn On Closed Captioning When Watching Videos

Many streaming video services and video player apps, such as Apple's own Videos app, offer closed captioning for the hearing impaired. You can typically enable closed captioning within the individual app, or universally via your iPad's general settings.

① Go to the Settings screen, select the General tab, tap Accessibility, and then scroll to the Media section and tap Subtitles & Captioning.

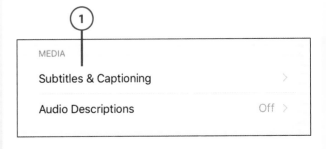

MEDIA

Subtitles & Captioning                           ⟩

Audio Descriptions                        Off ⟩

2  Tap "on" the Closed Captions + SDH switch.

3  Tap Style to select a closed-captioned style.

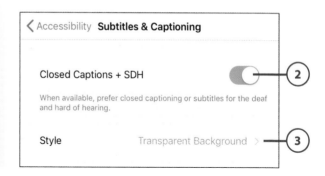

# Making the iPad Easier to Operate

If you have trouble performing the necessary touch gestures to operate your iPad, there are some options available to you. You can fine-tune how various gestures work, enable an assistive technology called AssistiveTouch, or just use the Siri personal assistant to operate your iPad via voice commands.

## Adjust the Touchscreen Display

Sometimes I find my iPad's touch-screen display to be a little too touchy. If you find yourself tapping or swiping things without meaning to, you can adjust the sensitivity of the display itself.

1  Go to the Settings screen, select the General tab, tap Accessibility, and then scroll to the Interaction section and tap Touch Accommodations.

(2) Tap "on" the Touch Accommodations switch.

(3) Adjust how long you must
touch the screen before that
touch is recognized by tapping
on the Hold Duration switch and
then setting a new time. (The
default is 0.10 seconds.)

(4) If your single touches sometimes register as double
touches, tap on the Ignore
Repeat switch and increase the
time limit.

(5) If you have trouble precisely
tapping onscreen elements,
enable Tap Assistance by
tapping either Use Initial
Touch Location or Use
Final Touch Location. Tap
Off to disable this feature.

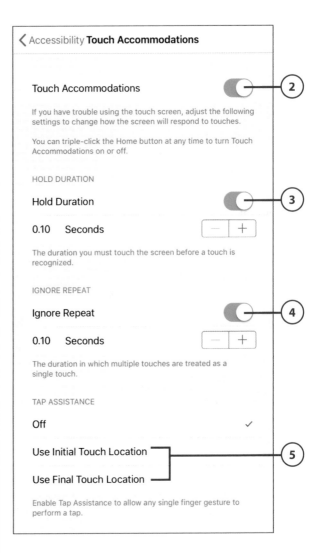

# Enable AssistiveTouch

Your iPad includes an accessibility feature dubbed AssistiveTouch that overlays a group of large icons onscreen for common functions. With AssistiveTouch enabled, just tap the AssistiveTouch icon and then tap an icon for Notification Center, Device, Control Center, Home, Siri, or Custom (any operation of your choice).

1. Go to the Settings screen, select the General tab, tap Accessibility, and then go to the Interaction section and tap AssistiveTouch.

2. Tap "on" the AssistiveTouch switch.

3. The AssistiveTouch icon now appears at the bottom-right corner of the iPad screen. Tap this icon to display the Assistive-Touch menu, and then tap the action you want to initiate. (Tap anywhere outside the Assistive-Touch menu to close the panel.)

## Use Siri

If you have trouble managing the gestures you need to operate your iPad, use voice commands instead. You can activate many accessibility features by talking to your iPad via the Siri personal digital assistant. Just say "Siri, turn on VoiceOver," for example, and that feature will be turned on. (Learn more in Chapter 7.

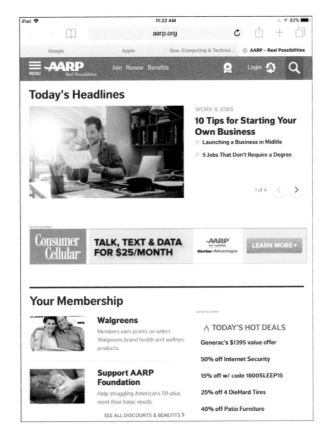

In this chapter, you learn how to connect your iPad to Wi-Fi networks and hotspots to access sites and information on the Internet. You also learn how to use the Safari web browser to surf the Web.

5

→ Connecting to a Wi-Fi Network
→ Using the Safari Web Browser
→ Making the Web More Readable
→ Searching the Web

# Connecting to the Internet and Browsing the Web

A lot of what you do with your iPad requires a connection to the Internet. Sending and receiving email, searching for information, video chatting with FaceTime, watching streaming videos or listening to streaming music—all of these activities require an Internet connection.

You connect your iPad to the Internet via a Wi-Fi wireless connection. Your iPad has built-in Wi-Fi, so it's just a matter of connecting to a private Wi-Fi network (like you probably have at home) or a public Wi-Fi hotspot. After you're connected, you can do all that fun Internet-related stuff—as well as use those apps that also require an Internet connection.

# Connecting to a Wi-Fi Network

To get the most out of your iPad, you need to connect it to the Internet, via a wireless network. You can connect to your home Wi-Fi network, or to any public Wi-Fi network or hotspot.

### Wi-Fi

Wi-Fi (short for *Wireless Fidelity*) is the consumer-friendly name for the IEEE 802.11 wireless networking standard. Most of today's wireless networks are Wi-Fi networks and use Wi-Fi-certified products.

## Connect to Your Home Wireless Network

Obviously, if you have a wireless network in your home you'll want to connect your iPad to that. Once you've initially connected, you won't need to manually reconnect in the future; your iPad remembers the network settings and reconnects automatically.

To connect to your home network, you need to know the name of the network (sometimes called an SSID, for *service set identifier*) and the network password (sometimes called a *security key*).

( 1 ) From the Dock or Home screen, tap the Settings icon to open the Settings screen.

( 2 ) In the left column, tap Wi-Fi. (If you're not yet connected, it should say "Not Connected.")

**3** Make sure the Wi-Fi switch is in the "on" position. If it isn't, tap to turn it on.

**4** You see a list of the wireless networks within range. Tap to select your home network. This displays the password panel.

## Public Versus Private Networks

Private wireless networks require a password to connect, and are indicated with a lock icon in the network list. Public networks (sometimes called *open networks*) let you connect without a password, and are not accompanied by the lock icon.

**5** Use the onscreen keyboard to enter the password for your network.

**6** Tap Join. You are now connected to the network and can access the Internet.

## Current Connection

If you're currently connected to a wireless network, you see that network's name in the Wi-Fi field in the left column of the Wi-Fi page. You can connect to a different network if you like; see the "Change Networks" task later in this section.

# Connect to a Public Wireless Hotspot

Most wireless networks and hotspots you find out in the real world are public networks—that is, you don't need a special password to connect. All you have to do is identify the network from the list and click to connect. (You'll know you're connected when you see the Wi-Fi icon in the status bar at the top of the screen.)

Some public networks, however, do require you to read through and agree to their terms of service after you connect but before you can use the network.

If this is the case, the site typically launches a connection page in your web browser. (In some instances, you may need to launch the Safari browser manually and try to access a web page; this will then launch the wireless connection page.) When you see the connection page from the wireless network or hotspot, you might need to check an "I read that" option or click a "connect" button.

For example, if you connect to the wireless networks at your local Starbucks or McDonald's, you need to manually log in from their respective log-in pages. In some instances, there may be a fee to use the wireless network, in which case you'll need to enter your credit card number to proceed.

---

### Hotel Wi-Fi

If you're connecting to the wireless network in a hotel without free Wi-Fi, you typically enter your room number to add the charges to your bill. Given that some hotels charge $10 or more per night, it's always a smart idea to shop around for hotels that offer free Wi-Fi.

---

(1) From the Settings screen, tap Wi-Fi in the left column.

**2** Make sure the Wi-Fi switch is in the "on" position. If it isn't, tap to turn it on.

**3** You see a list of the wireless networks and hotspots within range. Tap to select the desired network.

**4** If the hotspot requires you to sign in, it should launch a log-in screen and display a sign-in page. (If this doesn't happen automatically, you might need to manually launch the Safari web browser and then enter any web page address to open the sign-in page.) Check to agree to any terms and conditions and then click the "accept" or "sign in" button.

## Change Networks

Sometimes, especially out in public, you may have several different Wi-Fi networks available to you—and your iPad might automatically connect to one other than the one you wanted to connect to. If this is the case, it's easy enough to switch networks.

(1) From the Settings screen, observe the Wi-Fi field in the left column. The currently connected network is displayed. If you don't want to connect to this network, tap the Wi-Fi field to display a list of other available networks.

(2) Tap the network you want to connect to. Your iPad disconnects from the previous network and connects instead to the newly selected one.

## Connect to a Network You've Previously Connected To

This one's easier. When you're in range of a wireless network or hotspot you've previously connected to, your iPad automatically connects to it again. You don't have to choose it from the list; the iPad automatically discovers the network and makes the connection.

If it's a private network, like your home network, your iPad remembers the previously entered password and enters it for you. If it's a public network or hotspot that requires logging in via your web browser, you might be asked to agree to terms and click the "sign in" button again. (Or you might not; some sites allow reconnection without having to sign back in.)

## *It's Not All Good*

**Connection Problems**

Not all Internet connections are good. Sometimes the Wi-Fi network or hotspot you connect to has problems, which can keep your iPad from connecting to the Internet.

For example, the Wi-Fi hotspot I use at one of my local coffeehouses has a tendency to go missing every few hours. That is, I'll be connected one minute and the next minute find that I'm not connected—and that the hotspot itself is no longer visible on my iPad. Normally I wait a minute or two, the hotspot reappears, and my iPad reconnects. The best I can figure is that the coffeehouse's Wi-Fi router has rebooted, for some reason, which kicks everyone using it off until it powers back on.

You can also run into similar connection problems with your home Wi-Fi network. In many cases, the problem corrects itself automatically within a few minutes. If the problem persists, try turning off your iPad's Wi-Fi and then turning it back on. This forces your iPad to establish a new connection to the wireless network or hotspot, which often fixes the problem.

# Using the Safari Web Browser

After your iPad is connected to a Wi-Fi network or hotspot, you should have access (via that network) to the Internet. That's where all the fun stuff happens—including surfing the Web.

To surf the Web you need an app called a *web browser*. You're probably familiar with using a web browser on your computer or phone, and it works similarly on your iPad.

The browser that Apple includes with your iPad is called Safari. It works like most other web browsers, and it's ready for use whenever you are.

### Other Web Browsers

Safari is preinstalled on your iPad, but you can use other web browsers, if you like. The most popular non-Apple browser is Google Chrome, which is available for free from the iTunes App Store. Many people prefer Chrome to Safari, especially if they use Chrome on their computer or other devices.

## Launch the Safari Browser

The icon for the Safari browser is located by default in the Dock at the bottom of all Home screens.

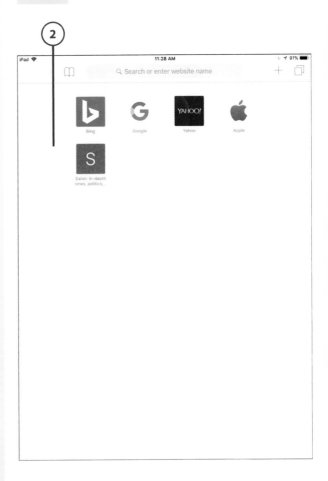

1 From the Dock or Home screen, tap the Safari icon to open the Safari browser.

2 The first time you launch Safari, it opens to a blank page, possibly with some website suggestions. If you've previously used the browser, it opens your last open page.

## Enter a Web Address

To go directly to a given website or web page, you must enter the web address of that page into the Address box at the top of the browser screen.

1 Tap within the Address box to display the onscreen keyboard.

**2** Enter the address of the web page you want to visit.

**3** As you type, Safari might suggest matching web pages. Tap any page to go to it. *Or…*

**4** Finish entering the full address and then tap Go on the keyboard to go to that page.

**5** The web page appears onscreen. Swipe up to scroll down the page.

**6** If a page has trouble loading, or if you want to refresh the content, you can reload the page by tapping the Reload button.

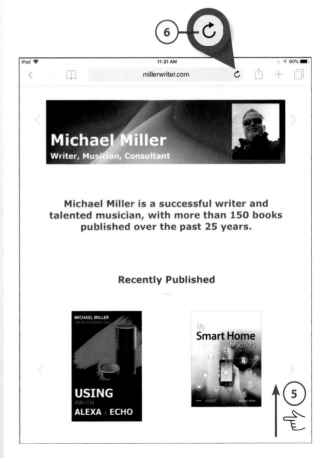

# >>>Go Further
## WEB ADDRESSES

A web address is called a Uniform Resource Locator, or URL. Technically, all URLs start with either http:// or (for secure sites) https://. You don't need to type this part of the URL, however; Safari assumes it and enters it automatically.

The main part of most web addresses starts with www followed by a dot, then the name of the website, then another dot and the domain identifier, such as com or org. As an example, my personal website is www.millerwriter.com. (You don't have to enter the "www."; Safari does this for you.)

## Use Web Links

Pages on the Web are often connected via clickable (on your iPad, tappable) links, called *web links*. A web link can be within a page's text (typically underlined or in a different color) or embedded in an image. Tap a link to go the linked-to page.

(1) On the current web page, tap the web link.

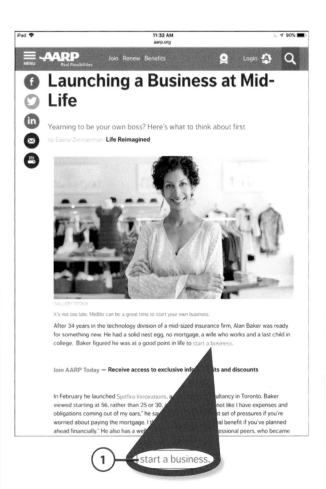

(2) The linked-to page displays.

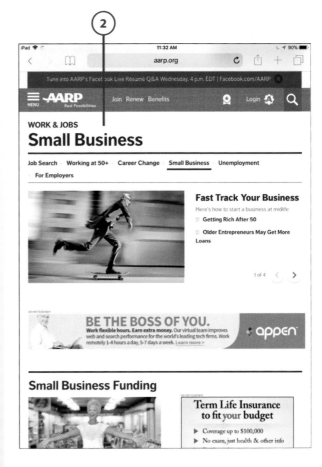

## View Multiple Pages in Tabs

Safari, like most modern web browsers, lets you open more than one page at a time, using *tabs*. You can open different web pages in different tabs, and easily switch between them.

(1) Tap the + icon to create a new tab.

2. Enter the desired web address into the new tab's Address box.

3. Tap a different tab to view that tab. *Or…*

4. Tap the tabs icon to view thumbnails of all open tabs.

5. Tap to switch to a different tab.

6. Swipe a tab to the left to close it. *Or…*

7. Tap the X on any tab to close it.

# Bookmark Pages

You can save any page you visit by *bookmarking* that page. It's easy, then, to revisit those pages you've bookmarked.

( **1** ) Navigate to the page you want to bookmark and then tap the Share icon. The Share panel displays.

( **2** ) Tap Add Bookmark.

( **3** ) Accept, edit, or enter the web page name in the Add Book-mark panel.

( **4** ) Tap Save. The page is now saved in your bookmarks.

## Favorites

Safari offers a special category of bookmarks, called Favorites. You save a page to your Favorites list by tapping Add to Favorites in the Share panel. All Favorites can be accessed by selecting Favorites in the Book-mark panel; Favorites are also displayed when you tap + to open a new empty tab.

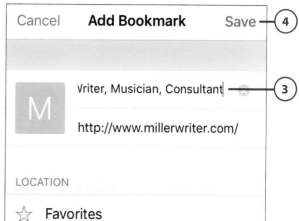

(5) Tap the Bookmark icon to open the Bookmark panel so you can view and revisit bookmarked pages.

(6) Make sure the Bookmarks tab is selected.

(7) Some bookmarks are organized into folders. Tap a folder name to view all bookmarks in that folder.

(8) Tap the name of a bookmark to open the corresponding web page.

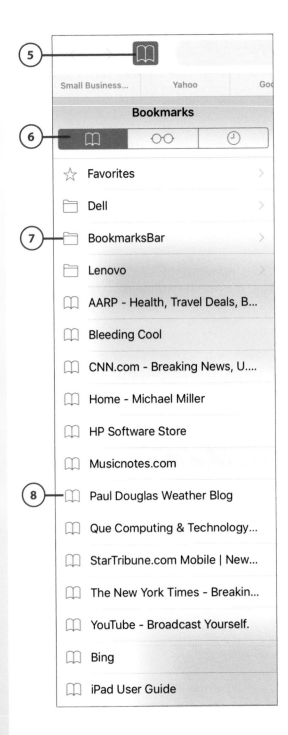

# >>>Go Further

## ADD TO HOME SCREEN

If you find yourself visiting a given web page with regularity, you might want to create a shortcut to it on your iPad's Home screen. When you add an icon for a page to the Home screen, tapping that icon launches Safari and opens that page.

To add an icon for a given web page, navigate to that page, tap the Share icon, and then tap Add to Home Screen. When the Add to Home panel appears, tap Add.

## Revisit Past Pages

How easy is it to return to a web page you've previously viewed? Safari keeps track of all your web browsing history, and revisiting a page is as easy as tapping it in the Bookmark panel.

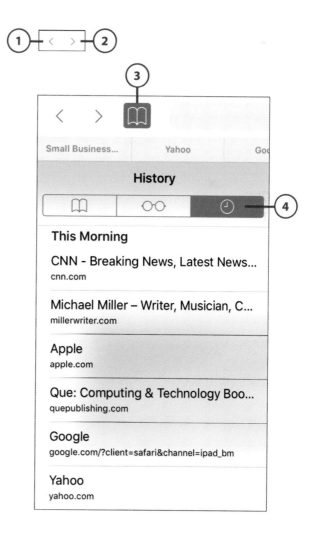

1. View the page you just visited by tapping the back (left arrow) icon.

2. Return to the next page by tapping the forward (right arrow) icon.

3. Tap the Bookmark icon to open the Bookmark panel.

4. Tap History to view pages you've visited, newest first.

# Browse the Web in Private

There are some web pages you might want to browse in private, and not let others know you've seen. When you want to browse anonymously, use Safari's Private mode. Pages you visit while in Private mode are not stored to your history, and are not otherwise tracked on your device or elsewhere.

1. From within Safari, tap the Tabs icon.

2. Tap Private.

3. Tap Done. You are now in private browsing mode.

4. Use Safari as normal. None of your activity will be tracked.

5. Tap the Tabs icon to exit private browsing mode.

6. Tap Private. You now see any tabs you had open before entering private browsing mode.

7. Tap Done.

## Configure Safari Settings

Safari is configured perfectly for most users by default, but there are a number of settings you can change to better personalize your Safari browsing experience. You access all these settings from your iPad's Settings screen.

① From the Dock or Home screen, tap the Settings icon to open the Settings screen.

② Scroll down the left column to the apps section and tap Safari.

③ Tap to edit any setting.

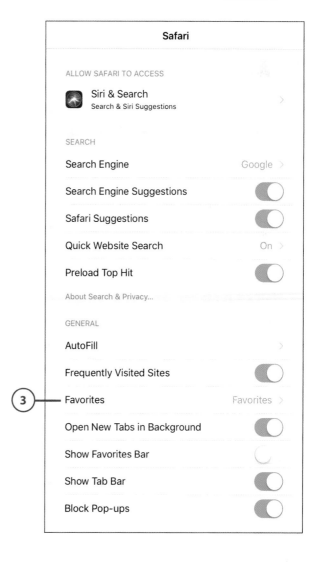

## >>>*Go Further*

### BLOCK ONLINE ADS

If you're like me, you quickly tire of all the online ads displayed on various web pages. (There are even ads on Facebook and many web-based email services!) Fortunately, you can block many if not all of these ads by installing an ad blocker extension in the Safari web browser. With an ad blocker installed, ads simply don't display on a web page—you see a blank space where the ad is supposed to be. Ad blockers don't hurt your browser or your iPad, and make browsing the Web that much more pleasant.

There are a variety of different ad blockers available in the iTunes App Store. Some are free; some aren't. The most popular ones include 1Blocker, Adblock, Norton Ad Blocker, and Weblock.

You may have to manually enable any ad blocker you install. From your iPad's Settings screen, tap Safari in the left column and then tap Content Blockers. (This option is not available until you install an ad blocker.) You can then enable or disable any ad blocker you've installed.

## Making the Web More Readable

Viewing web pages in Safari might not always be easy. Some pages, especially those not optimized for mobile viewing, may contain very small type or columns that wrap too far off the side of a page, making them less than readable.

Fortunately, there are ways to make small type on web pages a little larger—and web pages more readable, in general.

## Zoom into a Page

If you find a particular web page difficult to read, the first thing you can do
is try to zoom into the text—that is,
make the text larger onscreen.

1. Double-tap a block of text to
   make it fill the screen. (This
   works on some web pages, but
   not all.) Double-tap again to
   return the text to normal size.

2. Place two fingers together on
   the screen and then expand
   them. As you move your fingers
   apart, you zoom into that portion of the page. To zoom back
   out, pinch your two fingers back
   together.

GALLERY STOCK

Women age 65 and over are projected to make up 25 percent of the women's labor force in 2024.

Countering earlier trends of older women not participating in the workforce, the Bureau of
Labor Statistics (BLS) now projects that by 2024, women over 65 will make up roughly the
same percentage of the female workforce as older men do of the male workforce. Additionally,
BLS predicts that twice as many women over 55 will be in the labor force as women ages 16-
24, *Quartz* reports.

GALLERY STOCK

Women age 65 and over are projected to make up 25 percent

Countering earlier trends of older women not particip
Labor Statistics (BLS) now projects that by 2024, wor
same percentage of the female workforce as older me
BLS predicts that twice as many women over 55 will b
24, *Quartz* reports.

# Read Articles with Safari Reader

Safari Reader is a special reading mode that makes some web pages easier to read by removing ads, images, videos, and other extraneous elements. Not all web pages can be viewed with Safari Reader, but those that can are a lot easier to read than normal cluttered web pages. (Safari Reader is especially useful for reading articles on web news sites.)

1. If a page can be viewed with Safari Reader, it has a Reader icon in the Address bar. Tap this icon to switch to Reader mode.

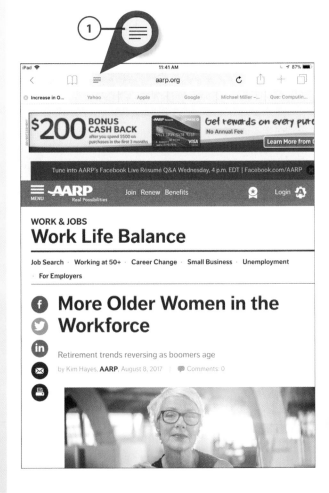

**2** Tap the Reader icon again to return to normal web page view.

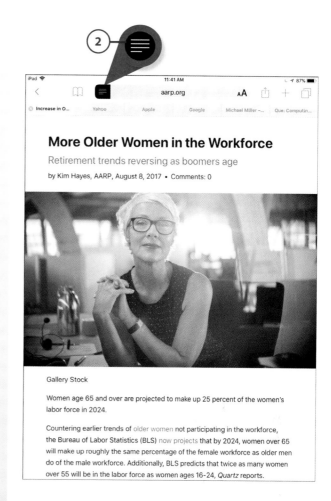

# Searching the Web

With so much information available on the Web, how do you find the stuff you want or need to know? It's easy, thanks to Google.

## Search the Web with Google

Google is the default search engine for the Safari web browser. You can search Google from within Safari, or from Google's own website.

**( 1 )** To search within Safari, tap within the Address box and enter your query.

**( 2 )** As you type, Safari displays several suggested searches. Go to the Google Search section and, if the search you want is listed, tap it.

**( 3 )** Otherwise, continue entering your query and tap Go on the onscreen keyboard. *Or....*

**( 4 )** Go directly to the Google web page at www.google.com, enter your query into the Search box, and tap the Search button.

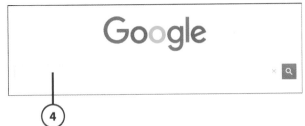

**5** Google displays a page of search results. Tap to open a given web page. *Or…*

**6** Display different types of results by selecting a results type along the top of the page—All, Images, Shopping, Videos, News, Maps, and so forth.

**7** Further refine your results by tapping Search. This displays a new search bar; tap to filter results by time and other options.

# Change Your Search Engine

If you'd rather use a different search engine with Safari, such as Microsoft's Bing or Yahoo!, you can do that.

( 1 ) From your iPad's Settings screen, tap Safari in the left column.

( 2 ) In the Search section, tap Search Engine.

( 3 ) Tap to select your desired search engine.

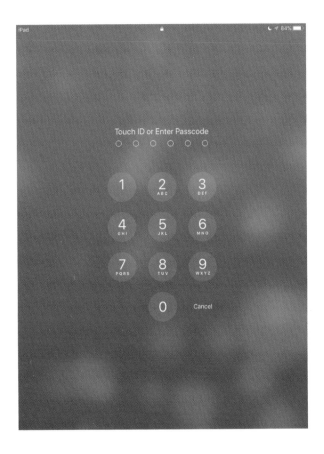

In this chapter, you learn how to keep your iPad safe from unwanted users.

→ Creating a Safer Lock Screen
→ Reducing the Risk of Theft
→ Staying Safe Online

6

# Keeping Your iPad Safe and Secure

Your iPad is a small portable device. That means that it could be relatively easy for someone to walk away with it while you're not looking. If someone takes your iPad—accidentally or on purpose—do you really want them digging around in everything you have stored inside?

Fortunately, there are ways to keep the information on your iPad safe from prying eyes. And there are lots of things you can do to minimize the risk of data theft if your iPad is lost or stolen.

In addition, there are things you can do to keep your information and identity safe when using your iPad to go online. The Internet can be a dangerous place, so it makes sense to be as safe as possible when you're connecting with your iPad.

# Creating a Safer Lock Screen

When it comes to keeping unwanted users away from the information stored on your iPad, your first and best line of defense is the device's Lock screen. If you play your cards right, strangers simply won't be able to get past the Lock screen to see anything else on your iPad.

## Set a Simple Passcode

By default, you unlock your iPad by simply pressing the Home button. That's convenient but far from secure; anybody picking up your device can unlock and see what you've stored inside.

A better approach is to establish a passcode (like a personal identification number, or PIN) to use to unlock your phone. Your passcode should consist of six numbers and be fairly random—or as random as you can remember.

When you've enabled passcode operation, you're prompted to enter your passcode after you've restarted your iPad or woken it from sleep.

( 1 ) From the Dock or Home screen, tap the Settings icon to open the Settings screen.

( 2 ) Tap Touch ID & Passcode in the left column.

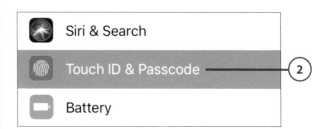

(3) Tap Turn Passcode On to display the Set Passcode panel.

(4) Enter your desired six-digit passcode.

## Creating a Passcode

Your passcode should be a series of digits you can remember but not something easily guessed. For example, you shouldn't use your birthdate as your passcode, nor should you set a common series of digits, such as 123456.

(5) When prompted, re-enter your six-digit passcode. Your passcode is now enabled, and you'll need to use it to unlock your device in the future—so write it down somewhere only you can find it!

## Data Encryption

Creating a passcode also turns on your iPad's data encryption. This uses your passcode as a key to encrypt Mail messages and all attachments stored on your device.

# Use Fingerprint Recognition with Touch ID

On all current iPads, you can employ even stronger security by using your fingerprint to unlock your device. This is called Touch ID, and you can also use it to make purchases in the iTunes Store and App Store, provide debit and credit card payment information, enter billing and shipping addresses, and provide contact info when making in-app purchases on apps that offer Apple Pay as a payment method.

To unlock your phone using Touch ID, all you have to do is press your thumb or finger (whichever fingerprint you registered) on the Home button, which doubles as the Touch ID sensor. When the iPad recognizes your fingerprint, it unlocks.

(1) From the Settings screen, tap Touch ID & Passcode in the left column.

(2) Tap Add a Fingerprint.

(3) Place your finger or thumb on the Home button.

(4) Follow the onscreen instructions to lift and place your finger as many times as necessary to register your fingerprint.

Cancel

# Touch ID

Use your fingerprint in place of your passcode or Apple ID password for purchases.

Start by placing your finger or thumb on the Home Button.

(3)

Cancel

# Place Your Finger

Lift and rest your finger on the Home button repeatedly.

(4)

5. When the process is complete, tap Continue. Your device is ready to use with Touch ID enabled.

## Erase Data After Too Many Passcode Attempts

As the ultimate "fail-safe" procedure, you can configure your iPad to erase all its stored data after ten failed passcode attempts. This ensures that none of your data will fall into the wrong hands, especially if your iPad is stolen.

1. From the Settings screen, tap Touch ID & Passcode in the left column.

2. Tap "on" the Erase Data switch.

3. Tap Enable in the confirmation box.

*It's Not All Good*

**Don't Forget Your Passcode**

If you forget your passcode and enter more than ten passcode attempts, you'll need to restore your iPad to use it again. Restoring your iPad to factory condition also deletes all the apps and data stored on the device. So don't forget your passcode—or you're in for a lot of unnecessary trouble!

# Reducing the Risk of Theft

As noted, your iPad (any size, from mini to Pro) is a relatively small device that's usually not plugged into anything, which means it can be easily heisted by those with impure hearts. (It's also easy to lose or leave behind, but that's another issue.) Given the attractiveness of the iPad to would-be thieves, how do you keep it away from sticky-fingered strangers?

## Keep Your iPad Safe

Your iPad is a particularly attractive target for thieves. Not only is it small and easy to steal, it's also a high-value item. All Apple products are considered luxury items, and thieves like items that can command a high price when sold or pawned.

Knowing this, you need to take extra care when you take your iPad out in public. If most crime consists of the criminally bent taking advantage of an opportunity, you want to reduce that opportunity as much as possible.

- Don't show it off. You may be very proud of your shiny new iPad, but don't make a big deal out of it. Don't show it off, don't make others aware of what you have. Treat it as low key as you can.

- Keep it hidden—especially when you're not around. An expensive iPad is not the sort of thing you want to leave sitting on the table at Starbucks when you go off to use the restroom. It's also not a good thing to leave visible on the front seat or dashboard of your car when you park. When you're not using it, put it away—in your purse or backpack or briefcase. Or just carry it around with you.

- Be aware of your surroundings. A near-empty coffeehouse with a table near the counter is safer than a crowded McDonald's filled with suspicious-looking characters. If the surroundings look unsafe, keep a firmer grasp on your iPad—or don't bring it out at all.

- Be cautious around strangers. Yes, there will be earnest individuals who see you using your new iPad and want to ask you all sorts of questions about it. There are also smooth-talking heisters who get you to show them your iPad purely as a ruse to grab it out of your hands. Beware the latter.

- Keep it safe even at home. You might think it would be okay to leave your iPad sitting out on the coffee table at your own house or apartment, but that's just tempting fate. If your house is broken into, small expensive items sitting in plain sight are the first things that thieves grab. And if your house has a lot of foot traffic (think friends of your kids or grandkids), a loose iPad on the table is pretty attractive for anyone with money or addiction problems. Even at home, keep your iPad in a safe and private place.

In other words, be smart about how you use and store your iPad, and you can remove a lot of the risk involved.

## Enable iPad Tracking

What do you do if your iPad is stolen or even just lost? Fortunately, your iPad includes an app, called Find My iPhone, that you can use to track a lost or stolen device.

---

### iPhone or iPad

The Find My iPhone app gets its name from its original target audience: iPhone users. (Statistically, there are more iPhones lost and stolen than iPads—probably because of the smaller size.) Don't get too hung up on the name, however; you can use the Find My iPhone app to find your lost or stolen iPad.

---

Before you can track a lost or stolen device, you first have to turn on Find My iPad.

( 1 ) From the Settings screen, tap Accounts & Passwords in the left column.

( 2 ) Tap iCloud.

( 3 ) Tap Find My iPad.

( 4 ) Tap "on" the Find My iPad switch. (This may be enabled by default.)

( 5 ) If you want the location of your iPad to be automatically sent to Apple before the battery dies, tap "on" the Send Last Location switch.

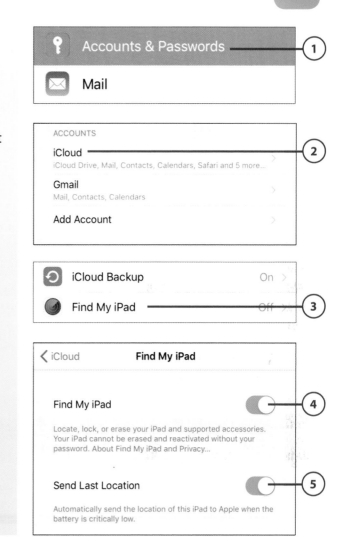

## Track a Lost or Stolen iPad

If your lost or stolen iPad is connected to a Wi-Fi network (or, for cellular models, to either a Wi-Fi or cellular network), and if you've enabled the app previously, Find My iPhone can locate your missing device. Naturally, you can't open Find My iPhone on your missing iPad, but you can use the app on another person's device or from the Web, at www.icloud.com/find.

Let's look at how you use Find My iPhone on another iPad, iPhone, or computer to find a lost or stolen device.

(1) From another iOS device, or from the www.icloud.com website, tap the Find iPhone icon. (You might need to sign into your iCloud account to proceed; you may also be prompted to allow access to your location while you're using the app.)

(2) Your device appears centered on the map. You should also see a panel of options for this device. (You might need to tap the device on the map to see this panel.)

(3) Tap Play Sound to play an alert sound on your iPad for two minutes. (This works even if the device has been muted.)

(4) Tap Lost Mode to immediately lock your iPad with a passcode and display a custom message onscreen, along with your contact number. (Lost Mode automatically enables Location Services, which is used to track your device's location.)

(5) Tap Erase iPad to delete all the data and media on your iPad and restore it to the original factory settings. Employ this option as a last resort to keep anyone from accessing your personal data or using your iPad to make unauthorized payments using Apple Pay.

# Staying Safe Online

Much of what you do on your iPad is done over the Internet, via either the Safari web browser or apps that use online resources. Unfortunately, the Internet can be a scary place. There are certain predators who target older users online, and for good reasons. Many older computer users are more trusting than younger users, and they're also less tech savvy. In addition, older people often have large nest eggs that are attractive to online predators, and older computer users are often ashamed to report being taken advantage of.

It all adds up to a potentially dangerous environment for older people—which means you need to learn how to protect yourself when you're online. You need to be able to identify the most common online threats and scams and know how to avoid becoming a victim.

## Protect Against Identity Theft

Online predators want your personal information—your real name, address, online usernames and passwords, bank account numbers, and the like. It's called *identity theft*, and it's a way for a con artist to impersonate you—both online and in the real world. If your personal data falls into the hands of identity thieves, they can use it to hack into your online accounts, make unauthorized charges on your credit card, and maybe even drain your bank account.

There are many ways for criminals to obtain your personal information. Almost all involve tricking you, in some way or another, into providing this information of your own free will. Your challenge is to avoid being tricked.

One of the most common techniques used by identity thieves is called *phishing*. It's called that because the other party is "fishing" for your personal information, typically via fake email messages and websites.

## It's Not All Good

**Phishing Means Phony**

A phishing scam typically starts with a phony email message that appears to be from a legitimate source, such as your bank, the postal service, PayPal, or other official institution. This email purports to contain important information that you can see if you tap the enclosed link. That's where the bad stuff starts.

If you tap the link in the phishing email, you're taken to a fake website masquerading as the real site, complete with logos and official-looking text. You're encouraged to enter your personal information into the forms on this fake web page; when you do so, your information is sent to the scammer, and you're now a victim of identity theft.

How can you avoid falling victim to a phishing scam? There are several things you can do:

- Look at the sender's email address. Most phishing emails come from an address different from the one indicated by the (fake) sender.

- Look for poor grammar and misspellings. Many phishing schemes come from outside the U.S. by scammers who don't speak English as their first language. As such, you're likely to find questionable phrasing and unprofessional text— not what you'd expect from your bank or other professional institution.

- If you receive an unexpected email, no matter the apparent source, do *not* tap any of the links in the email. If you think there's a legitimate issue from a given website, go to that site manually in Safari and access your account from there.

- Some phishing messages include attached files that you are urged to open to display a document or image. Do *not* open any of these attachments; they might contain malware that can steal personal information from your device. (While malware isn't as much of a threat to iPads as it is to personal computers, you still want to avoid opening unexpected email attachments.)

**Malware Threats**

If you're a long-time computer user, you're probably familiar with the threat posed by computer viruses, spyware, and other malicious software (malware). Computers are easily infected by these harmful programs. Fortunately, your iPad is not as easily infected; due to technological safeguards built into the iOS operating system, the malware risk for iPad users is extremely low. So don't worry too much about malware on your iPad—but still remain vigilant, nonetheless.

# Keep Your Private Information Private

Identity theft can happen any time you make private information public. This has become a special issue on social networks, such as Facebook, where users tend to forget that most everything they post is publicly visible—and often share information about birthdays, schools attended, and even phone numbers.

None of this might sound dangerous, until you realize that all of these items are the type of personal information many companies use for the "secret questions" their websites use to reset users' passwords. A fraudster armed with this publicly visible information could log onto your account on a banking website, for example, reset your password (to a new one he provides), and thus gain access to your banking accounts.

The solution to this problem, of course, is to enter as little personal information as possible when you're online. For example, you don't need to—and shouldn't—include your street address or phone number in a comment or reply to an online news article. Don't give the bad guys anything they can use against you!

# Protect Against Online Fraud

Identity theft isn't the only kind of online fraud you might encounter. Con artists are especially creative in concocting schemes that can defraud unsuspecting victims of thousands of dollars.

Most of these scams start with an email or social media message that promises something for nothing. Maybe the message tells you that you've won a lottery, or you are asked to help someone in a foreign country deposit funds in a U.S. bank account. You might even receive requests from people purporting to be far-off relatives who need some cash to bail them out of some sort of trouble.

The common factor in these scams is that you're eventually asked to either send money (typically via wire transfer) or provide your bank account information—with which the scammers can drain your money faster than you can imagine. If you're naïve or gullible enough then the damage can be considerable.

Protecting yourself from the huge number of these online scams is both difficult and simple. The difficulty comes from the sheer number of scams and their amazing variety. The simplicity comes from the fact that the best way to deal with any such scam is to use common sense—and ignore it.

Most online fraud is easily detectable by the simple fact that it arrives out of the blue and seems too good to be true. So if you get an unsolicited offer that promises great riches, you know to tap Delete—pronto.

Savvy Internet users train themselves to recognize scam messages at a glance. That's because most scam messages come from complete strangers, and often don't even address you by name. Most of these messages are rife with spelling and grammatical errors, as scammers frequently operate from foreign countries and do not use English as their first language.

A typical scam email promises you large sums of money for little or no effort on your part. Either in the first or subsequent messages (if you respond), you will be asked to provide your bank account number, credit card number, or other personal information—or are asked to provide money upfront for various fees, or to pay the cost of expediting the process.

If you receive a message that you think is a scam, delete it. In fact, it's a good idea to ignore all unsolicited messages, of any type. No stranger will send you a legitimate offer via email or Facebook; it just doesn't happen.

Also, and this should go without saying, but you just shouldn't give in to greed. If an offer sounds too good to be true, it is; there are no true "get rich quick" schemes.

# >>>Go Further

## WHAT TO DO IF YOU'VE BEEN SCAMMED

What should you do if you think you've been the victim of an online fraud? There are a few steps you can take to minimize the damage:

- If the fraud involved transmittal of your credit card information, contact your credit card company to put a halt to all unauthorized payments—and to limit your liability to the first $50.

- If you think your bank accounts have been compromised, contact your bank to put a freeze on your checking and savings accounts—and to open new accounts, if necessary.

- Contact one of the three major credit reporting bureaus to see if stolen personal information has been used to open new credit accounts—or max out your existing accounts.

- Contact your local law enforcement authorities—fraud is illegal, and it should be reported as a crime.

- Report the fraud to your state attorney general's office.

- File a complaint with the Federal Trade Commission (FTC) via the form located at www.ftccomplaintassistant.gov.

- Contact any or all of the following consumer-oriented websites: Better Business Bureau (www.bbb.org), Internet Crime Complaint Center (www.ic3.gov), and the National Consumers League's Fraud Center (www.fraud.org).

Above all, don't provide any additional information or money to the scammers. As soon as you suspect you've been had, halt all contact and cut off all access to your bank and credit card accounts. Sometimes the best you can hope for is to minimize your losses.

# Shop Safely

Many people use their iPads to shop online. It's convenient, and you don't have to bother with driving to the store and dealing with all those crowds.

Despite the huge upsurge in online shopping, many users are still reticent to provide their credit card information over the Internet. It is possible, after all, for shady sellers to take your money and not deliver the goods, or even for high-tech thieves to intercept your credit card information over the Internet—or from a public Wi-Fi hotspot.

All that said, online shopping remains immensely popular, and is generally quite safe. You can make your online shopping even safer by following this advice:

- Don't shop in public. While you can shop over any wireless connection, public connections (like the kind you find at coffeehouses and restaurants) aren't as secure as the private connection you have on your home network. It's possible for individuals with the right equipment to intercept public wireless signals, and thus skim your credit card and other personal information. While this sort of data theft doesn't happen often, it's better to make your online purchases over a safer private connection.

- Shop only at secure websites. Whatever you're shopping for online, make sure you're using a website that offers secure connections. (A secure web address starts with https:, not the normal http:.) A secure website encrypts the data you send to it, so even if it is intercepted by a third party, that party can't read it. Most major online retailers have secure sites.

- Don't leave your credit card number on file with online retailers. As tempting as it is to have your favorite retailer store your credit card info for future purchases, that also means they have a copy of it on their servers—and anyone breaking into their servers can then steal your information. Instead, enter your credit card number fresh with each new purchase; it's just safer.

If you shop at major online retailers, you're probably going to be safe. Same thing if you buy from smaller sellers on eBay or Etsy; those sites have their own robust security mechanisms in place. If it's a retailer you haven't heard of before, check them out by doing a Google search and reading online reviews; if the reviews trend toward the negative, shop elsewhere. And always, always shop from a merchant that offers a toll-free number for customer support, just in case something goes wrong.

Do all of these things and shopping with your iPad will be not only convenient but also safe.

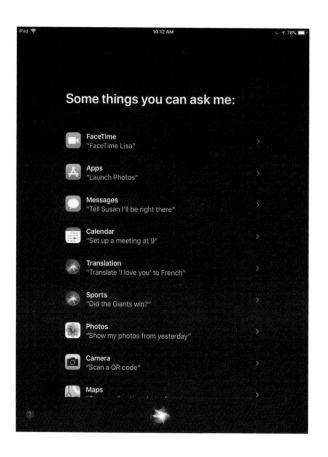

In this chapter, you learn how to use Siri to control iPad operations and query for specific information.

→ Getting to Know Siri, Your iPad's Virtual Personal Assistant
→ Using Siri to Control Your iPad and Apps
→ Using Siri to Find Interesting and Useful Information

7

# Controlling Your iPad— and More—with Siri

Siri isn't a person; it's a thing, sort of. To be precise, Siri is a piece of software that functions as a virtual personal assistant on your iPad and other Apple devices. It's a way of both operating your iPad using voice commands and searching the Internet for relevant information.

Siri understands natural speech, so all you have to do is talk to your iPad using plain-English questions and commands and Siri knows what you're asking and responds accordingly. You can use Siri not just to ask questions and find information, but also to control the operations of your iPad.

# Getting to Know Siri, Your iPad's Virtual Personal Assistant

Siri functions as a high-tech personal assistant on your iPad. In reality, Siri is nothing more than an app on your device, albeit one that's highly functional and very high tech. The Siri app essentially serves as a voice-controlled interface between you and various operations on your iPad, enabling you to perform many operations via voice commands.

You can use Siri to initiate most operations on your iPad. Use Siri to compose and send messages, schedule events, watch videos, and listen to music, as well as launch apps, turn on Do Not Disturb mode, and raise and lower your iPad's volume levels.

Siri can also keep you updated on current sports scores, news events, and weather conditions. You can even ask Siri factual questions, such as "How many miles is it to the moon?" or "How much is five times seven?"

## Configure Siri

There are several things you can change to personalize your own experience with Siri. You can change Siri's voice, the language she speaks, and even whether you can summon Siri merely by saying, "Hey Siri!"

1. From the Dock or Home screen, tap the Settings icon to open the Settings screen.

2. In the left column, tap Siri & Search.

(**3**) To summon Siri without first tapping the Home button, tap "on" the Listen for "Hey Siri!" switch. You are prompted to set up Siri to recognize your voice; follow the onscreen instructions. ("Hey Siri!" only works when your iPad is connected to external power.)

(**4**) By default, you can summon Siri by pressing and holding your iPad's Home button. To disable Home button activation, tap "off" the Press Home for Siri switch.

(**5**) By default, you can summon Siri from any screen, including the Lock screen (before you unlock it). If you don't want Siri available to your locked device, tap "off" the Allow Siri When Locked switch.

(**6**) Tap Language and then make a selection to change the language that Siri speaks.

(**7**) To change Siri's speaking voice, tap Siri Voice and make a new selection. Choose from American (default), Australian, or British accents, in either Male or Female (default) voices.

(**8**) By default, Siri provides voice and onscreen feedback. To disable this in favor of onscreen feedback only, tap Voice Feedback and then tap Hands-Free Only.

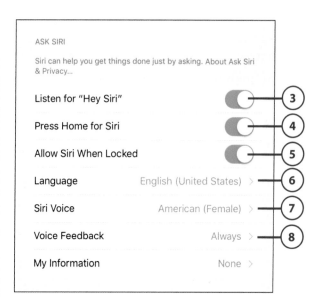

ASK SIRI

Siri can help you get things done just by asking. About Ask Siri & Privacy...

| | |
|---|---|
| Listen for "Hey Siri" | ⬤ — (3) |
| Press Home for Siri | ⬤ — (4) |
| Allow Siri When Locked | ⬤ — (5) |
| Language | English (United States) > — (6) |
| Siri Voice | American (Female) > — (7) |
| Voice Feedback | Always > — (8) |
| My Information | None > |

( 9 ) Siri can operate more effectively if it knows more about you. Tap My Information and select your name from the resulting contacts list.

( 10 ) By default, Siri offers suggestions when you use your iPad's Search function. If you find this too intrusive, tap "off" the Suggestions in Search switch.

( 11 ) Also by default, Siri offers suggestions when you use your iPad's Look Up function. To disable this, tap "off" the Suggestions in Look Up switch.

( 12 ) Siri can also function within individual apps. To change how Siri works within a given app, tap the name of that app and then tap "off" the Search & Siri Suggestions switch.

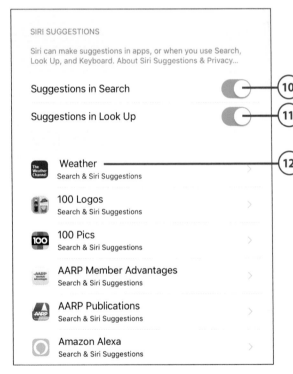

## Summon Siri

(**1**) Press and hold the iPad's Home button. *Or...*

(**2**) If you've enabled "Hey Siri!" functionality (and your iPad is plugged into external power), simply speak the words "Hey Siri!" into the device.

(**3**) You'll see the words "What can I help you with?" onscreen. Speak your question or command.

### Louder or Softer

To adjust the volume level of Siri's voice, use the volume up and down buttons on the side of your iPad.

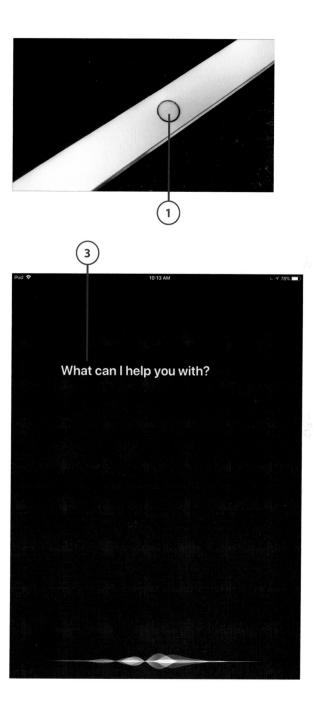

# Using Siri to Control Your iPad and Apps

Instead of tapping onscreen icons or controls, you can use Siri's voice commands to perform many operations on your iPad. This makes Siri essential for using the iPad for those with accessibility issues—and just more convenient for the rest of us.

### Connect to Query

To use Siri, your iPad must be connected to the Internet.

## Launch Apps

The first thing you can do with Siri is launch apps on your iPad. To do so, say something like

*Launch app name.*

For example, to launch the Facebook app, say

*Launch Facebook.*

## Control System Functions

You can use Siri to enable, disable, and control various system functions on your iPad. Say the following:

*Turn Wi-Fi on.*

*Turn Bluetooth off.*

*Increase the brightness.*

## Send and Receive Messages

Siri is useful if you want to send or receive messages via the Messages or Mail apps. To read messages, say the following:

*Read my messages.*

*Read messages from Bob.*

*Read my last message from Sally.*

To reply to a message, say the following, and then say "Send":

*Reply I'll see you then.*

*Reply okay.*

To create a new message, say any of the following, and then say "Send":

*New email to John Jones.*

*Send a message to Oliver saying I'm free tomorrow.*

*Email Clark and say I received the pictures, thanks.*

You can also use Siri to initiate FaceTime conversations. Say something like

*FaceTime Hayley.*

*End conversation.*

## Manage Meetings, Events, and Reminders

If you use your iPad to manage your meetings, events, and reminders, Siri definitely can come in handy.

Here are a few commands to try regarding meetings and appointments:

*What's on my calendar tomorrow?*

*Do I have a meeting at noon?*

*Where is my ten o'clock meeting?*

*Set up a meeting with Hal at two.*

*Cancel my eleven o'clock appointment.*

*Reschedule my meeting with Dinah to next Friday at ten.*

You can even create complex events, complete with other attendees. Just tell Siri as much as possible about the event, like this:

*Make an event for nine forty-five tomorrow called Neighborhood Association with Randy Jones, Don Emory, Betsy Griffin, and Samuel Hancock.*

Then there are reminders, of which Siri can be quite helpful. Say something like

*Remind me to pay the electric bill by the fifteenth.*

*Remind me to stop at the drug store when I leave here.*

*Remind me to buy milk.*

*Remind me to feed the fish when I get home.*

You can also use Siri to create notes. Say something like

*Create a new note* or *Make a note named Parts List*, and then dictate your note.

*Find my note about plumbers.*

You can even use Siri to set alarms and timers. Say something like

*Set an alarm for six am.*

*Set an alarm for three hours from now.*

*Turn off all alarms.*

*Set a timer for fifteen minutes.*

## Take and View Pictures

If you use the camera in your iPad, you can control it via Siri voice commands. Say something like

*Open camera.*

*Take a picture.*

*Take a selfie.*

To view pictures you've taken, say something like

*Show me photos from October.*

*Show me photos I took last year.*

*Show me photos of Dave.*

*Show me photos of Florida.*

*Show me photos from my Family album.*

## Listen to Music

If you use your iPad's Music app to listen to music, you can control what you listen to via Siri's voice commands. Try the following:

*Play music.*

*Pause music.*

*Stop.*

*Next song.*

*Previous song.*

To play specific music, say something like

*Play James Taylor.*

*Play "Proud Mary."*

*Play* Abbey Road.

*Play the playlist My Favorites.*

*Play the radio station Classic Rock.*

You can even shuffle the music you call up:

*Play Classic Soul shuffled.*

To find out more about the currently playing song, say something like

*What's playing?*

*Who sings this song?*

*Who is this song by?*

## >>>Go Further

### SMART HOME CONTROL

If you use Apple's Home app to control HomeKit-enabled devices in your home, you can use Siri to control those devices via voice commands. For example, you can tell Siri to do the following:

*Turn off the lights.*

*Turn down the dining room lights.*

*Dim the lights.*

*Set brightness to 50 percent.*

*Set the temperature to 72 degrees.*

*Turn on the coffeemaker.*

After you get a device set up, experiment with different commands to see just what Siri can control. Learn more in Chapter 18, "Controlling Your Smart Home."

# Using Siri to Find Interesting and Useful Information

Siri isn't just about controlling apps and settings on your iPad. You can also use Siri to find information—like searching the Web with voice commands.

## Find Information

Probably one of the most used functions for Siri is to find information. It's like using Google, but Siri returns a real answer to any question you ask.

You can ask Siri about the weather:

*What's the current temperature?*

*Is it going to rain today?*

*What's the weather like this weekend?*

Or about sports:

*What's the score of the Vikings game?*

*Who's in first place in the National League West?*

Or the stock market:

*How is the stock market doing today?*

*What is Apple's stock price?*

Interested in a new movie?

*Is the new* Avengers *movie any good?*

*What time is the* Star Trek *movie playing?*

Or just ask Siri about anything in which you're interested. Here are a few queries to try:

*How far is it to the moon?*

*How old is Tom Hanks?*

*Who is prime minister of Canada?*

*Who wrote* War and Peace*?*

# Solve Equations and Make Conversions

Siri is also great for converting various measurements. Here's a sampling of what you can ask:

*How many kilometers are there in a mile?*

*How many dollars in a Euro?*

*Convert 2.7 ounces to grams.*

*Convert $47 to pounds.*

Conversions are fun, but what about basic math problems? Siri can handle all sorts of equations, such as

*What is a 20 percent tip on $83?*

*What is 238 times 72?*

*What is 22 divided by 2?*

*What is the square root of pi?*

# Find Businesses and Get Directions

Siri can help you find nearby businesses (and information about them). Say something like

*Where is the nearest gas station?*

*Are there any good Chinese restaurants nearby?*

*How late is Home Depot open?*

*Is CVS open right now?*

You can also use Siri to find and make reservations via the Yelp and OpenTable apps:

*Find me a table for two for dinner tomorrow.*

*Book me a table for four at noon on Thursday at The Fancy Pear.*

Then there are directions, of which you can ask Siri:

*Show me how to get to the history museum.*

*Find directions to 10223 Main Street.*

You can even ask Siri other travel-related questions, such as

*Check flight status of United 231.*

*When does Southwest 72 arrive?*

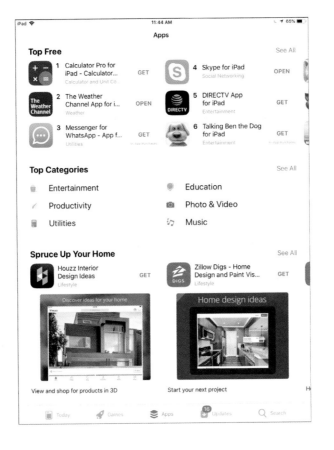

In this chapter, you learn how to find, purchase, install, and use apps on your iPad.

→ Working with Apps

→ Finding New Apps in the App Store

→ Managing Installed Apps

→ Multitasking on Your iPad

# Installing and Using Apps

Most of what you do on your iPad you do via *applications*, or *apps*. An app is a self-contained program designed to perform a particular task or serve a specific purpose. There are apps for news and weather, apps for email and text messaging, apps for Facebook and Pinterest, even apps for listening to music and watching videos. Whatever you want to do on your iPad, there's probably an app for it.

Your new iPad came with more than a dozen apps preinstalled, but these aren't the only apps you can use. There are tens of thousands of additional apps available, most for free or low cost, in Apple's online App Store. It's easy to find new apps and install them on your iPad—and then use them every day.

# Working with Apps

To do just about anything on your iPad, you have to learn how to work with apps. All the apps currently installed on your iPad are displayed on the various Home screens. Each icon on the screen represents a different app. When you install a new app, an icon for that app appears on the Home screen.

## Launch an App from the Home Screen

You open apps from the iPad's Home screen.

1. Press the Home button to return to the main Home screen.

2. Navigate to the Home screen that displays the icon for the app you want to open.

3. Tap the icon to open the app.

# Launch an App from the Dock

You can also launch apps from the Dock, which floats at the bottom of every screen on your iPad. (Chapter 3, "Personalizing the Way Your iPad Looks and Works," explains how to customize the apps on the Dock.)

( 1 ) The Dock floats above every Home screen and many apps. If the Dock is hidden, display it by swiping up slightly from the bottom of the screen.

( 2 ) Tap an icon on the Dock to open that app.

( 3 ) If you've recently viewed files or documents with a given productivity app, long-press the app's icon on the Dock to view a panel that displays those files.

( 4 ) Tap Show More to display even more recent files.

( 5 ) Tap a file to open that file within the app.

## Search for an App

If you have a ton of apps installed on your iPad, it may be challenging to find a specific app you want. (Which Home screen did you put it on?) If this is the case, use your iPad's search function to find that one app you're looking for.

1. From the main Home screen, swipe from left to right to display the Cover Sheet. *Or...*

2. Swipe down from the center of the Home screen to display the Search panel.

3. Enter the name of the app you want into the Search box.

4. As you type, your iPad suggests matching apps. Tap the name of an app to open it.

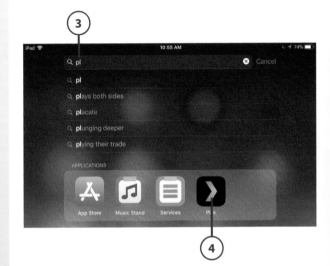

# Switch Between Apps

You can have multiple apps open at the same time, and easily switch between them.

(1) Press the Home button twice. *Or…*

(2) Swipe up from the bottom of any Home screen.

(3) You see Apple's App Switcher, which displays all your open apps. Swipe left or right to focus on other apps.

(4) Tap an app to switch to that app.

## Close an App

Apps remain open until you manually close them. When you're not using an app, it remains paused in the background, but it doesn't consume system resources. Because of this, you don't have to close an app when you're done with it—although you can if you want.

( 1 )  Press the Home button twice. *Or…*

( 2 )  Swipe up from any Home screen.

( 3 )  You now see the App Switcher, with all open apps displayed. Tap and drag the app up and off the screen until it disappears.

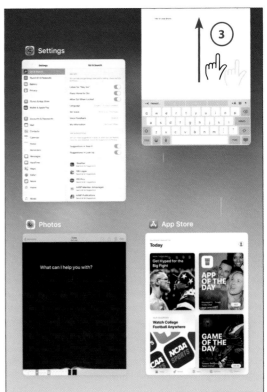

# Finding New Apps in the App Store

Where do you find new apps to use on your iPad? There's one central source that offers apps from multiple developers—Apple's App Store.

## Browse and Search the App Store

Apple's App Store is an online store that offers apps and games for iPads and iPhones. Most apps in the App Store are free or relatively low cost. It's easy to find new apps by either browsing or searching.

1. Tap the App Store icon to open the App Store.

2. Tap the Today tab to view stories and recommendations about featured apps and games.

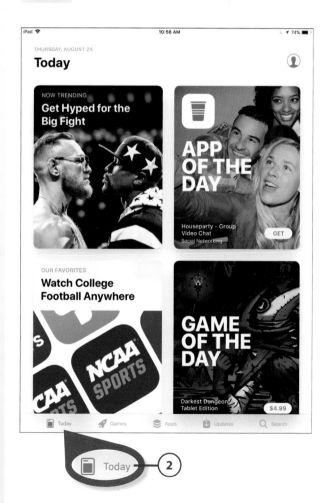

**3** Tap the Search tab to search for apps or games by name.

**4** Tap the Games tab to view new, top, and featured games for your iPad.

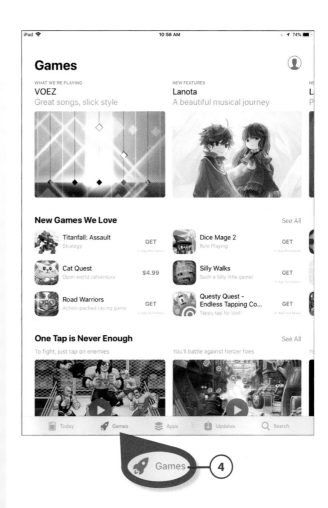

5. Tap the Apps tab to view new, top, and featured apps.

6. Swipe from right to left to see more apps/games in each list.

7. Scroll down to the Top Categories section to view apps/games by category.

8. Tap See All to view all categories.

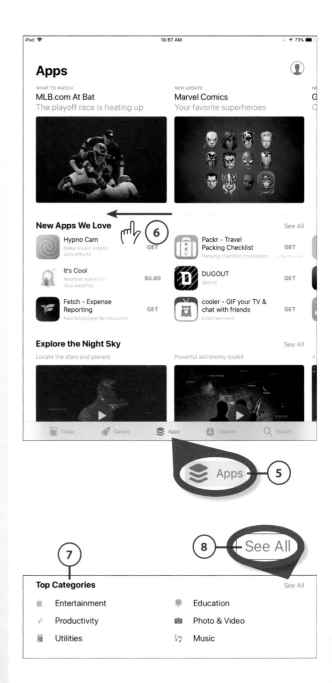

**9** Tap a category to view apps/ games in that category.

**10** Tap an app/game to view more about that item.

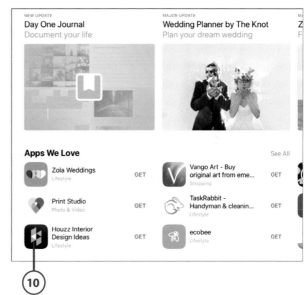

# Purchase and Download Apps

Many apps in the App Store are free. Others you have to pay for.

(1) Download a free app from the app panel by tapping the Get button.

(2) You see the details panel for that app; tap Install and, if prompted, enter the password for your Apple ID. The app is downloaded to and installed on your iPad.

## Locating and Moving Apps

When you install a new app, the icon for that app appears in the first empty space on the second or later Home screen. (New apps are not added to your main Home screen.) You can then move that icon to another position or screen if you like. (Learn more about moving and managing app icons in Chapter 3.)

(3) Instead of a Get button, a paid app displays a price button. Tap this button to initiate the purchase.

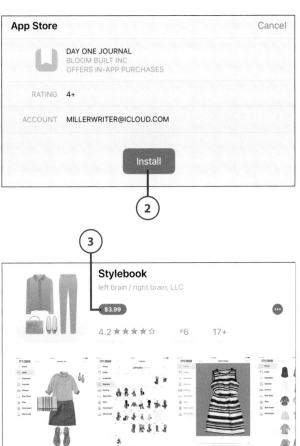

( **4** )  The details panel for a paid app displays the app's price. Tap the Purchase button.

( **5** )  The iTunes Store should recognize your Apple ID and then ask you for your password; if not, you need to enter both your Apple ID and password to sign in. The app is purchased and the download begins.

>>>*Go Further*
## PAYING FOR APPS

Naturally, you have to pay for those apps that have a price. Payment is automatic when you tap the Buy button, provided you're signed into the iTunes Store and have a credit card on file for your Apple ID.

You may have provided credit card information when you first set up your iPad or created your Apple ID. If not, you can add a credit card to your account at any time by using the Safari app to go to https://appleid.apple.com and signing into your Apple account. On the main page, scroll down to the Payment and Shipping section and tap Edit Payment Information. Enter your credit card number, expiration date, billing address, and the like, and then tap Save. This credit card will then be used for all your App Store purchases.

# Managing Installed Apps

Your iPad offers a variety of functions you can employ to better manage the apps you have installed on your device.

## View and Manage Purchased Apps

All the apps you've ever purchased are listed in the App Store app. Even if you've deleted an app from your device, you can still see that app and reinstall it on your iPad at any time.

1. From the Today tab in the App Store, tap the Profile icon to display the Account panel.

(**2**) Tap Purchased to display the Purchased panel.

(**3**) Tap the All tab to view all apps you've purchased.

(**4**) Apps that are currently installed on this device have an Open button. Tap the Open button to launch that app.

(**5**) Apps you've purchased but have yet to install or that you've since deleted (so they're not currently installed) have a cloud icon. Tap this Download icon to install an app on your device.

(**6**) The App Store even keeps track of apps you've installed on other devices (such as your iPhone) that you can also install on your iPad. Tap Not on This iPad at the top of the page.

(**7**) Tap the Download icon to install an app on your iPad.

# Update Your Apps

From time to time the apps on your iPad get updated. Some apps add new features, some merely include bug fixes. In any case, you need to keep your apps up to date, which you do from the App Store app. All updates are always free.

1. If you have apps that need updating, you see a number on the App Store icon. This number indicates how many apps you need to update. Tap the App Store icon to open the App Store.

2. From within the App Store, tap the Updates tab. All apps awaiting update are listed here.

3. To update an individual app, tap that app's Update button.

4. To update all apps with pending updates, tap Update All.

# Delete an App

Over time, you'll probably find that you've installed some apps that you no longer use. You may want to delete these apps to clear up any Home screen clutter and to free up storage space for new apps.

( 1 ) Navigate to the Home screen that contains the app you want to delete; then press and hold the app you want to delete. All the app icons start to wiggle.

( 2 ) Tap the X next to the app icon you want to delete.

( 3 ) Tap Delete at the prompt.

( 4 ) Press your iPad's Home button to return to the normal, non-wiggly Home screen.

## No X

If, when you press and hold an app's icon, you don't see a little X in the top-left corner that means you're looking at a system app that can't be deleted. Apps with Xs can be deleted; those without can't.

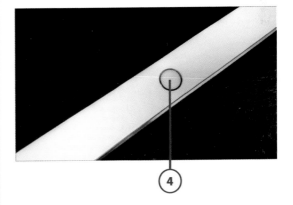

# Multitasking on Your iPad

Your iPad enables you to have multiple apps open simultaneously. Normally, you use one app full screen while the other apps hide in the background; you then use the App Switcher to change from one app to another.

You can also choose to run two apps onscreen at the same time. This type of multitasking is enabled by the Slide Over and Split View functions—both of which work better when you hold your iPad horizontally.

## Open a Second App with Slide Over

Slide Over enables you to open a second app onscreen without closing the one you're currently in. The second app (called the *side app*) appears in a narrow panel that floats on top of the first app on the right or left side of the screen.

### Designed for iOS 11

To use an app with Slide Over or Split View, that app must be specifically designed to work with iOS 11. Almost all of Apple's built-in apps work with these views, but not all third-party apps have been appropriately updated. If you try to move into Slide Over or Split View with a given app and it doesn't work, that's because the app is not yet compatible with these new iOS 11 features.

① With the first app open, drag the icon from the Dock for the app you want in the Slide Over panel up onto the main screen, then release. *Or…*

(2) From any Home screen, tap and slightly drag the icon for the app you want in the Slide Over panel.

(3) While still dragging, use a second finger to tap the icon for the app you want full-screen. The full-screen app opens, and you can finish dragging the other icon to create the Slide Over panel.

(4) You can interact with the main app and the Slide Over app at the same time; they're both "live."

(5) Sometimes the Slide Over panel hovers over important information on the full-screen app, and you might need to move it to use the other app. To move the Slide Over panel to the other side of the screen, press the handle at the top of the panel and drag it to the other side.

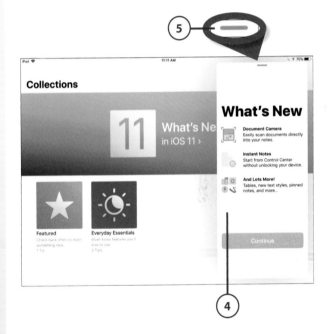

6. To display a different app in the Slide Over panel, tap and drag that app's icon from the Dock onto the screen.

7. To turn the Slide Over panel into a Split View app, flick down the handle at the top of the panel.

8. To hide the Slide Over panel, press the handle at the top of the panel and drag it off the right side of the screen.

9. To redisplay the Slide Over panel, swipe in from the right side of the screen.

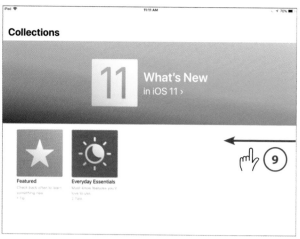

# Display Two Apps at Once with Split View

The Slide Over feature lets you see two apps at once, although the second app is in a narrow panel. If you want to display two apps on the screen in more equally sized panels, use iPad's Split View.

① With the first app open, tap and drag the icon for the second app from the Dock.

② Drag the icon to the right edge of the screen; the first app should shrink to the left. You can now drop the icon for the second app into the blank space at the right side of the screen.

(3) The two apps are displayed side by side. To change the space assigned to each app, drag the handle between the two apps left or right, as necessary.

(4) To turn a Split View app into a Slide Over panel, flick down the app handle at the top of that app.

(5) To return to single-app view, drag the app divider handle to the right edge of the screen (to close the right-hand app) or to the left (to close the left-hand app).

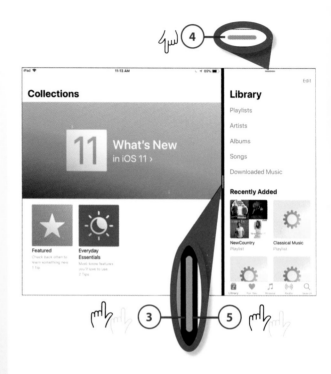

# Drag and Drop Text and Pictures Between Apps

Apple's new iOS 11 lets you easily copy text and pictures between apps using either Slide Over or Split View. You do this with simple drag and drop.

(1) In either Slide Over or Split View, press to select the text or picture you want to copy.

( 2 ) Still holding down the selection, drag it to the point in the other app where you want to copy it.

( 3 ) Release your finger, and the item is placed in the second app.

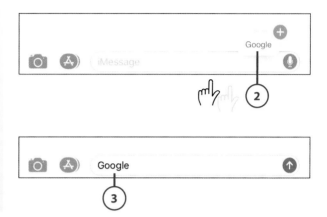

# >>>Go Further

## PICTURE IN PICTURE

Your iPad also offers a picture in picture mode for use with certain apps. If you're watching a TV show or movie, or conducting a FaceTime video chat, you can keep that video or chat playing in a separate window while you do other stuff on the iPad screen. The video or chat appears in a small window that floats on top of the active app, so you can keep watching while you work.

To activate picture in picture mode, tap the Picture in Picture icon (in the video app) or press the iPad's Home button (when using FaceTime). The video screen shrinks to a corner of your display. Your Home screen or other apps appear beneath the video window, and you can then use whatever app you want while the video or chat keeps playing.

When you display the picture in picture window, you can make the window bigger by expanding two fingers on the window. Pinch two fingers together to make the video window smaller. And, if you want, you can use your finger to drag the video window to a different corner or position on the screen.

To return the video window to full screen, tap the window to display the control icons and then tap the Picture in Picture icon.

‹ Mailboxes Edit

# All Inboxes

🔍 Search

**Fred Miller** 2:19 PM
Jackson
Here's a pic of Jackson I took last week at the park. Love that smile!

**Google Analytics** Yesterday
Ask a question, get an answer in Googl...
Get instant answers to your marketing and analytics questions in Google Anal...

**Screen Time** Yesterday
Screen Time Daily Summary for Augus...
Summary for August 22 Hayley: 4 hr 21 mins 6 apps used: Minecraft · Pocket...

**WordPress** Tuesday
[Michael Miller] Please moderate: "Onl...
A new comment on the post "Online Content for Music Books Available Aga...

**Fred Miller** Friday
Lunch next week?
Are you free for lunch any day next week? My schedule's open, let me kno...

● **Fred Miller** Friday
Cable problems?
Are you having trouble with your cable

Checking for Mail...

From: Fred Miller ›
To: molehillgroup@gmail.com › Hide

M

## Jackson

Today at 2:19 PM

Here's a pic of Jackson I took last week at the park. Love that smile!

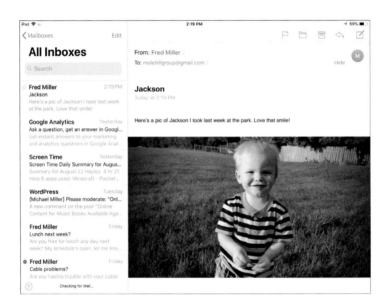

In this chapter, you learn how to use your iPad's Mail app to send and receive email messages.

→ Configuring the Mail App
→ Sending and Receiving Messages

9

# Sending and Receiving Email

For the past several decades, email has been an important means for people to communicate with each other. Whether you're trading messages with friends and family members, receiving messages from groups to which you belong, or receiving confirmation messages after you've purchased merchandise online, it's important to have an email address and master the workings of a full-featured email program.

The email app included with your iPad is called Mail. You can use Mail to send and receive emails using your Apple email account, or configure the app to work with other email services, such as Yahoo! Mail and Google's Gmail.

## Configuring the Mail App

You use your iPad's Mail app to send and receive email messages. It works like most other email apps, and can work with your Apple iCloud email, Microsoft Outlook, Google's Gmail, Yahoo! Mail, and other email services.

# Add an Email Account

When you set up your iPad with your Apple ID, that information was automatically added to the Mail app. So if you have an Apple or iCloud email address, that account is already set up in the Mail app—there's nothing more you need to do to get started.

If you have an email address with a different service, however, you can add that account to the Mail app and check that email from the app. The Mail app lets you add multiple accounts and check messages from multiple addresses and inboxes. It's convenient to be able to check all your emails in one place.

While you can still go to the Gmail website for your email, for example, it's just as easy to check your Gmail messages from within the Mail app. All you have to do is configure the Mail app for the new account.

( 1 )  From the Dock or Home screen, tap the Settings icon to open the Settings screen.

( 2 )  Scroll down the left column and tap Accounts & Passwords.

( 3 )  In the Accounts section, tap Add Account to display the Add Account screen.

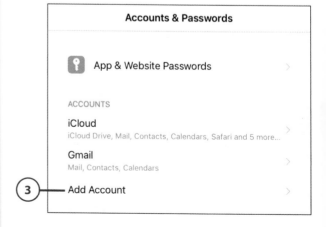

( 4 ) Tap the type of email account you want to add—iCloud, Exchange, Google, Yahoo!, AOL, or Outlook.com. (If you have another type of email, tap Other.)

( 5 ) When prompted, sign into the email account you selected with that account's email address and password.

( 6 ) If prompted to enable various aspects of your email account (such as calendar or contacts), select those options you want and tap Save. This account is now added to the Mail app.

## >>>*Go Further*
### SELECT A DEFAULT ACCOUNT

Although Mail receives messages from all accounts you add, you need to select which account is used when you send messages. This is important if you have, say, both iCloud and Gmail accounts added in the app; you have to decide whether the new emails you send come from your iCloud or Gmail address.

To do this, open the Settings screen, tap Mail, and then scroll down to the Composing section. Tap Default Account and select the account you want to use to send new messages.

You're not stuck with this one account, however. You can select a different sending account when creating a new message. When you create a new message, tap within the From field to display a panel with all your accounts listed, then select a different email account.

## Get Notified of New Messages

The Mail app can notify you when you receive new messages.

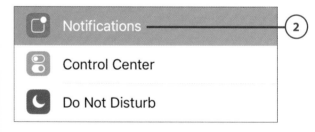

1. Tap the Settings icon on the Dock or Home screen to open the Settings screen.

2. Tap Notifications in the left column.

3. Tap Mail.

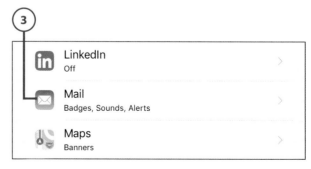

(4) Tap "on" the Allow Notifications switch.

(5) Tap the account from which you want to receive notifications.

(6) Indicate that you want to show notifications from this account on the Lock screen by tapping "on" the Show on Lock Screen switch.

(7) To display previews of message contents in the alerts, tap Show Previews.

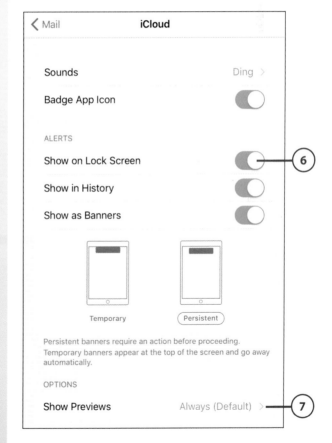

(**8**) Select when you want to show message previews: Always, When Unlocked, or Never.

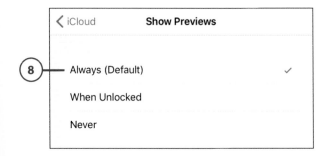

## Create a Signature

By default, when you send email from the Mail app, it automatically attaches a line of text to the bottom of each message stating "Sent from my iPad." This line is called a *signature*, and you can customize what text you include in yours.

(**1**) From the Settings screen, scroll down the left column to the list of apps and tap Mail.

(**2**) Scroll down the Mail screen to the Composing section and tap Signature.

(**3**) Tap All Accounts to create a signature for use with all your email accounts. *Or…*

(**4**) Tap Per Account to create a signature for a specific email account.

(**5**) Tap within the text box or the text box for a specific account, delete the default signature ("Sent from my iPad"), and type a new one.

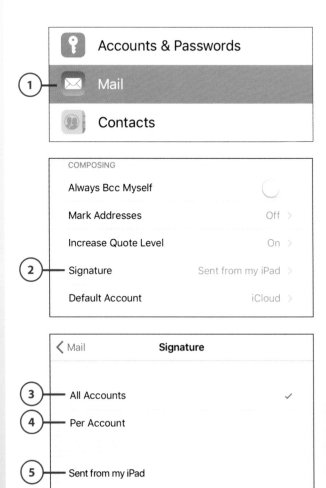

SIGNATURES

Your email signature should be used to tell your recipients something about you. It can contain useful or fun information.

Many people use their signatures to display additional contact information, such as a phone number or Twitter handle. Others display their job title or professional qualifications in their signature.

A signature doesn't have to be serious, however. Some people end their emails with a favorite quotation, or even a personal statement of some sort. Just keep it short—nobody wants to read a six-line signature in every email they receive from you!

# Sending and Receiving Messages

The whole point of the Mail app is to let you send and receive email messages to and from your friends and family. (And any other person or organization who uses email, as well.) To that end, it's relatively easy to use—just like most other email apps and services.

## Select an Inbox

If you've configured the Mail app for more than one email account, you have more than one inbox to deal with. The Mail app includes inboxes for each account you use, as well as a master inbox (All Inboxes) that displays messages from all your accounts in a single place. There's also a VIP inbox, which lists messages from people you've decided are very important.

(1) From the Dock or Home screen, tap the Mail icon to open the Mail app. (If you have unread email, you'll see a number on the Mail icon, which signifies how many messages you have waiting.)

2. Tap All Inboxes to view all your incoming messages from all accounts. *Or…*

3. Tap the name of an account to view messages from that specific account. *Or…*

4. Tap VIP to view messages from your most important contacts.

# >>>Go Further

## ADDING A VIP

To add the first person to the Mail app's VIP list, so that their incoming messages automatically appear in the VIP inbox, tap to open the VIP inbox, then tap Add VIP. You now see a list of all your contacts; tap the name of the person you want to add to your VIP list. After the first person has been added, tap the Information (i) icon next to VIP in the Mailboxes pane and then tap Add VIP.

## Read a Message

Reading a message in the Mail app is subtly different depending on how you hold your iPad. When you hold the device horizontally, you see a split screen, with inbox contents on the left and the selected message on the right. When you hold the device vertically, so the screen isn't quite as wide, you see only the selected message; the inbox list slides offscreen to give more room to the selected message.

In this and the following tasks, I show you how Mail works in horizontal mode—which works best for reading emails.

**1** From within the Mail app, tap the inbox you want to view. (Or tap All Inboxes to view all your messages from all your email accounts.) The left column slides offscreen to reveal all the messages in this inbox.

**2** Unread messages are displayed with a blue dot next to the subject line; messages you've read don't have this blue dot. Each message displays the sender's name and/or email address, the date received, message subject, and the first line or so of the message. Tap the message you want to read; the selected message header is shaded.

**3** The selected message displays on the right side of the screen. (Or, if the iPad is held vertically, it fills the entire screen.) The name of the sender appears at the top, with the message subject beneath that. The text of the message fills the bottom of the message pane; if this message is in reply to a previous message, the previous message is "quoted" beneath that.

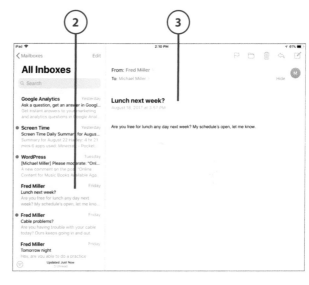

**4** If the sender has attached photos to the message, those photos are automatically down-loaded and displayed within the message text. (If a photo is not automatically displayed, tap the Download link to display it.)

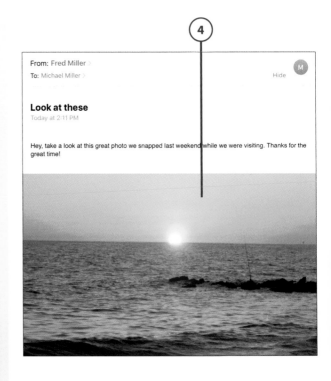

## Reply to a Message

When you reply to an email message, the original message is "quoted" beneath your reply.

**1** Open the original message and then tap the Reply icon at the top of the screen.

**2** Tap Reply to open the Reply pane.

**3** The original sender is listed as the recipient in the To field, and the subject is also automatically filled in (although you can edit the subject, if you want). Enter your reply into the main text box.

**4** Tap Send to send your reply to the original sender.

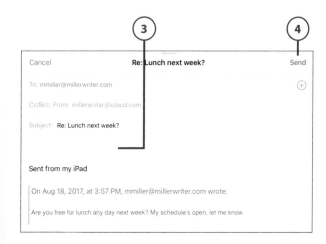

## Create and Send a New Message

Writing and sending a new email message is similar to replying to an existing message. All you need to know is who you're sending it to!

**1** From within the Mail app, tap the New Message icon at the top-right corner of the screen. This displays the New Message pane.

**2** Tap within the To field and start typing the name or email address of the intended recipient. As you type, the Mail app displays matching names from your contacts list. If this person is listed there, tap their name.

**3** If you're sending an email to someone not in your contacts list, continue entering the person's email address manually.

## Contacts

Learn more about your contacts and the Contacts app in Chapter 10, "Managing Your Contacts."

**( 4 )** Add another recipient by tapping again within the To field and repeating steps 2 and 3.

**( 5 )** Add Cc or Bcc recipients by tapping Cc/Bcc and adding the desired names.

## Cc and Bcc

Cc stands for *carbon copy*, and sends a copy of your message to additional recipients. Bcc stands for *blind carbon copy*, and sends a copy of your message to additional recipients but hides their names and addresses from the main recipients.

**( 6 )** Tap within the Subject field and enter the subject of this email.

**( 7 )** Tap within the main text box and enter your email message.

**( 8 )** Tap Send to send the message.

# Attach a Photo to a Message

The Mail app lets you attach photos and other files to your email messages. This makes it easy to share pictures with your friends and family.

## Attachments
A file of any sort attached to an email message is called an *attachment*.

1. From within the Mail app, tap the New Message icon to create a new message.

2. Tap within the main text box to display the icons beneath the New Message pane, and then tap the Camera icon. (To attach a different kind of file, tap the Paperclip icon instead.) The Photos pane displays.

3. Tap the photo album that contains the photo you want.

4. Tap to select the photo you want to attach.

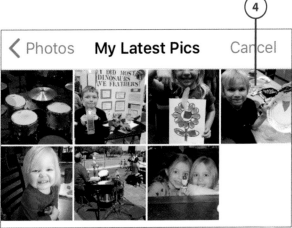

## It's Not All Good

### Keep It Small

Many digital photos, especially ones you take with your iPad camera, can create fairly large image files. If an image file is too large, your email service (or your recipient's email service) may reject it. For this reason, the Mail app may prompt you to resize any large photo you attach. If you're so prompted, choose a new size before proceeding (Note, however, that a smaller image size won't look as good if printed.).

⑤ Tap Use. The photo is added to your new message.

⑥ Complete your email as normal and tap Send.

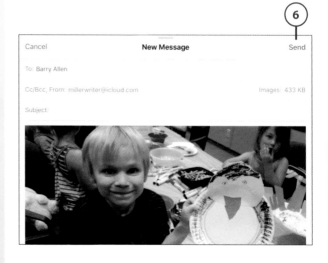

## It's Not All Good

**Unwanted Attachments**

If you receive an attachment via email that you weren't expecting—especially from someone you don't know—do *not* tap to open it! Attachments can contain viruses and other malware that can infect or damage your iPad. Unwanted file attachments, and the emails they come attached to, should be deleted!

## Delete a Message

When you're done reading a message, you may want to delete it. You may even want to delete a message before you read it, if it's from some entity you don't want to hear from. Fortunately, you can delete messages from the inbox itself, or from the reading pane.

1. To delete a message after you've read it, display the message and then tap the Trash icon.

2. To delete one or more messages from the inbox, tap Edit.

3. Tap to select the message(s) you want to delete.

4. Tap Trash.

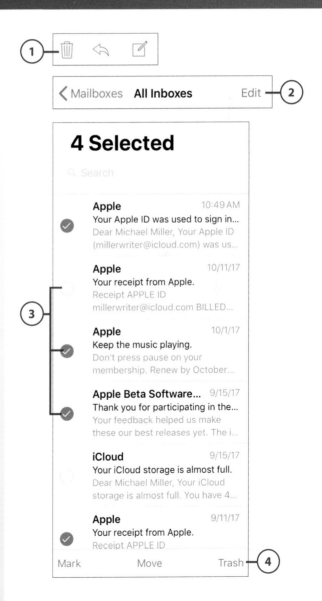

## Organize Messages in Files

What do you do with your old messages after you've read them? You may want to delete some of them (and you just learned how), but you may want to keep some around for future reference. Instead of letting old messages clog up your inbox, create folders to organize and store your old messages.

1. From the Mailboxes list, tap Edit.

2. Tap New Mailbox. (The Mail app refers to folders as *mailboxes*.)

3. Tap within the Name field and enter a name for this new folder/mailbox.

4. Tap Mailbox Location.

5. Tap the account where you want to store this folder.

6. You can also select a master folder for this new folder; the new folder then becomes a subfolder within that folder.

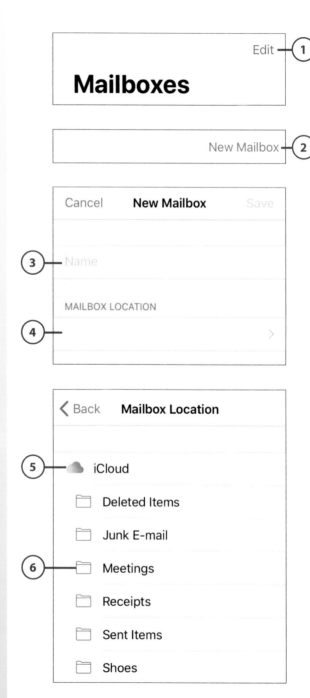

**7** Tap Save.

**8** Tap Done. The new folder/mailbox is now created.

**9** Move an email message to a folder by opening the message and then tapping the Folder icon at the top of the screen.

**10** Tap the folder you want to move this message to. The message is moved to that folder.

**11** Tap a folder/mailbox in the Mailboxes pane to view the contents of that folder/mailbox.

# Deal with Junk Email (Spam)

One of the more annoying things about email is the amount of junk email, or spam, you sometimes receive. Fortunately, the Mail app includes a spam filter that attempts to identify junk email and automatically send it to a special Junk E-mail folder.

1. View messages in the Junk folder by going to a given account in the Mailboxes pane and tapping Junk.

2. Send a spam message you've received to the Junk E-mail folder by opening the message and tapping the Flag icon.

3. Tap Move to Junk.

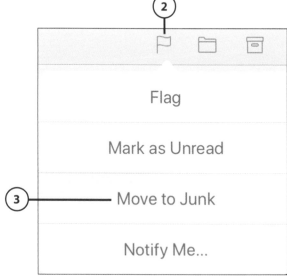

# >>>*Go Further*

## OTHER EMAIL APPS

Although Apple's Mail app is a very good email app, and it's included free with your iPad, there are other email apps available for your use. If you use a different email service, such as Gmail or Outlook.com, you may want to use the specific app for that service instead. You can find apps for most of the major email services in Apple's App Store; just search by the name of your email service.

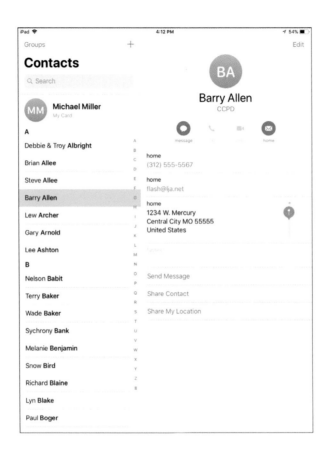

In this chapter, you learn how to manage contacts on your iPad for email, messaging, and video chatting.

→ Using the Contacts App
→ Viewing and Contacting Your Contacts

# Managing Your Contacts

When you use the Mail app to send an email to someone, you can enter that person's email address manually. That's not a big deal. Unless you send a lot of emails to that person, of course, in which case re-entering that same email address each time gets pretty annoying.

It's also annoying to try to remember the email address of each and every person you communicate with. Or their phone numbers. Or their street addresses. If you have a lot of friends and family, all that information becomes overwhelming.

In the real world, you might keep people's names and addresses in a physical card file or address book. On your iPad, you can do the same thing, by storing all their key information in the Contacts app. It's a lot easier to have the Contacts app remember all these names and addresses than trying to do it yourself!

# Using the Contacts App

The Contacts app is preinstalled on your new iPad. You use the Contacts app to store the names, email addresses, street addresses, phone numbers, and other important information of the people you contact most often.

## Add a New Contact

To add a new contact to the Contacts app, all you need to know is that person's name and any contact information about that person.

(1) Tap the Contacts icon to open the Contacts app. All your existing contacts are listed in alphabetical order.

(2) Tap the + icon to display the New Contact panel.

(3) Enter the person's first and last name into the First Name and Last Name fields. (Or, if you're entering a company or organization, enter that entity's name into the Company field.) Past this point, any information you enter is optional—that is, you only need to enter the contact's name.

(4) Tap the + next to Add Phone and enter the contact's phone number.

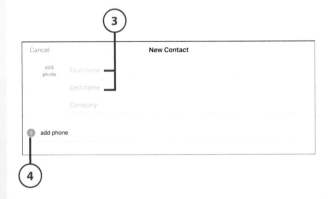

**5** The Contacts app assumes this is the person's home phone number. If this is not the case, tap Home and then select another type of phone from the list—Work, Mobile, and so forth.

**6** Add another phone number by tapping the + next to Add Phone and repeating steps 4 and 5.

**7** Tap the + next to Add Email, and enter the contact's email address.

**8** Scroll down, tap the + next to Add Address, and enter the contact's address.

**9** Add other information by tapping the + next to that field and then entering the appropriate data.

**10** Include a photo of this person (if you have one) by tapping Add Photo and selecting a picture from your iPad photo library.

**11** Tap Done to save the contact.

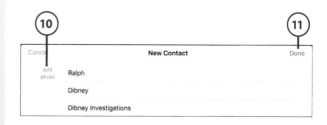

## >>>Go Further

### IMPORT CONTACTS

Although you can manually enter new contacts into the Contacts app, you can also import any existing contacts you have in other apps. This way you don't have to re-enter information you may have entered previously.

You do this by enabling contact sharing with those apps that have their own contacts, such as the Facebook and Mail apps. You do this from your iPad's Settings page. Tap Contacts, tap Siri & Search, and then make sure the Find Contacts in Other Apps switch is on. (If it's not, tap it "on.")

## Edit a Contact

Sometimes you may want to add new information about a given contact, or change existing info.

(1) From within the Contacts app, tap the name of the contact you want to edit.

(2) Tap Edit.

( **3** ) Tap within any field you want
to edit and make the necessary
changes.

( **4** ) Tap Done.

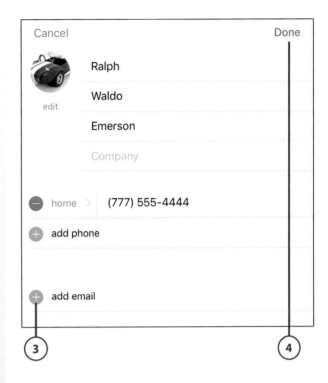

# Delete a Contact

You can also delete contacts you're
no longer interested in.

( **1** ) From within the Contacts app,
tap the name of the contact you
want to delete.

( **2** ) Tap Edit.

( **3** ) Scroll down to the bottom of
the contact information and tap
Delete Contact.

( **4** ) When asked to confirm this
deletion, tap Delete Contact.

# Consolidate Contacts from Multiple Sources

When you import contacts from various sources, you might end up with multiple entries for a single person. Let's say, for example, that you've manually entered Bob Smith's contact information, but also imported that person's info from Facebook and Gmail. You end up with three entries in the Contacts app for Bob Smith, with lots of duplicated information.

What you need to do is to consolidate these multiple contacts into a single contact—what Apple calls a *unified contact*. You do this by "linking" all the individual contacts together.

## Automatic Linking

The Contacts app might attempt to automatically link contacts that it thinks are similar. You'll probably still need to manually link some contacts, however.

(1) From within the Contacts app, tap to select one of the contacts you want to link.

(2) Tap Edit.

(3) Scroll to the bottom of the screen and tap Link Contacts. This displays your entire contacts list.

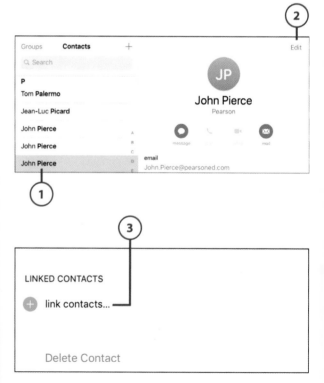

**4** Tap the other contact you want to link.

**5** You now see information about the other contact. Tap Link to return to the original contact screen.

**6** Tap Done. The two contacts are combined.

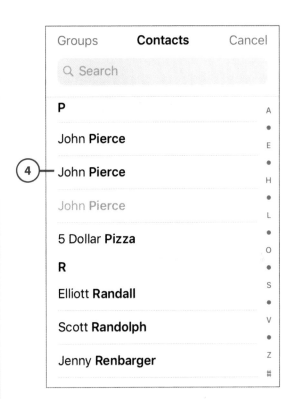

Groups    **Contacts**    Cancel

🔍 Search

P

John **Pierce**

John **Pierce**

John Pierce

5 Dollar **Pizza**

R

Elliott **Randall**

Scott **Randolph**

Jenny **Renbarger**

A
E
H
L
O
S
V
Z
#

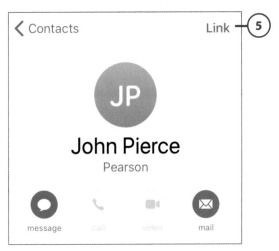

❮ Contacts                    Link

JP

John Pierce
Pearson

message    call    video    mail

Cancel                    Done

# Viewing and Contacting Your Contacts

The Contacts app displays the names of all your contacts in the left column onscreen. When you select a contact, information for that person or entity is displayed on the right side of the screen.

## Display a Contact

By default, your contacts are listed in alphabetical order by last name.

(1) From within the Contacts app, on the left side of the screen, tap a letter on the right edge of the list to display all contact names that start with that letter.

(2) Tap a contact name to display that contact's information on the right side of the screen.

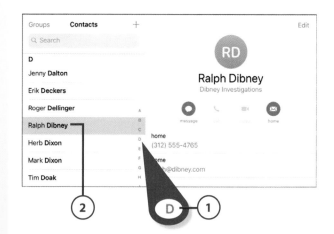

## Search for a Contact

If you have a lot of names in your contacts list, it might be quicker and easier to search for a specific person instead of scrolling through all your contacts.

(1) From within the Contacts app, tap within the Search box. Use the onscreen keyboard to begin typing the person's first or last name.

(2) As you type, the Contacts app displays matching names. Tap to select the contact you want.

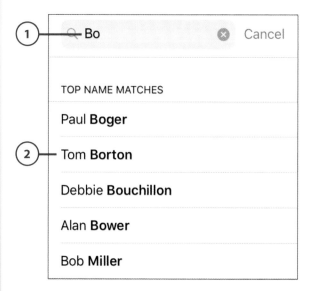

# Change How Contacts Are Displayed

By default, your contacts are sorted by last name, but displayed as first name then last name, like this:

Bob Smith

You can change the way your contacts are both sorted and displayed.

1. From the Dock or Home screen, tap the Settings icon to display the Settings page.

2. In the left column, scroll down and tap Contacts.

3. Tap Sort Order.

4. Select either Last, First (the default) or First, Last.

5. Tap Contacts to return to the previous screen.

6. Tap Display Order.

7. Select either First, Last (the default) or Last, First.

8. Tap Contacts to return to the previous screen.

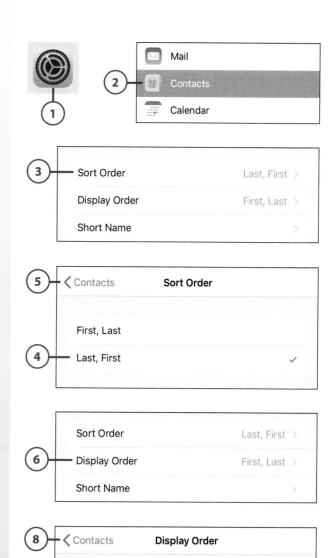

**9** Tap Short Name.

**10** Make sure the Short Name switch is in the on position.

**11** Tap how you want the app's "short names" to display. (Short names are used when space onscreen is at a premium.)

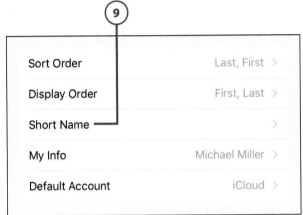

| | |
|---|---|
| Sort Order | Last, First > |
| Display Order | First, Last > |
| Short Name | > |
| My Info | Michael Miller > |
| Default Account | iCloud > |

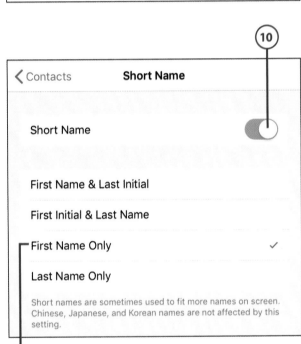

**‹** Contacts        **Short Name**

Short Name

First Name & Last Initial

First Initial & Last Name

First Name Only        ✓

Last Name Only

Short names are sometimes used to fit more names on screen. Chinese, Japanese, and Korean names are not affected by this setting.

## Contact a Contact

Many apps—including Mail, Messages, and FaceTime—use your contacts list to help you easily email or message your contacts. You can also send email to, message, or call (via FaceTime) a person directly from the Contacts app.

( **1** ) From within the Contacts app, tap to select the person you want to contact.

( **2** ) Tap the Mail icon to send an email to this person. (The icon might say "Home" or "Work," if you've specified that person's home or work email address.)

( **3** ) Tap Message to send a text message to this person.

( **4** ) Tap the Call icon to initiate a FaceTime voice call with this person.

( **5** ) Tap the Video icon to initiate a FaceTime video call with this person. (This icon is grayed out if the person isn't currently online and capable of receiving FaceTime calls.)

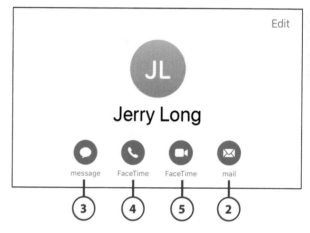

### FaceTime and Messaging

To learn more about FaceTime and text messages, turn to Chapter 11, "Video Chatting and Texting."

Messages app

FaceTime

In this chapter, you learn how to communicate with friends and family using the Messages and FaceTime apps.

→ Text Messaging with the Messages App
→ Video Chatting and More with FaceTime

# Video Chatting and Texting

You've learned how to communicate with friends, family, and businesses with email. But email is slow (relatively) and not at all like having a conversation in real time.

For that, we turn to text messaging and video chatting. Text messaging, using the iPad's Messages app, is great for sending short thoughts and notes. Video chatting, using the FaceTime app, is better when you want one-on-one, face-to-face conversation.

## Text Messaging with the Messages App

Let's start with text messaging, like you do on your phone. On your iPad, you use the Messages app to send text messages over Wi-Fi via Apple's iMessage service. Your messages can include photos, videos, and other files you attach to the basic text.

## >>>Go Further
### iMESSAGE

The Messages app utilizes Apple's iMessage service, which connects Apple devices via Wi-Fi. (It also connects iPhones via cellular service, if they're not connected to a wireless network.) iMessage is a lot like phone-based SMS/MMS text messaging, but is an Apple-only service.

At present iMessage is not available to users of Windows computers or Android phones or computers. Nor can you use iMessage to contact cell phone users via their text message services; you can only connect to other iPad and iPhone users via the Messages app.

## Send and Receive Text Messages

The Messages app lets you send text messages to any of your friends and family who have an iPad, iPhone, or Mac computer. It's as easy as tapping out a message on the onscreen keyboard and then tapping the Send button.

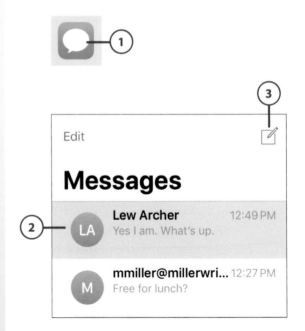

1. Tap the Messages icon to open the Messages app.

2. Previous conversations are listed in the left column. Tap a conversation to send another message to this person.

3. Tap the Compose icon to start a new conversation.

**4** Tap in the To field and use the onscreen keyboard to begin entering the name or email address of the person you want to talk with.

**5** As you type, the Messages app displays a list of matching people from your contacts list. Tap the name of the person you want to text with or finish entering the email address of the person.

### Group Messages

To send a message to a group of people, enter multiple names into the To box. Everyone listed here will receive and be able to respond to your message—and all subsequent responses.

**6** Type your message into the iMessage box.

**7** Tap the blue Send icon.

### Emoji

To include an emoji character in your text, tap the Emoji (smiley face) button on the onscreen keyboard and make a selection from there.

**8** Your message appears on the right side of the message pane.

**9** Messages from the other person appear on the left.

**10** Continue typing to continue the conversation.

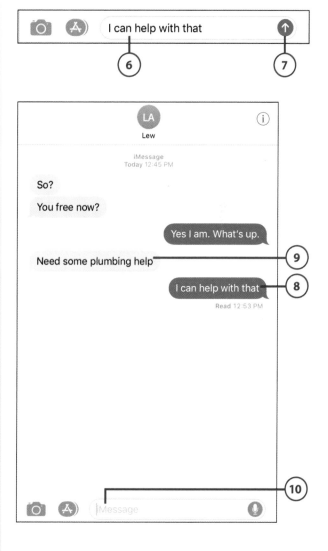

## Send an Audio Message

Instead of sending a plain text message, you can record and send a short audio message. Just tap the Record button and start talking!

(1) From within the Messages app, resume an existing conversation or start a new conversation and enter the recipient's name into the To field.

(2) In the iMessage box, press and hold the Microphone icon.

(3) Begin talking. While you talk, make sure you keep pressing the Microphone icon. You see the waveform of your voice in the iMessage box.

(4) When you're done talking, lift your finger from the screen.

(5) Tap the Play button to hear what you recorded.

(6) Tap the Send button to send the recording to the other person.

# Send a Photo

Just as with phone-based MMS (multimedia messaging), you can send photos to people you're messaging in the Messages app. You can send photos stored in your iPad's photo library, or take a new photo (like a selfie) and send it.

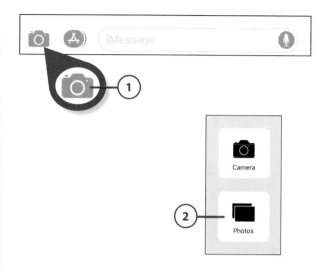

( **1** ) From within a conversation, tap the Camera icon next to the iMessages box to display a new panel at the bottom of the screen.

( **2** ) To send a photo stored on your iPad, tap Photos. (If you want to take and send a new photo, skip to step 7.)

( **3** ) Tap the album that contains the photo you want to send.

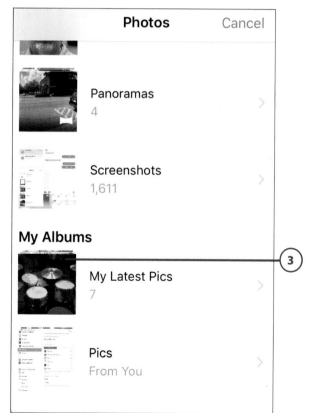

( 4 ) Tap the desired photo or photos.

( 5 ) Tap Use.

( 6 ) Tap the Send icon to send the photo(s) to the person you're texting with.

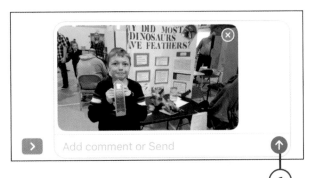

(7) To take and send a new photo, tap Camera. This displays the camera screen.

(8) Make sure that Photo is selected.

(9) If necessary, tap the Flip icon to switch from the rear camera to the front camera.

(10) Aim your iPad and then tap the big round icon to take the picture.

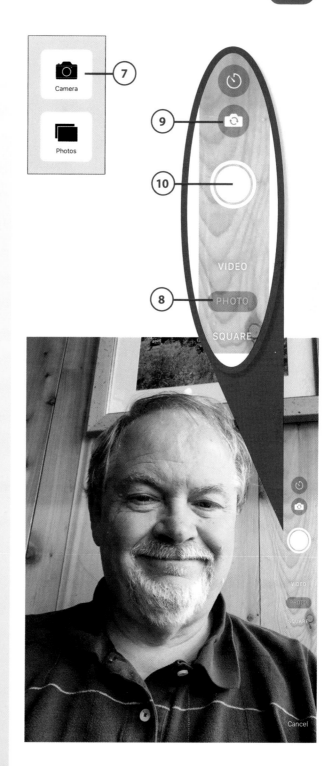

(11) You now see the picture you just took. If you like it, tap Done. (Otherwise, tap Retake and do it again.)

(12) You see the picture you took in the conversation pane. If you like it, tap the Send icon. (If not, tap the X to delete it.) The picture is now sent to the person you're texting with.

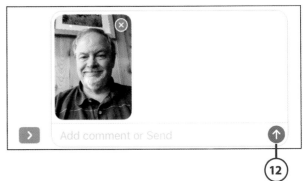

## Send a Video Message

Just as you can send photos and short audio messages, you can also record and send short video messages, using your iPad's front-facing FaceTime camera.

**(1)** From within the Messages app, resume an existing conversation or start a new conversation and enter the recipient's name into the To field.

**(2)** Tap the Camera icon next to the iMessage box to display the photo/video panel at the bottom of the screen.

**(3)** Tap the Camera icon to display the camera screen.

④ Tap Video.

⑤ If necessary, tap the Flip icon to switch to the front-facing camera.

⑥ Look into the camera and tap the red Record button. Start talking!

⑦ When you're done talking, tap the Record button again.

**8** You now see the video you recorded. Tap the Play button to play the video.

**9** If you like the video you recorded, tap Done. (If not, tap Retake.)

**10** The video is now added to the message page. Tap the Send icon to send the message to the recipient.

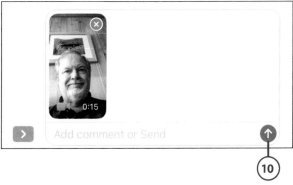

# Video Chatting and More with FaceTime

Text messaging is nice, but sometimes you want a face-to-face conversation with someone. Maybe you're snowbirding down south while your grandkids are still in school up north. Maybe your siblings live in a different part of the country than you do. Maybe you or one of your family members is stuck at home and you just want to check in or keep in touch.

When a text message or phone call isn't good enough, use Apple's FaceTime app to video chat in real time with your friends and family. All you need is your iPad—and its built-in camera and microphone. Every call you make is free!

## Apple Users Only

FaceTime is only available on Apple devices—iPads, iPhones, and Mac computers. You can't use FaceTime to chat with anyone who doesn't have an Apple device.

## Start a Video Chat

You can use FaceTime to video chat with anyone who has an iPad, iPhone, or Mac that includes a front-facing camera.

1. Tap the FaceTime icon to open the FaceTime app.

2. You see yourself, via your iPad's front-facing FaceTime camera. Overlaid on the left side of the screen is a list of people with whom you've recently chatted. Tap Video at the top of this pane.

3. To chat again with one of the people listed, tap their name.

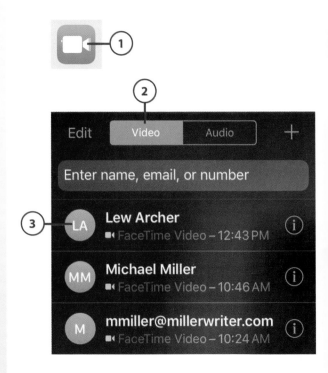

( **4** ) To chat with someone new, enter that person's name, email, or phone number into the text box. (Alternatively, tap the + icon to select a person from your contacts list.)

( **5** ) As you type, matching contacts are displayed. Those that are online and available to chat have a bright camera and/or phone icon next to their names. Select the person you want from this list, or finish typing the person's email address or phone number.

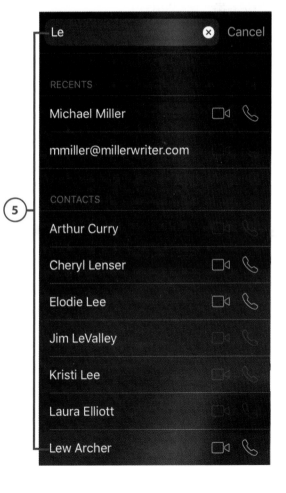

**6** You now see the person's contact pane. Tap the FaceTime video Camera icon, and FaceTime dials the other person.

**7** If that person is available and answers, you see that person onscreen. A small thumbnail in the corner of the screen displays what the other person is seeing (you). Have a nice conversation!

**8** Tap the screen to show the control icons at the bottom.

**9** Tap the Mute icon to mute the sound. Tap the button again to resume normal conversation.

**10** Tap the red End icon to end the chat.

## Answer a Video Chat Request

Just as you can call others via FaceTime, they can also call you. How do you answer a video call? By pressing an icon and talking, of course!

( 1 ) When someone calls you via FaceTime, your screen changes to the FaceTime screen.

( 2 ) You see two icons at the bottom. Tap Accept to accept the call. (Tap Decline to not answer.)

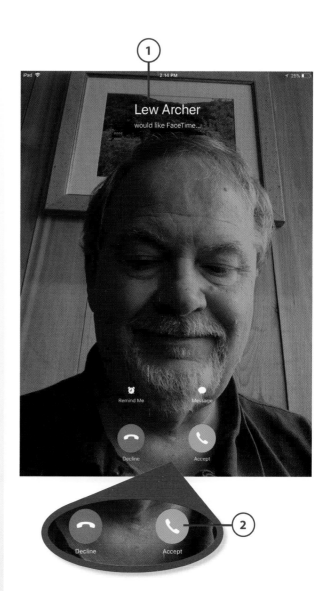

(3) Your call starts—so start talking!

(4) Tap the screen to display the control icons at the bottom.

(5) Tap the End icon to end the chat.

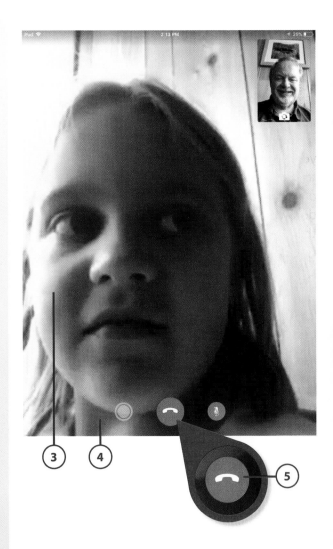

# Make an Audio Call

FaceTime also lets you participate in audio calls—like phone calls but from your iPad to other Apple devices. This is good if you just want to talk and don't need to see the other person, if you're not quite presentable enough to show yourself to the other person, or if you're talking to someone who doesn't have a front-facing camera in their device.

1. From within the FaceTime app, tap Audio at the top of the left pane.

2. Enter or select the person you want to call.

3. FaceTime dials the other person. If that person is available and answers, you see the FaceTime controls onscreen. Start talking!

4. Tap the Mute icon to mute the sound. Tap the icon again to resume normal conversation.

5. Tap the FaceTime icon to turn this audio call into a video call.

6. Tap the red End icon to end this call.

# >>>*Go Further*

## CALLING OTHER FRIENDS WITH SKYPE

As convenient and easy-to-use as FaceTime is, it only lets you call people who have Apple devices. How can you chat with friends and family who have Samsung or Nexus smartphones or tablets, or Windows PCs?

The answer is to use Skype, a similar video-calling service that operates across all platforms. There are Skype apps not only for Apple's iPad and iPhones, but also for Android phones and tablets, Windows and Mac computers, and Xbox One game systems. You can use Skype to call just about anybody on any device—not just Apple devices. Just make sure the person you're calling also has the Skype app installed. (And, as with FaceTime, your user-to-user calls on Skype are free.)

To use Skype, you must download the Skype app from Apple's App Store (it's free) and have a Skype account (also free). You can create a new Skype account or sign in with an existing Microsoft ID (but not an Apple ID).

To call someone on Skype, that person has to be added to your Skype contacts list. (This is separate from your normal iPad contacts list.) You have to invite someone to be a contact, and they need to accept your invitation.

From there, making a video call is as easy as tapping the name of the person you want to call, starting a conversation, and then tapping either the Video (for video calls) or Phone (for voice calls) icons. If you initiate a video call, you see the other person full-screen and yourself in a smaller thumbnail image. Start talking!

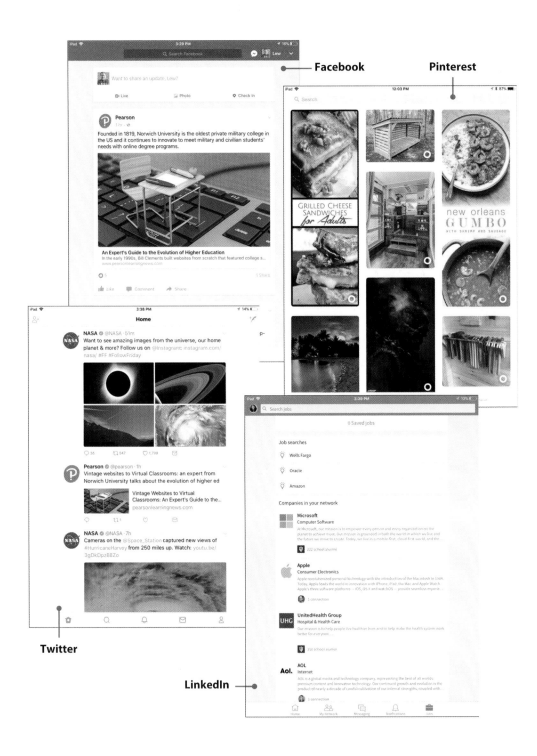

**Facebook**

**Pinterest**

**Twitter**

**LinkedIn**

In this chapter, you learn how to share your thoughts and experiences online via Facebook, Pinterest, Twitter, and other social networks.

→ Understanding Social Networking
→ Using Facebook on Your iPad
→ Using Pinterest on Your iPad
→ Using Twitter on Your iPad
→ Using LinkedIn on Your iPad

# 12

# Getting Social with Facebook, Pinterest, and Other Social Networks

Social networking is all the rage. We're talking online communities like Facebook, Pinterest, and Twitter, places where you can go to share what you're doing with your online friends, and find out what they're up to, too.

If you've never used a social network before, it's a whole new world to explore—and you can do it from the comfort of your iPad. If you have used Facebook or another social network, you need to install the appropriate app(s) on your iPad and learn how they work.

# Understanding Social Networking

A *social network* is an Internet-based service that hosts a community of users and makes it easy for those users to communicate with one another. Social networks enable users to share experiences and opinions with one another, and thus keep in touch with friends and family members, no matter where they're located.

The goal of a social network is to create a network of online "friends," and then share your activities with them via a series of message posts. These posts are short text messages, sometimes called *status updates*, which can be viewed by all your friends on the site. A status update can be text only, or contain photos, videos, and links to other web pages.

Your online friends read your posts, as well as posts from other friends, in a continuously updated stream. On Facebook, this stream is called the *News Feed* (other sites call it different things), and it's the one place where you can read updates from all your online friends and family; it's where you find out what's really happening.

There are many social networks on the Internet, and Facebook is the largest and most popular among users of all ages, including older users. Other social networks popular among those 50+ include LinkedIn, Pinterest, and Twitter.

---

### More About Social Media

Learn more about Facebook, Pinterest, Twitter, and other social networks in my companion book, *My Social Media for Seniors*, available online and in bookstores everywhere.

---

# Using Facebook on Your iPad

With more than two billion users worldwide, chances are many of your friends and family are already using Facebook.

Although Facebook started as a network for college students, today it's the social network of choice, especially for older users. In fact, half of all people aged 65 or older who are online make Facebook their hub for online social activity—and browse the site for at least an hour each day.

People of all ages use Facebook to connect with current family members and reconnect with friends from the past. If you want to know what your friends from high school or the old neighborhood have been up to over the past several decades, chances are you can find them on Facebook.

In addition, Facebook helps you keep your friends informed about what you're doing. Write one post and it's seen by hundreds of your online "friends." It's the easiest way I know to connect with almost everyone you know.

Like all the social networks discussed in this chapter, Facebook is completely free to use. You access Facebook from its iPad app, which you can download from Apple's App Store.

## Navigate Facebook's iPad App

The first time you launch the Facebook app, you're prompted to either sign into an existing account (if you have one) or create a new account. Follow the onscreen instructions to proceed from there.

Whenever you open the Facebook app, you see the News Feed screen. The News Feed is where you view status updates from all your Facebook friends, and it looks different depending on how you're holding your iPad.

( 1 ) Tap the Facebook icon to launch the Facebook app.

( 2 ) In landscape mode (held horizontally), you see the News Feed on the left with a sidebar on the right side of the screen that displays upcoming events, the Chat panel (with favorite friends listed), trending topics, and more. Scroll down the screen to view more updates in the News Feed; refresh the News Feed by pulling down from the top of the screen and then releasing.

**News Feed**    **Trending topics**

( 3 ) In portrait mode (held vertically), you see the normal screen
with no additional sidebars. All
the navigation icons are at the
bottom of the screen; tap News
Feed to display the News Feed.

( 4 ) Tap the down arrow in the
top-right corner to access app
settings.

( 5 ) When a person you know sees
you on Facebook, she might
send you a friend request. You
have to be friends with someone on Facebook to see their
posts in the News Feed. To view
your friend requests, tap the
Requests icon.

( 6 ) Tap the Marketplace icon to see
items for sale from Facebook
members in your area.

( 7 ) Tap the Notifications icon
to view notifications from
Facebook.

( 8 ) Tap the More icon to view your
favorite pages and groups, and
to configure Facebook settings.

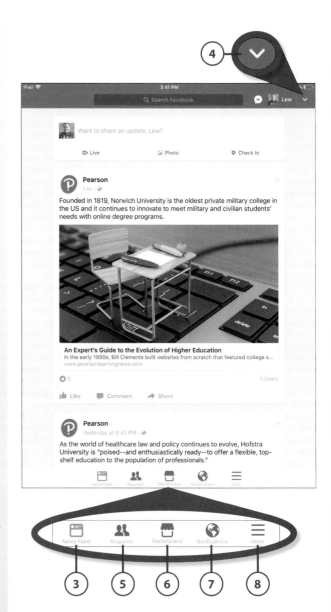

## Pages and Groups

In addition to posts from individuals,
Facebook also offers official "pages"
from companies and celebrities, as
well as topic-specific groups. You can
"like" a public page to receive posts
from that page, or join a group to
post and receive messages from other
members of that group.

# Read and Respond to Posts

The messages people post to Facebook are called *status updates* or *posts*. You read and respond to posts from your friends on the News Feed screen.

1. For any given post, tap the Like icon to like that post. Tap and hold the Like icon to choose from a range of responses, from Love to Sad to Angry.

2. Tap the Comment icon to comment on a post.

3. Tap the Share icon to share this post.

4. Tap the poster's name to view that person's Timeline page. (The Timeline page serves as a person's home base, displaying her personal profile, posts she's made, and photos she's uploaded.)

5. If the post includes a photo, tap the photo to view it full screen.

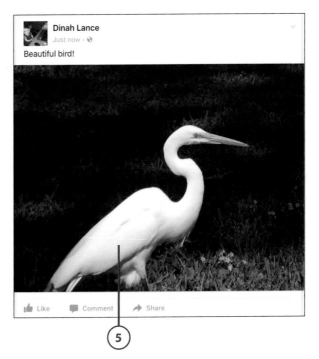

**6** If the post includes a video, tap the video thumbnail to begin playback. (Some videos may play back automatically when you scroll to them.)

**7** If the post includes a link to another web page, tap the link or thumbnail to view that page on a new screen.

# Post a Status Update

You create new status updates from the Facebook app's News Feed screen. The status updates you post are displayed on your friends' News Feeds.

1. Tap within the status update box at the top of the page to display the Update Status panel.

2. Type the text of your message into the big text box.

3. Tap Photo/Video to include a photo or video with your post.

4. Tap Live Video to shoot live (real-time) video and share with your friends.

5. Tap Check In to include your location in your post.

6. Tap Feeling/Activity/Sticker to share how you feel, tell others what you're doing, or add a small graphic sticker image to your message.

7. Tap Tag People to tag another person in your post.

8. Change who can see the post by tapping the Privacy button beneath your name.

9. Tap Post to post the status update.

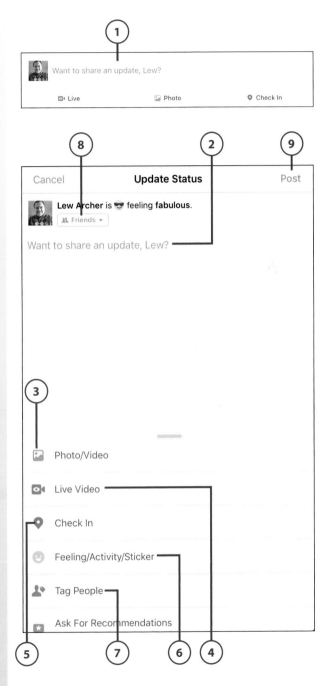

**More About Facebook**

Learn more about Facebook in my companion book, *My Facebook for Seniors*, available online and in bookstores everywhere.

# Using Pinterest on Your iPad

Facebook isn't the only social network that may interest you. Pinterest is a newer, different type of social network with particular appeal to middle-aged and older women—although there are a growing number of male users, too.

Unlike Facebook, which lets you post text-based status updates, Pinterest is all about images. The site consists of a collection of virtual online boards that people use to share pictures they find interesting. Users "pin" or save photos and other images to their personal message boards, and then they share their pins with online friends.

You can save images of anything—clothing, furniture, recipes, do-it-yourself projects, and the like. Your Pinterest friends can then "repin" your images to their boards—and on and on.

Like Facebook, Pinterest is totally free to use. You access Pinterest from the Pinterest app.

## View and Save Pins

You can download the Pinterest app, for free, from Apple's App Store. The first time you launch the app, you're prompted to either sign into an existing account (if you have one) or create a new account. Follow the onscreen instructions to proceed from there.

(1) Tap the Pinterest icon to launch the Pinterest app. You see a variety of pins.

**2** The pins in your feed include items pinned by people you follow, as well as recommended pins from Pinterest. Tap a pin to view it full screen.

**3** Press and hold a pin to display the command icons.

**4** Keep your finger pressed to the screen and move it to the Save icon to save this item to one of your boards.

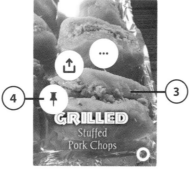

( 5 ) Accept or edit the current description of the item.

( 6 ) Scroll down and select which board you want to save to (or tap Create Board to pin to a new board). The item is then saved to that board.

## Not Always Welcome

Some websites don't want people to pin their images, and code their pages to prohibit pinning. If you try to pin from one of these pages, you get a message that no pinnable images have been found. If you happen to pin an image that some entity owns and doesn't want you to pin, they can ask Pinterest to take down the pin. (Legally, Pinterest says it's not responsible for any copyright claims for items saved to its site. Pinning images other than your own can infringe on copyright laws.)

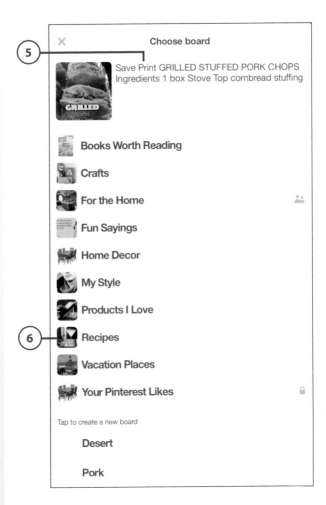

## Pin from a Website

Many Pinterest users find images outside of Pinterest to pin to their boards. When you see an image on a website, you can easily pin it to a Pinterest board.

( 1 ) From the Safari web browser, navigate to the web page that contains the image you want to pin and then tap the Share icon in the browser to display the Share panel.

**2** Tap Pinterest to display the Pick an Image panel. (If you don't see the Pinterest icon, tap More to display it.)

**3** You see thumbnails of all available images on that web page. Tap the thumbnail you want to pin.

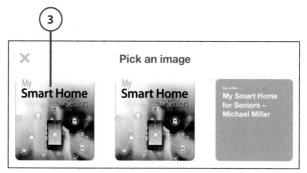

( 4 ) Accept or edit the description for this pin.

( 5 ) Tap the board you want to pin to (or tap Create Board to pin to a new board). The selected image is pinned to that board on Pinterest.

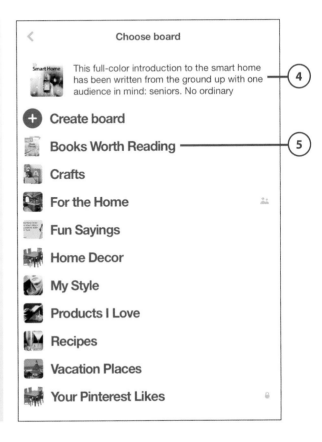

# Using Twitter on Your iPad

You may have heard of Twitter, even if you haven't used it yourself. It's one of the more popular social media networks out there, although it isn't that widely used by those 50 and up. It's most popular among users in their twenties and thirties—and among politicians and celebrities reaching out to large audiences.

Twitter is kind of like Facebook, but with only posts—called *tweets*—and no groups or pages or any of that. Tweets are short posts (280 characters or less), kind of like text messages, although they can include photos, videos, and links to pages on the Web.

As happens with the other social networks, you identify people you want to follow, then you see all of their tweets in your feed. People who follow you see your tweets in their feed.

# Read Tweets

Twitter is completely free to use. You have to sign up to use it, however, which you can do from the Twitter app, available for free from Apple's App Store.

1. Tap the Twitter icon to open the Twitter app.

2. Tap the Home icon to display your feed. Tweets from people you follow are listed here.

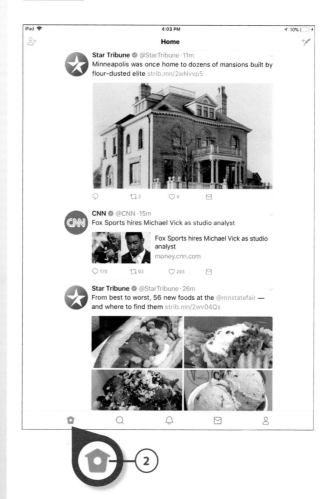

③ To "like" a tweet, tap the Heart icon.

④ To retweet a tweet (that is, post it to the people who follow you), tap the Retweet icon, and then tap Retweet.

## Create a New Tweet

Tweets can be a maximum of 280 characters long. You can include photos, videos, and web links in your tweets.

① From the Twitter app, tap the New Tweet icon at the top of the screen.

**2** Use the onscreen keyboard to enter the text for your tweet. Remember to make it no more than 280 characters long!

**3** To tweet a photo or video, tap the Photo icon and then select a photo or video stored on your phone. (The photo or video doesn't count toward the 280-character limit.)

**4** Tap the Tweet button to post your tweet.

### Hashtags

Twitter encourages the use of *hashtags* in their tweets. A hashtag is a word or phrase (with no spaces between words) preceded by the hash (#) character, like this: **#hashtag**. Use hashtags to link your tweet to other tweets with the same hashtag; click a hashtag to see other tweets with that hashtag.

# Using LinkedIn on Your iPad

LinkedIn is a social network with a business bent. It's designed primarily for business professionals, and it's a good way to keep in touch with others in your profession, including people you've worked with in the past. LinkedIn is particularly useful if you're in the market for a new job; it's easy to make new contacts and do your business networking online.

# Navigate the LinkedIn App

Like all the other social networks, LinkedIn is free to use; all you have to do is create an account and enter a little information about yourself. You access LinkedIn on your iPad from the LinkedIn app, which is available for download (for free) from Apple's App Store.

1. Tap the LinkedIn icon to open the LinkedIn app.

2. Tap Home to view posts from people or businesses you follow.

3. Tap My Network to connect with other users and view suggestions of people to follow.

4. Tap Messaging to exchange private messages with other LinkedIn users.

5. Tap Notifications to view recent activity from the people you follow.

6. Tap Jobs to look for employment opportunities.

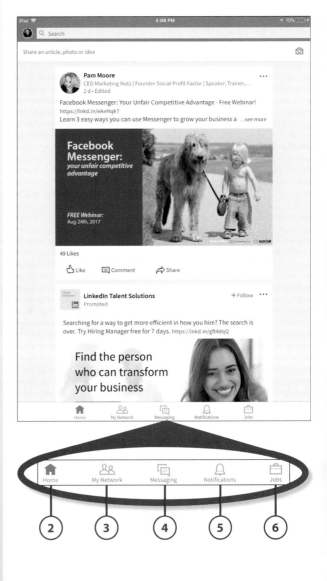

# Create a New Post

You can share notes, articles, photos, and more with the people you're linked to on LinkedIn.

(**1**) From the app's Home screen, tap within the Share an Article, Photo, or Idea box to display the Post screen.

(**2**) Enter the text of your message within the text box.

(**3**) Tap the Photo icon to include a photo with your post.

(**4**) Tap the Post button to post your update.

## >>>*Go Further*

## PRIVACY ON SOCIAL NETWORKS

It's important, when using any social network, to be aware of your privacy. It's easy to think of Facebook or any social network as a personal diary, but it's not. These social networks are extremely public; when you post a message or photo, it could be viewed by millions of people you don't even know.

If you value your privacy, you want to configure your settings on each network so that what you post is seen only by select people. Ideally, you want only your friends to see what you post; that means changing the posting privacy options from public to another more private setting. In addition, some networks (such as Facebook) let you adjust your privacy on a post-by-post basis. This way you could post something that you want your family members to see but don't want to show to co-workers or other friends.

How you adjust a network's privacy settings differs from network to network. In the Facebook app, for example, tap the Menu button (down arrow) at the top-right corner and then tap Privacy Shortcuts; everything you need to configure, privacy-wise, is listed there.

Of course, the best way to keep some things private on a social network is to not post them at all. You're old enough to know when to be discreet; resist the urge to post private information, private thoughts, and photos that ought to stay private. If you don't post 'em, nobody'll see 'em.

Finally, never, ever post your private contact information on a social network—or anywhere online, for that matter. If you don't want strangers calling you up or showing up at your door, don't share your phone number or street address with them. In addition, never post about going out of town (or even out on the town); it's not unheard of for burglars to troll the social networks so they'll know when a house is empty and ripe for the looting.

Bottom line: Be careful out there!

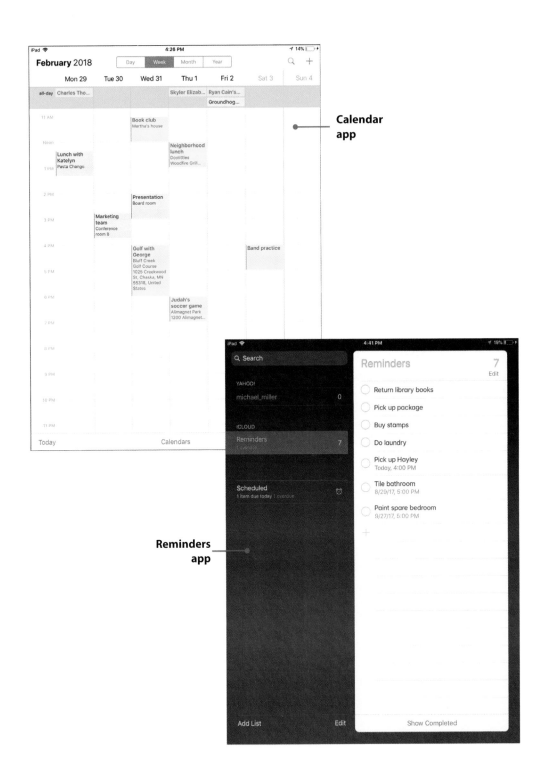

Calendar
app

Reminders
app

In this chapter, you learn how to use the iPad's Calendar and Reminders apps to manage your schedule and to-do lists.

→ Using the Calendar App
→ Using the Reminders App

# Staying Organized with Calendar and Reminders

Sometimes it's tough to keep track of your time. How are you supposed to juggle all the various things you're supposed to do—appointments, events, and everything that's on your to-do list?

Fortunately, you can use your iPad to help you manage just about everything on your schedule. Use the Calendar app to manage your appointments and events, and the Reminders app to track all the items on your to-do list.

## Using the Calendar App

Apple's Calendar app was included with your iPad. Use the Calendar app to track everything you have on your schedule—what the app calls *events*.

# View Events

You can view your calendar by day, week, month, or year.

1. From the Home screen, tap the Calendar icon to open the Calendar app.

2. Tap the Day tab to view a daily schedule. Scroll down to view times later in the day.

3. Swipe the calendar to the left to view the next day.

4. Swipe the calendar to the right to view the previous day.

5. Tap a specific date at the top of the calendar to view events for that day.

6. Tap a specific event on the calendar to view details about that event.

7. Tap Delete Event to delete the selected event.

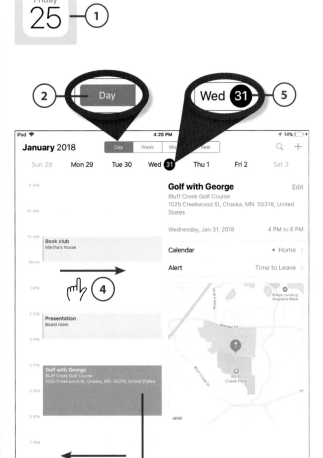

**8** Tap the Week tab to view all events this week.

**9** Swipe the calendar to the left to view the next week.

**10** Swipe the calendar to the right to view the previous week.

**11** Tap an event to view details about that event.

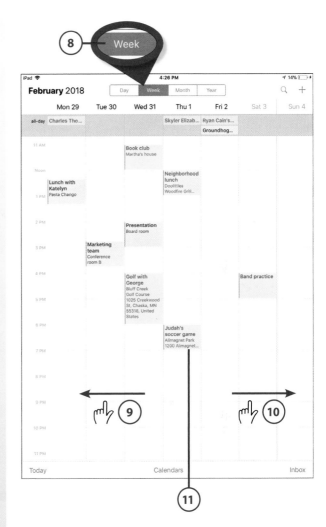

**12** Tap the Month tab to view all events this month.

**13** Scroll down the page to view events in the future.

**14** Tap an event to view details about that event.

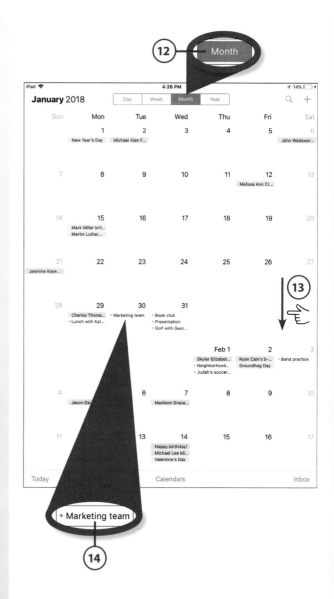

(15) Tap the Year tab to view a yearly calendar.

(16) Tap within a given month to view that monthly calendar.

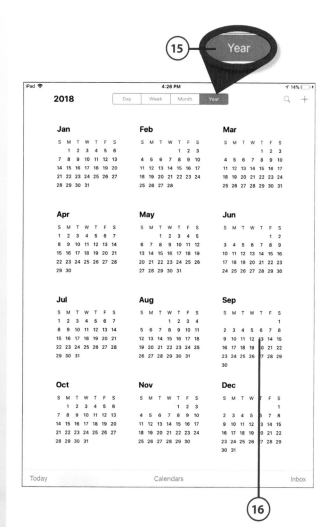

## Add a New Event

By default, the Calendar app imports important dates from your contacts list—birthdays, anniversaries, and the like. It also creates events for major national holidays. (These show up in color shading.)

The real value of the Calendar app, of course, is evident when you add your own events to the calendar. You can add events for meetings, parties, sports games—you name it.

( 1 ) From within the Calendar app, navigate to the day, week, or month you want and then tap the New (+) icon.

( 2 ) Tap within the Title field and add the name of this event.

( 3 ) Tap within the Location field and enter the location of this event. (This information is optional; the more detail you include—such as the street address—the better.)

( 4 ) If this event lasts all day, tap on the All-Day switch. Otherwise…

( 5 ) Tap the Starts field to expand the panel.

| Cancel | **New Event** | Add |
|---|---|---|

Title

Location

All-day

| Starts | Feb 6, 2018 | 4:00 PM |
|---|---|---|

| Ends | | 5:00 PM |

**6** Use the spin control to select the date of the event.

**7** Use the spin control to select the start time of the event. (The date, hour, minutes, and AM/PM controls spin separately.)

**8** If necessary, select the appropriate time zone for the event.

**9** Tap the Ends field to select the end date and time for the event.

**10** If you need to travel to this event, tap Travel Time and add the appropriate travel time.

**11** Tap Add to add this event to your calendar.

| Cancel | **New Event** | | Add |
|---|---|---|---|
| All-day | | | |
| Starts | Feb 6 | 2018 | 2:20 PM |
| | Sun Feb 4 | 12 | 10 |
| | Mon Feb 5 | 1 | 15 AM |
| | Tue Feb 6 | 2 | 20 PM |
| | Wed Feb 7 | 3 | 25 |
| | Thu Feb 8 | 4 | 30 |
| Time Zone | | | Chicago > |
| Ends | | | 3:20 PM |
| Repeat | | | Never > |
| Travel Time | | | None > |

## Create a Recurring Event

Some events repeat. For example, you might have a standing golf match every Saturday morning, or a neighborhood meeting the first Monday of each month. Fortunately, the Calendar app lets you create recurring events.

**1** From within the Calendar app, create a new event as normal and then tap the Repeat field.

| Cancel | **New Event** | Add |
|---|---|---|
| All-day | | |
| Starts | Feb 6, 2018 | 2:20 PM |
| Ends | | 3:20 PM |
| Repeat | | Never > |
| Travel Time | | None > |

(2) Tap how often this event recurs—Every Day, Every Week, Every 2 Weeks, Every Month, or Every Year.

(3) If the occurrence is more complex, tap Custom.

(4) Tap Frequency to select how often the event recurs—Daily, Weekly, Monthly, or Yearly.

(5) Tap Every to determine how the event recurs—every 1, 2, 3, or so days, weeks, months, or years.

(6) If you selected Weekly frequency, select which day(s) of the week this event recurs.

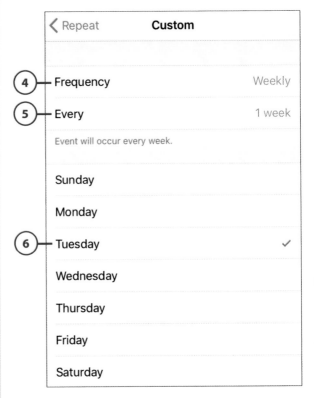

**7** If you selected Monthly frequency, select which day(s) of the month this event recurs. *Or…*

**8** Tap On The and select which day(s) you want (First Sunday of the month, Second Thursday of the month, and so forth).

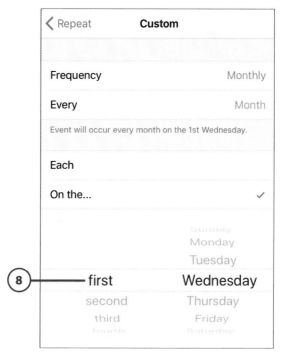

**9** If you selected Yearly frequency, select which month(s) of the year and days of the week this event recurs.

**10** Tap the back arrow to return to the Repeat panel, then again to return to the New Event panel.

**11** Tap the End Repeat field, unless the event is ongoing. (If it's ongoing—that is, if it doesn't have a set end date—don't tap End Repeat, and skip steps 12 and 13.)

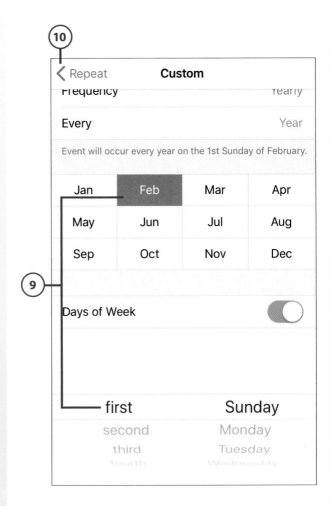

**12** Tap On Date.

**13** Use the spin controls to select the last date this event occurs. (If the event is ongoing, skip steps 12 and 13.)

**14** Tap the back arrow to return to the New Event panel and finish creating the event. Tap Add when done.

**14** ‹ New Event    **End Repeat**

Never

**12** On Date    ✓

December    3
January    4    2016
February    5    2017
**13** March    6    2018
April    7    2019
May    8    2020
June    9    2021

## Create an Alert for an Event

Sometimes you want to be notified when an event is coming up. Maybe you need a full day to prepare for a big event, or just a five-minute reminder to let you know what you need to do next. You can add alerts to any event you create in the Calendar app.

**1** From within the Calendar app, create a new app as normal and then tap the Alert field.

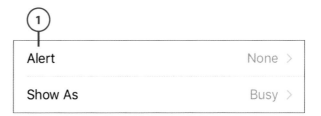

Alert    None  ›

Show As    Busy  ›

② Tap when you want to be alerted, anywhere from at the time of the event to 1 week before. Your iPad displays an alert for this event at the designated time.

**‹ New Event**          **Alert**

None

At time of event

5 minutes before

15 minutes before

30 minutes before

②— 1 hour before

2 hours before

1 day before

2 days before

1 week before

## Invite Others to an Event

Some events are personal. Others are quite public, involving lots of other people. (We're talking meetings, parties, and the like.) With the Calendar app you can invite your friends and family to new events you create, so they'll have these events on their calendars, too.

① From within the Calendar app, create a new event as normal and then tap the Invitees field.

Calendar                    ● Home ›

Invitees                        None ›

①

(2) From within the Add Invitees panel, tap the To field and enter the name or email address of the person you want to invite.

(3) Alternatively, tap the + to display and select from people in your contacts list.

(4) This person is added to the invite list. Repeat steps 2 and 3 to add more invitees.

(5) Tap Done. Each invitee is sent an email inviting them to your event.

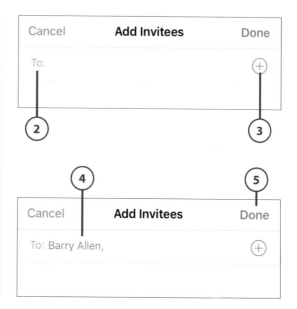

# Using the Reminders App

I have trouble remembering things. Always have—it's not an age thing. As such, I can use all the help I can get to help me track all the various things I need to do.

Apple's Reminders app, included with your iPad, lets you create a digital to-do list containing all the various tasks and chores you need to remember. Add an item to the Reminders list and you'll be prompted (or nagged, as the case may be) to complete that task.

# View and Manage Your Reminders

By default, upcoming and past-due reminders are displayed in the Reminders widget on your iPad's Cover Sheet screen (on your Lock screen). You can also review them all in the Reminders app itself.

( 1 ) From the Cover Sheet screen, tap a reminder to view it in the Reminders app. *Or...*

( 2 ) From the Home screen, tap the Reminders icon to open the Reminders app.

( 3 ) Tap Reminders to view items you have not yet completed.

( 4 ) Tap Scheduled to view items you want to complete by a given date.

( 5 ) Tap the circle next to a given item to mark that item as completed.

## Change the Order

To change the order of the items in your Reminders list, tap Edit at the top of the list and then tap and drag any item to a new position.

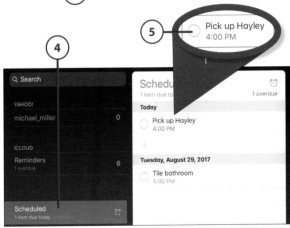

## Add a New Reminder

Adding a new item to your reminders list is as easy as adding a new event to your calendar.

1. From within the Reminders app, tap Reminders.

2. Tap next to the + within the reminders list and enter the item you need reminding of.

3. Tap Done.

4. To add an item that has a set completion date, tap Scheduled.

5. Tap next to the + within the scheduled list and enter the item you need reminding of.

6. Tap the Information (i) icon to display the Details pane.

7 Tap the Alarm field and select a day and time for the completion of this item.

8 If this is a high-priority item, go to the Priority section and tap from one to three exclamation marks (!).

9 Tap Done.

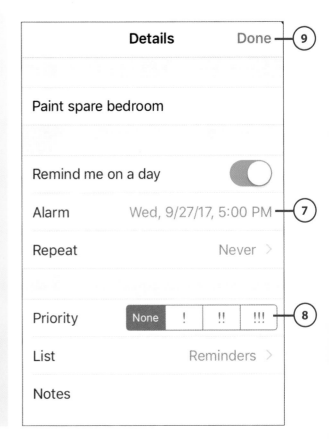

**Details**        Done — 9

Paint spare bedroom

Remind me on a day

Alarm       Wed, 9/27/17, 5:00 PM — 7

Repeat       Never >

Priority    | None | ! | !! | !!! | — 8

List       Reminders >

Notes

# >>>Go Further

## USE SIRI

Instead of entering events and reminders manually, you can use Siri to create new items for both the Calendar and Reminders apps.

To add a calendar event, activate Siri and speak as much information as you know about the event. Say something like, "Schedule a meeting Monday at 3:00 at the Mounds Conference Center" or "Create an event on Tuesday the 29th at 4 pm."

To add a reminder, activate Siri and speak about the task. Say something like, "Remind me to pick up milk on the way home" or "Remember to pay the rent on the first of the month."

# Delete a Reminder

As you've seen, it's easy enough to mark an item as completed; when completed, the item no longer shows in the Reminders list. But what about items that you haven't completed and don't want to show any more? Fortunately, they're easy to delete.

1. From within the Reminders app, tap Reminders.

2. Tap Edit at the top of the reminders list.

3. Tap the red – next to the item you want to delete. The event slides left and you see additional controls.

4. Tap Delete. The item is deleted.

**iBooks app**

USING AMAZON ALEXA AND ECHO

# Chapter 2: Choosing the Right Amazon Echo Device

The Alexa personal digital assistant is built into many different devices. The first of these was the Amazon Echo smart speaker, quickly followed by other devices in the Echo line—the smaller, more affordable Echo Dot, the touchscreen-enabled Echo Show, the webcam-enabled Echo Look, and the battery-operated Amazon Tap. (Okay, that last one didn't have the word "Echo" in its name, but it's clearly part of the same line.) Amazon also builds Alexa capability into its line of Fire TV devices as well as its Fire tablets. And now there are a multitude of third-party devices that license Alexa technology from Amazon, from smart TVs to smart thermostats to smart baby monitors.

In other words, you can get Alexa functionality in just about any type of device you want. But which configuration is best for your personal needs?

## Amazon Echo

The Amazon Echo is the original Alexa-enabled device. De-... ...nally sold as a so-called "smart speaker," the ...and more – and remains Amazon's best-sell-

**Kindle app**

**News app**

# THURSDAY AUGUST 31

67°
Lakeville

# FOOD NETWORK

Food Network

### Rachael Ray's Best Recipes for Kicking Off Labor Day Weekend

Labor Day has a way of sneaking up. One day it's the 4th of July, and then, all of a sudden, it's Labor Day weekend and you're faced with prepping for the last cookout of the summer. Thanks to Rachael Ray's 30-...

1h ago

Food Network
**The Sweet Side of Life: Creme Brulee Without a Torch**
17h ago

Food Network
**Gear Up for Football Season with These Buffalo-Flavored Foods**
21h ago

Food Network
**Take the Day Off: Low-Labor Recipes for Labor Day**
1d ago

Food Network
**Keep the Heat Off with Easy No-Cook Breakfasts**
1d ago

MORE FROM FOOD NETWORK ▸

For You    Spotlight    Following    Search    Saved

In this chapter, you learn how to use your iPad to read various types of publications.

→ Reading eBooks on Your iPad
→ Reading News Stories with the News App

**14**

# Reading eBooks, Magazines, and Newspapers

Your iPad is a great device for reading. You can use your iPad, and the appropriate apps, to read books, newspapers, magazines, and other articles—all in electronic format, all in the palms of your hands.

## Reading eBooks on Your iPad

Electronic books, also known as eBooks, are a convenient way to read your favorite books. You can store multiple eBooks on your iPad and read any of them whenever and wherever you want. No more bulky paper books to haul around; no more losing your place among the dog-eared pages. Everything fits on and is viewed on your iPad.

Apple's iBooks app is preinstalled on your new iPad. You use the iBooks app to purchase eBooks from Apple's iBooks Store—and to read those eBooks you purchase.

# Find and Purchase Books with the iBooks App

Before you can read eBooks with iBooks, you have to buy something to read—which you do directly from the iBooks app, from Apple's iBooks Store.

1. From the iPad's Home screen, tap the iBooks icon to open the iBooks app.

2. Tap Featured to view books featured in the iBooks Store.

3. Tap NYTimes to view books on the *New York Times* bestseller list.

4. Tap Top Charts to view top books in various categories.

5. Tap Top Authors to view books by best-selling authors.

6. Tap Categories to view and select a category and see the best-selling titles in that category.

7. Type within the Search box to search for books by title or author.

8. Tap a book to view more details.

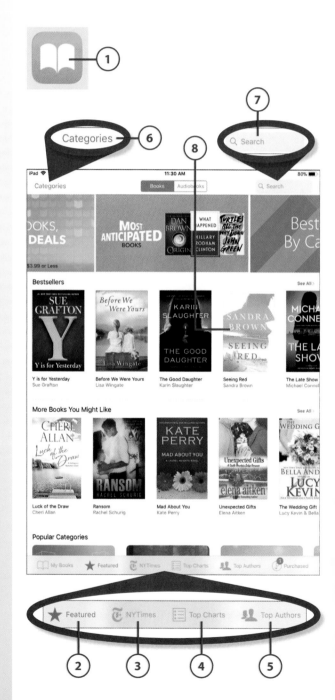

9. Tap Sample to download a short sample of this book.

10. Tap the price button to purchase the book. You see an iBooks Store panel.

11. Tap the Purchase button.

12. You're prompted to sign into the iBooks Store with your Apple ID. Enter your password and click OK to complete the purchase using the payment method you've previously supplied. (If you haven't yet provided a payment method, you're prompted to do so now.)

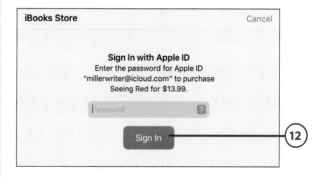

# Read a Book with the iBooks App

All the books you've purchased are downloaded to your iPad and displayed on the My Books screen.

1. From within the iBooks app, tap My Books to view the books and samples you've downloaded to your iPad. *Or…*

2. Tap Purchased to view all books you've purchased from the iBooks Store, even those not currently on this device.

3. Tap a book cover to open that book.

**4** Swipe from right to left (or tap the right side of the screen) to turn to the next page.

**5** Swipe from left to right (or tap the left side of the screen) to turn to the previous page.

**6** Drag the slider at the bottom of the page to move to another section in the book.

**7** Tap the Fonts icon to change the look and feel of the page.

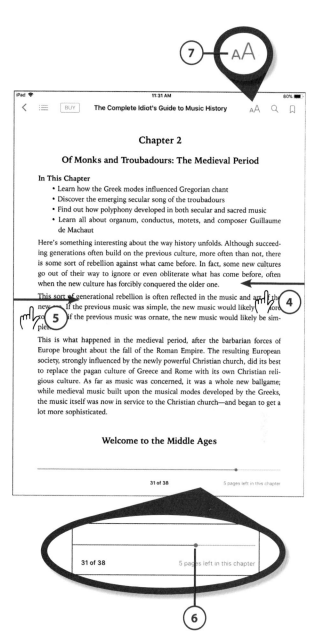

**8** Tap the right A to make the text larger. Continue tapping to make the text even larger.

**9** Tap the left A to make the text smaller. Continue tapping to make the text even smaller.

**10** Tap Fonts to display and select a different font for the book's text.

**11** Tap one of the colored circles to change the display theme for the book pages.

**12** Tap "off" the Auto-Night Theme switch if you don't want the screen to change in low-light conditions. (Leave it on for better reading in bed at night.)

**13** Tap "on" the Scrolling View switch if you'd prefer to scroll through instead of flip through pages.

**14** Tap the Search (magnifying glass) icon to display the Search box.

**15** Type within the Search box to search for a given word, phrase, or page number.

**16** Tap the Bookmark icon to bookmark this page in the book.

**17** Tap the Contents icon to view the book's table of contents.

**18** Tap the left-arrow icon to return to the My Books screen.

## >>>*Go Further*

## LISTENING TO AUDIOBOOKS IN iBOOKS

In addition to reading eBooks, you can also use the iBooks app to listen to audiobooks on your iPad. To purchase an audiobook, tap the Featured or Top Charts tabs and tap to select Audiobooks at the top of the screen. You can then purchase and download any audiobook just as you would an eBook.

To listen to an audiobook, tap that book on the My Books page. Use the playback controls at the bottom of the screen to pause or resume playback, skip 15 seconds back or forward, and even change the speed of the playback.

## Find and Read Books with the Kindle Book Browser

Apple provides its iBooks app for reading eBooks, but let's be honest—when you think about books and booksellers, Apple is not the first company that comes to mind. When you want a larger selection of eBooks, you might want to check out Amazon, the world's largest online bookstore, and Amazon's Kindle eReader app. You can download the Kindle app (it's free) from Apple's App Store.

### Amazon Account

When you first launch the Kindle app, you're prompted to sign into your existing Amazon account. Do so and the app will remember who you are. If you don't yet have an Amazon account, tap Are You New to Kindle? and follow the onscreen instructions from there.

(1) From the iPad's Home screen, tap the Kindle icon to launch the Kindle app. You see your book library.

(2) Tap All to view all books you've purchased. (Book purchases are not automatically downloaded to your iPad; they're stored online in the "cloud" until you're ready to read them.)

(3) Tap Downloaded to view those books that are stored on your iPad.

(4) Tap and type within the Search Kindle box to search for a specific book—both in your library and on Amazon.

(5) Tap the book you want to read. (If the book was in the cloud, it is now automatically downloaded to your iPad.)

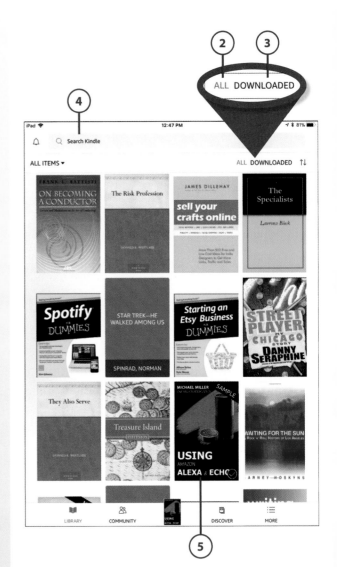

**6** Swipe from right to left (or tap the right side of the screen) to turn to the next page.

**7** Swipe from left to right (or tap the left side of the screen) to turn to the previous page.

# Chapter 1: Getting to Know Amazon Alexa and Echo

Amazon's Echo and Echo Dot are so-called "smart" speakers that have taken the tech industry—and households across the nation—by storm. These unobtrusive devices use a built-in personal digital assistant, dubbed Alexa, to find information, answer questions, and operate all manner of **7** household devices, all with plain-English voice commands. **6**

## What is Alexa?

The success of Amazon's Echo devices is due primarily to the voice and artificial intelligence behind the scenes. Alexa is that voice and AI; she is what (or who?) you interact with, and drives virtually everything that your Echo does.

Of course, Alexa isn't a real human being. She's just a disembodied voice driven by a piece of software, residing in the cloud and speaking (and listening) through your Echo device. You interact with Alexa with voice commands— that is, you talk to her and she talks back. There are no keyboards or touchscreens to tap (aside from the Echo Show device, that is). All your interactions with Alexa are vocal.

If you've ever used Siri on an Apple iPhone or iPad (or,

(8) Tap anywhere on the screen to slightly shrink the page and display controls at the top and bottom of the screen.

(9) Drag the slider at the bottom of the screen to move to another section of the book.

(10) Tap the Menu icon to display the menu pane.

(11) Tap the View Options (font) icon to change font size, font type, color scheme, and more.

(12) Tap the Bookmark icon to bookmark the current page.

(13) Tap the Search (magnifying glass) icon to search within this book.

(14) Tap anywhere on the page to hide the page controls and return to normal reading mode.

## Free eBooks Online

Some eBooks are free. Amazon, Barnes & Noble, and the iBooks Store offer some older books for free download. If you're an Amazon Prime member, you get a variety of free eBooks as part of that subscription. Free eBooks are also available at sites such as Project Gutenberg (www.gutenberg.org) and Open Library (www.openlibrary.org). You can also find many free eBooks at your local library—ask your librarian how to access them.

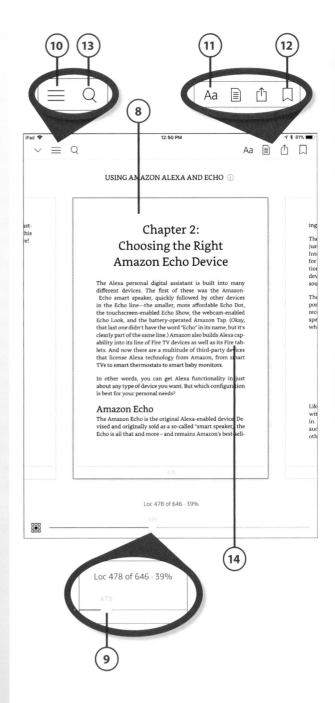

## It's Not All Good

**No In-App Purchases**

Unlike with the iBooks app, you can't purchase books from within the Kindle or Nook apps. That's because Apple doesn't allow third parties to sell books directly from within the Kindle app. (Well, they do, but they require the retailers to share their profits with Apple—which Amazon and Barnes & Noble don't really want to do.)

Instead, you have to make your purchases from the retailer's website, using the Safari web browser. All eBooks you purchase from the retailer's site automatically display within that retailer's eReader app.

## >>>Go Further

### BARNES & NOBLE NOOK

If you buy a lot of books from Barnes & Noble, you might want to check out the Nook eReader app for reading ebooks you purchase from B&N's online store (www.bn.com). The Nook app works similarly to the iBooks and Kindle apps, and is available for free from the Apple App Store.

# Reading News Stories with the News App

Books aren't the only things you can read on your iPad. You can also read online newspaper and magazine articles, using Apple's News app.

The News app aggregates stories from a variety of news sources, based on your reading habits. You see stories about topics you're most interested in, from those sources you like the best.

# Personalize What News You Receive

When you first launch the News app, you're prompted to select news sources (Apple calls them Channels) you'd like to include in your news feed. A handful of sources are already listed, just in case you don't have any preferences yet. You can select additional news sources now or do so at any later time.

1. From the iPad's Home screen, tap the News icon to launch the News app.

2. Tap Following at the bottom of the screen.

3. You see a list of news sources you're currently following. To remove any of these sources, tap Edit.

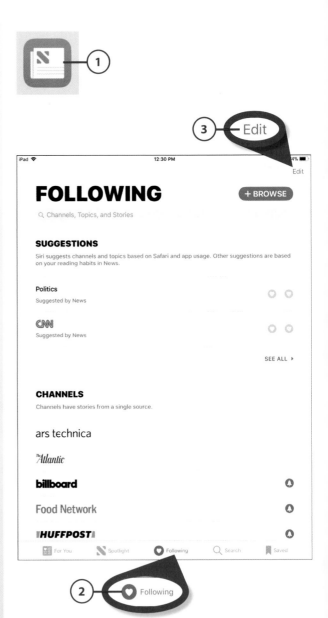

**4** Tap the red – next to any source you want to remove, and then tap Remove.

**5** Tap Done to return to the previous screen.

**6** Tap Browse to view additional news sources to add to your feed.

**7** Tap the Heart icon to add any news sources you want to follow.

**8** Tap Done when you're done.

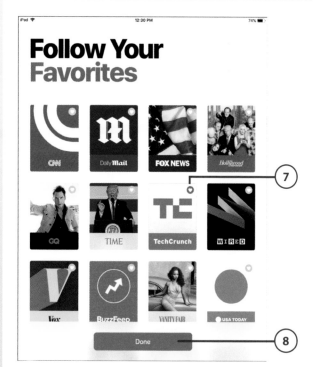

## Read News Stories

The News app assembles stories based on the sources and topics you select, and then fine-tunes those selections based on what you actually read over time. Stories are displayed on the main For You page.

(1) From within the News app, tap For You to view stories in your news feed.

(2) Stories are organized by news source and topic. Scroll down the screen to view additional sources and topics.

(3) Tap a story to read it.

**4** Swipe right to left to go to the next story.

**5** Swipe left to right to go to the previous story.

**6** Tap the Font icon to change the size of the onscreen text.

**7** Tap the Like (heart) icon to like this story.

**8** Top the Don't Like icon to dislike this story.

**9** Tap the Share icon to share this story via instant message, email, or social media.

**10** Tap the Back icon to return to the previous screen.

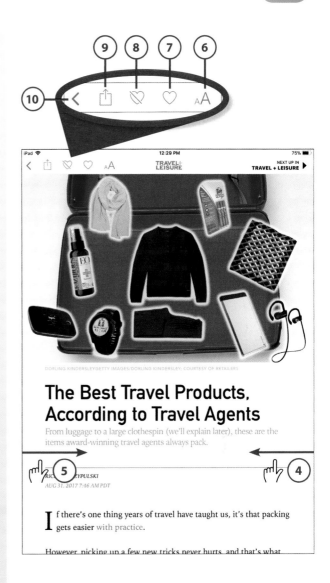

The Best Travel Products, According to Travel Agents

From luggage to a large clothespin (we'll explain later), these are the items award-winning travel agents always pack.

*RIC___ ___YPULSKI*
*AUG 31, 2017 7:46 AM PDT*

If there's one thing years of travel have taught us, it's that packing gets easier with practice.

However, picking up a few new tricks never hurts, and that's what

In this chapter, you learn how to use your iPad to shoot photos and videos, and then edit and share what you shot.

→ Shooting Digital Photos
→ Viewing and Editing Your Photos
→ Shooting and Editing Videos
→ Sharing Photos and Videos

# Shooting, Editing, and Sharing Photos and Videos

Your iPad is much like an iPhone or other smartphone in terms of the features it offers. (But with a much bigger screen, of course.) This is especially true when it comes to photography, as your iPad features two built-in cameras—one facing outward and one pointing toward your face. You can use these cameras to shoot still photos and videos, and then use various apps to edit and share those items with others.

## Shooting Digital Photos

Yes, you can use your iPad to shoot digital photos. You can take a picture of anything in front of you, or switch to the front-facing FaceTime camera and take a picture of yourself. (That's called a *selfie*.) You use the iPad's screen to preview the picture, then aim the camera at whatever it is you're shooting and press the Shutter button. You can then edit the pictures you take to crop them, rotate them, adjust brightness and color, and even apply filters for special effects.

# Launch the Camera App

Since you never know when a good photo op will present itself, Apple offers three different ways to quickly launch your iPad's camera.

1. From the iPad's Home screen, tap the Camera icon.

2. From any screen, swipe up from the bottom to display the Control Center and then tap the Camera icon.

3. From the Lock or Cover Sheet screen, swipe from right to left. (That's right—you don't have to unlock your iPad to use the camera!)

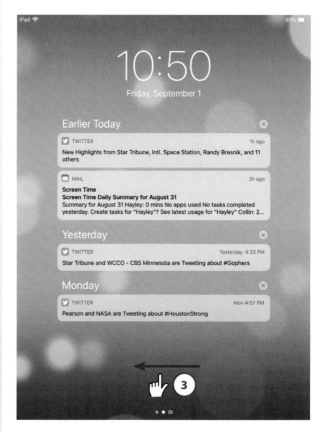

# Take a Picture

When it comes to taking pictures
with your iPad, you can shoot in the
16:9 aspect ratio that mirrors the iPad
screen or in a square format better
suited for some types of web uploads
(such as your profile picture in Facebook). Use the rear-facing iSight
camera to take pictures of things in
front of you or (as discussed in the
next task) the front-facing FaceTime
camera to take selfies.

1. Open the Camera app and make
   sure the rear-facing camera is
   selected. If not, tap the Switch
   button.

2. Hold your iPad vertically to take
   a portrait photo, or horizontally to take a landscape photo.
   The onscreen controls rotate
   accordingly.

**(3)** Tap Photo in the lower right to shoot 16:9 ratio photos.

**(4)** Tap Square in the lower right to shoot square photos.

**(5)** To enable HDR photos, which provide higher contrast results, tap to enable the HDR button.

## HDR

HDR stands for *high dynamic range*, which combines the results of three photos automatically shot in rapid succession (with different exposure settings) to create more detail in high-contrast photos.

**(6)** To use the timer (good if you want to include yourself in the shot—set the timer and run around in front of the camera!), tap the Timer button and select either a 3- or 10-second timer. The timer activates when you press the Shutter button.

**(7)** Drag the zoom slider on the left side of the screen to zoom into a shot. Alternatively, expand two fingers onscreen to zoom in.

**(8)** Optionally, tap the subject of the photo onscreen to focus on that person or object. This displays a box around the selected area, and an Exposure slider; drag the slider up to increase the exposure (makes the shot brighter) or down to decrease the exposure (darkens the shot).

## Auto Focus and Exposure

Your iPad's iSight camera includes auto focus and auto exposure, which uses face-recognition technology to identify the subject of the picture and focus and set exposure automatically. You can override these automatic controls by tapping to select a person or object onscreen different from the one your iPad selects.

( **9** )  Use the iPad's display to aim the camera and compose your picture, then press the Shutter button to take the photo. Alternatively, press either Volume button on the side of your iPad to take the picture.

( **10** )  Tap the preview thumbnail to view the picture you just took.

## Burst Shots

To take a series of rapid-fire ("burst") shots, press and hold the Shutter button. Release the button to stop shooting. (Not available on older iPad minis.)

## >>>Go Further

### CONFIGURING THE CAMERA APP

Your iPad's Camera app works just fine "out of the box," as it were, but there are a few options you can configure to personalize the way it works. To configure the Camera app, tap the Settings icon on the Dock or Home screen, then select Camera in the left column.

Here are a few of the settings you might want to change:

- To have the Camera app remember the last type of picture you took (Photo, Video, or Square), tap Preserve Settings and then tap "on" the Camera Mode switch.

- Tap "on" the Grid switch to display an onscreen grid, to help you better compose your photos.

- By default, the Camera app can shoot and read the QR codes you see on many products and items. To turn off this feature, tap "off" the Scan QR Codes switch.

- By default, the iSight camera records video at 1080p HD resolution, with a frame rate of 30 fps. This works fine in most instances, but if you want to record at a slightly lower resolution (which creates smaller files and saves space on your device), tap Record Video and select 720p HD at 30 fps.

- When you shoot HDR photos, the Camera app by default stores all three photos used to create the final HDR photo. If you'd rather save on storage space, tap off the Keep Normal Photo switch in the HDR section.

The default settings work fine in most cases, but if you need to change any of them, that's how to do it.

## Take a Selfie

Use the front-facing FaceTime camera on your iPad to take selfies of yourself. (Is that redundant?) When you use the FaceTime camera, you have fewer shooting options available—for example, you can't shoot HDR photos, or zoom into the shot.

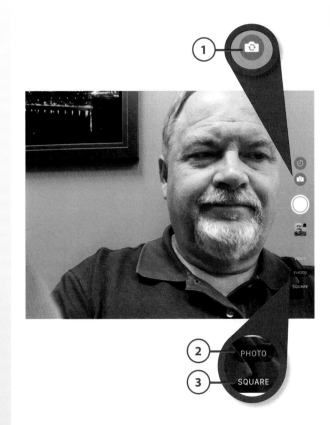

1. Open the Camera app and tap the Switch button to switch to the front-facing FaceTime camera. Rotate the iPad vertically to take a portrait picture (most common for selfies) or horizontally to take a landscape photo.

2. Tap Photo to take a 16:9 ratio photo.

3. Tap Square to take a square photo. (Great for profile pictures on many websites.)

(4) Smile at the camera (and look at your smiling face onscreen) and then press the Shutter button to take the picture.

(5) Tap the preview thumbnail to view the selfie you just took.

### Screen Capture

To take a screenshot of what's currently displayed on your iPad's screen, simultaneously press and release the Sleep/Wake and Home buttons on your iPad. Screenshots are stored in the Photos app or iCloud Photo Library.

# Take a Panoramic Photo

Apple's Camera app also lets you take panoramic photos that include a wide expanse not normally captured in a single photo. To create a panoramic photo, you shoot multiple photos from left to right, then the Camera app digitally stitches them together.

Panoramic photos are great for capturing outdoor landscapes, as well as "panning" a room indoors.

Panoramic photo

**1** From within the Camera app, make sure the iSight (rear-facing) camera is selected, then tap Pano in the lower-right corner.

**2** Hold the iPad vertically (portrait mode) and tap the Shutter button. (If you hold the iPad horizontally, the Photos app takes a vertical panoramic photo that stretches from the bottom to the top.)

**3** As directed onscreen, move or pan the iPad slowly in the direction of the arrow. The progress of your pan appears in an inset over the main display.

**4** Tap the Shutter button when you're done panning.

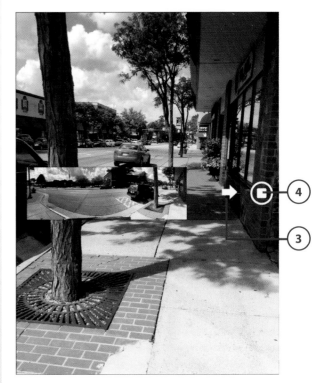

# Viewing and Editing Your Photos

While the iPad may be a little inconvenient as a day-to-day digital camera, it's actually pretty good for viewing and editing photos. The large screen, combined with handy touchscreen operation, makes it easy to look at the photos you've taken and make minor changes to them, if necessary.

You use Apple's Photos app to both view and edit your photos. In fact, you can use the iPad's Photos app to view and edit not only pictures taken with your iPad, but also photos taken by any of your Apple devices. When you use the iCloud Photo Library, all photos you take with your iPad *and* iPhone are automatically uploaded and stored online, and available to all your Apple devices. So take a picture with your iPhone and edit it with your iPad—it's the best way to use both devices!

## >>>Go Further
### CONFIGURING THE PHOTOS APP

Just as you might want to configure a few settings in your iPad's Camera app, you also might want to customize a handful of settings in the accompanying Photos app. Go to your iPad's Settings page and tap Photos in the left column, then look at the following settings in the right column:

- Tap "on" the iCloud Photo Library control to automatically upload your pictures to your iCloud account. To share these photos with others, scroll down and tap "on" iCloud Photo Sharing, too.

- To automatically beam the photos you take to other Apple devices in your home (when they're all connected to the same Wi-Fi network), tap "on" the Upload to My Photo Stream switch.

- To save storage space on your iPad, select Optimize iPad Storage; full-resolution photos will still be stored online in your iCloud account. If you'd rather keep full-resolution versions on your iPad, select Download and Keep Originals instead.

There are even more settings you can configure, but these are the main ones you want to pay attention to.

# View Your Photos

You can view photos you've just taken from within the Camera app or from Apple's Photos app.

1. From within the Camera app, tap the preview thumbnail to display the photo full screen. (Tap the back arrow to return to the camera to shoot some more photos.) Or…

2. From the Home screen, tap the Photos icon to open the Photos app.

3. You can let the Photos app organize your photos, by "smart" groups, or you can organize them yourself, in albums. To view the app's smart groups, tap Photos.

4. The largest type of smart group is called a Year; this simply organizes your photos by year taken. The next smallest group is called a Collection, which is typically a group of photos that share a time range or topic in common. The smallest group is called a Moment, which is typically photos within a Collection taken on a given date. The heading of a given screen indicates which type of smart group you're viewing. To move to the next smallest smart group, tap a Year or Collection.

5. To move to the next largest group, tap the Back icon at the top of the screen.

**6** Tap Memories to view photos and videos curated by the Photos app into collages and short videos.

**7** Tap a memory to view it.

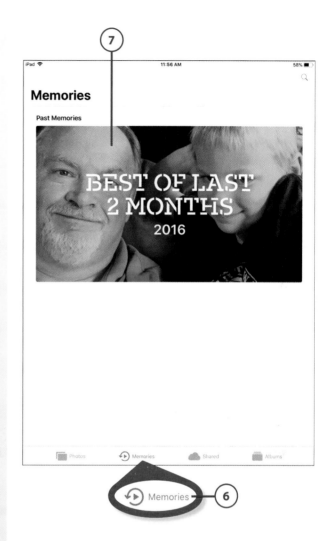

**8** Tap Shared to view photos from this and other devices stored in the iCloud Photo Library.

**9** Tap to view a specific photo.

(**10**) Tap Albums to view your photos organized by album.

(**11**) Tap an album to view the photos stored within.

(**12**) Tap to view a specific photo.

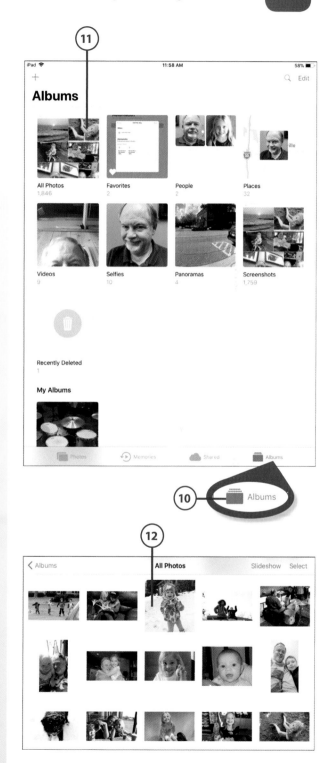

(13) Tap the Heart icon to add this photo to your Favorites album.

(14) Tap the Trash Can icon to delete the photo.

(15) Additional photos in this group or album are displayed as thumbnails in a strip along the bottom of the screen. Drag the strip left or right to see additional photos.

(16) Tap the Back icon to return to the previous group or album.

# >>>Go Further

## USING THE iCLOUD PHOTO LIBRARY

While you can store your photos (up to 1,000 of them, anyway) locally on your iPad, you can store many more photos online in Apple's iCloud Photo Library. When you enable the iCloud Photo Library on your device, all photos and videos you shoot are automatically uploaded to and stored on Apple's iCloud online storage service.

You can then access your photos and videos from any connected computer or device, just by going to the iCloud website (www.icloud.com) and logging in with your Apple ID. Any edits or changes you make to the stored photos are visible on all your devices.

To enable iCloud Photo Library storage, tap the Settings icon, select Photos, and then tap "on" the iCloud Photo Library switch. You're ready to go.

(Note that if you use the iCloud Photo Library, you no longer use the iTunes software to synchronize photos and videos between your iPad and your computer.)

## Organize Photos in Albums

The Photos app does a good job automatically organizing your photos into smart groups. That said, you might want to organize your photos your own way, by creating virtual photo albums to group photos by type, activity, location, and so forth.

1. From within the Photos app, tap Albums to display your existing albums. (If you're within a given album, tap the Back icon to return to the main Albums screen.)

(2) Tap an album to view the photos stored within. *Or...*

(3) Tap the + icon to create a new album.

(4) From the New Album panel, enter a name for this album.

(5) Tap Save.

(6) You're prompted to add photos to your new album. Tap to select those photos you want to add. (You can select multiple photos; as you select each photo, a blue check mark appears on each item you select.)

(7) Tap Done. The selected photos are added to your new album.

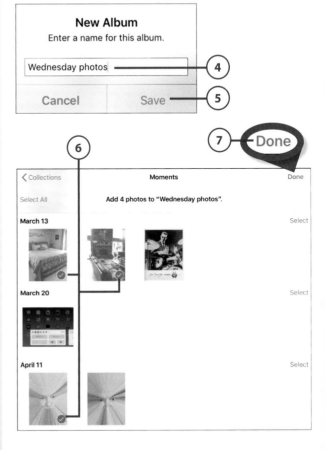

**8** To add additional photos to an album, open the group or album that contains the photo(s) you want to add.

**9** Tap Select.

**10** Tap to select the photos you want to add.

**11** Tap Add To.

**12** Tap to select the album you want to add these pictures to. The pictures are now added.

## Slideshows

The Photos app enables you to play a slideshow of photos from any given album. Just open the album, then tap Slideshow in the top-right corner of the screen.

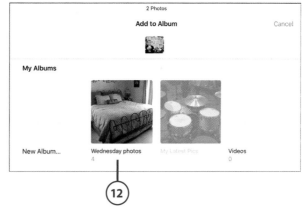

## >>>Go Further

## WORKING WITH SMART ALBUMS

The Photos app in iOS 11 includes several "smart" albums that are automatically filled with appropriate photos, as best as the app can determine.

Let's start with the People album. This album uses facial recognition technology to identify and include photos that have people's faces in them. It also groups photos by like faces, so that all photos of a given person should be grouped together. Tap a group to view all photos of that person.

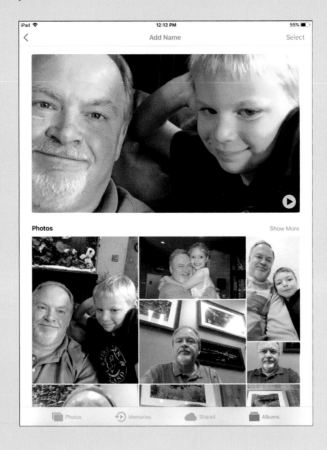

The Places album attempts to organize your photos by where they were taken. (That's if your iPad knows this; you have to take a photo with your device's location services enabled for this to work.) Open the Places album and you see a map of the U.S. with one or more places pinpointed; tap a location to view photos taken at that location. (And if the grouping is too vague—for example, all photos taken within a state are grouped together—just zoom into the map to display more local locations.) If the map is too confusing to you, tap Grid to display location photos in a traditional grid listing.

The Photos app also groups photos by type, so you'll see albums for Selfies, Panoramas, Screenshots, and the like. Just tap an album to view its contents.

# Crop and Straighten a Picture

Not every picture you take is perfect. Fortunately, digital pictures can be easily edited. You use the Photos app to make any necessary corrections to your photos.

1. From within the Photos app, open the photo you want to edit.

2. Tap Edit to display the editing screen.

3. Tap the Crop button.

4. To crop the picture, drag the corners of the screen until you like what you see.

5. To rotate the picture 90 degrees counterclockwise, tap the Rotate button at the top of the screen.

6. To straighten or rotate the picture in smaller increments, drag your finger on the rotation dial until the picture is as you like it.

7. Tap Done when you're satisfied with the results. (If you don't like the changes, tap Cancel in the lower-right corner to undo them and return to the original photo.)

## Apply Auto-Enhance

Sometimes a picture doesn't look quite right, but you don't want to do a lot of manual fine-tuning to fix it. In these instances, use the Photo app's Auto-Enhance control and let the app do the fixing for you. Auto-Enhance adjusts brightness, contrast, color, and other controls to try to make your picture look better.

( 1 ) From within the editing screen for a photo, tap the Auto-Enhance (magic wand) button.

( 2 ) If you like what you see, tap Done. (If you don't like the results, tap the Auto-Enhance button again to turn off the auto enhancement.)

## Apply a Filter

Another easy way to change the way a picture looks is to apply a photo filter. The Photos app comes with more than a half-dozen filters that can change the mood of a picture.

( 1 ) From within the editing screen for a photo, tap the Filters button.

( 2 ) You now see the available filters. Tap a filter to apply it to your photo.

( 3 ) If you like this filter, tap Done. (If you don't like this filter, select another or tap Cancel.)

# Adjust Brightness and Color

The Photos app also offers more traditional editing controls you can use to enhance your photos—brightness and contrast (what the app calls Light), color saturation (Color), and more.

1. From within the editing screen for a photo, tap the Adjustments button.

2. Tap Light to adjust brightness.

3. Tap the thumbnail that best represents the brightness/contrast you want. *Or...*

4. To more precisely adjust brightness characteristics, tap the More button.

5. Tap to adjust any of the following characteristics: Brilliance, Exposure, Highlights, Shadows, Brightness, Contrast, and Black Point.

6. Use the slider to adjust the selected adjustment.

7. Tap the More button to return to the previous screen, then tap Close.

8. Tap Color to adjust color saturation (how much color there is in the photo).

**9** Tap the thumbnail that best represents the desired color saturation. *Or…*

**10** To more precisely adjust color characteristics, tap the More button and then tap to adjust any of the following characteristics: Saturation, Contrast, and Cast (tint).

**11** Tap the B&W button to turn your picture into a black-and-white photo, and make appropriate adjustments.

**12** Tap the thumbnail that best represents the black-and-white look you want. *Or…*

**13** To more precisely adjust black-and-white characteristics, tap the More button and tap to adjust any of the following characteristics: Intensity, Neutrals, Tone, and Grain.

**14** Tap Done when you're done editing. (Or tap Cancel to undo your changes and return to the original photo.)

## Revert to Original

When you make changes to a photo, the Photos app keeps a copy of the original photo. You can discard any changes and revert back to the original photo at any time by re-opening the photo for editing and tapping Revert. When prompted, tap Revert to Original, and that's what you get.

## Mark Up a Photo

You can also, if you want, "mark up" a photo by drawing on it or adding text to the picture.

1. From within the editing screen for a photo, tap the More button.

2. Tap Markup.

3. Tap the Pen icon to draw on the photo. (Alternatively, tap the Highlighter icon to highlight an area, the Pencil icon to draw a fine line, or the Eraser icon to erase something you've previously drawn.)

4. Tap a color to select the pen color.

5. Drag your finger across the screen to draw.

6. To add text to a picture, tap the More (+) icon.

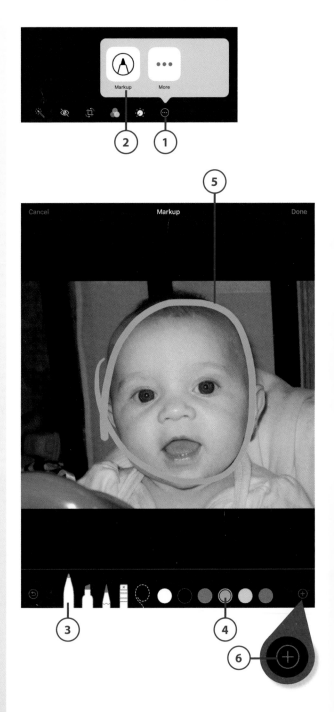

( 7 ) Select Text. This places a text box on the screen.

( 8 ) Double-tap the text box to display the onscreen keyboard, and then type the text you want. Close the keyboard to see other text options.

( 9 ) To change the text color, tap the text box and then select the color you want.

( 10 ) To change the size and other characteristics of the text, select the text box and then tap the Font button.

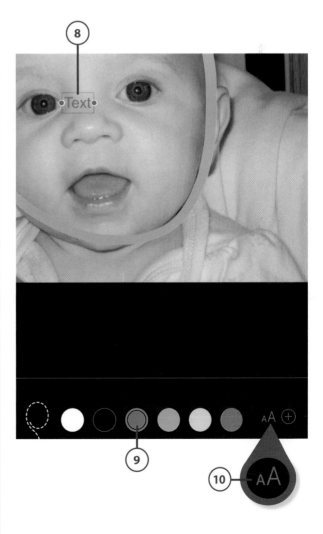

**11** Tap to select a different font family.

**12** Use the slider to change the size of the text.

**13** Tap one of the alignment buttons to change how the text is aligned (left, center, justified, or right).

**14** Tap Done when you're done.

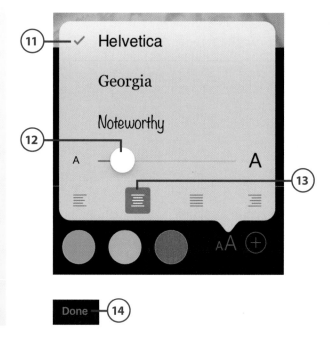

# Shooting and Editing Videos

The rear-facing and front-facing cameras in your iPad can also be used to shoot videos. That means you can shoot videos of family gatherings, vacations, sporting events, and more—even selfie videos of yourself!

## Shoot a Video

Shooting a video with your iPad is almost as easy as shooting a still photograph.

**1** Tap the Camera icon to open the Camera app.

( **2** ) Hold your iPad vertically to take a portrait video, or horizontally to take a landscape video. The onscreen controls rotate accordingly.

( **3** ) Tap Video in the lower-right corner of the screen.

( **4** ) Tap the Switch button to switch between the rear-facing (iSight) and front-facing (FaceTime) cameras.

## Widescreen Videos

Most videos are shot in landscape format, which requires you to hold your iPad horizontally. This is the orientation used by all movies and TV shows; it produces a 16:9 ratio widescreen picture, which fits perfectly on your TV screen.

( **5** ) Drag the zoom slider on the left side of the screen to zoom into a shot. Alternatively, expand two fingers onscreen to zoom in.

( **6** ) Optionally, tap the subject of the video onscreen to focus on that person or object. This displays a box around the selected area, and an Exposure slider; drag the slider up to increase the exposure (makes the video brighter) or down to decrease the exposure (darkens the video).

**7** Use the iPad's display to aim the camera and compose your picture and then press the red Record button to start recording. Alternatively, press either Volume button on the side of your iPad to initiate recording.

**8** As you record, the elapsed time is displayed at the top of the screen.

**9** Tap the Record button again to stop recording.

## >>>Go Further
### SLO-MO AND TIME-LAPSE VIDEOS

The Photos app enables you to take two special types of videos. You can shoot video for slow-motion playback or record a series of still photographs as a time-lapse video.

To shoot in slow motion, select Slo-Mo as the recording type. Your video is then shot at a super-fast 120 frames per second (fps). When a fast fps video is played at a normal (30 fps) frame rate, you get crystal-clear slow motion. You select which parts of your video to play in slow motion when you edit the video.

To record a time-lapse video, you have to keep your iPad perfectly still over the period of time you're shooting. Select Time-Lapse as the recording type, tap the Record button, and the Camera app starts capturing individual shots. Tap Record again to end the recording, and the individual shots are compiled into a short video.

# Trim a Video

After you've shot a video, you can trim the beginning and end to make the video shorter and focus on the important parts. You can do this editing from within the Camera or Photos apps.

**1** After you've shot the video in the Camera app, tap the thumbnail to display the video playback screen. *Or…*

**2** From within the Photos app, tap to open the video you want to trim.

**3** Tap Edit.

**4** In the series of thumbnails (called a *timeline*) beneath the video, touch and drag either of the arrows until a yellow border appears in the timeline.

**5** Drag the yellow left and right arrows until you've selected the portion of the video you want to keep. (Everything outside the yellow selected section will be trimmed.)

**6** Tap the Play button to play the selected (yellow) section of the video.

**7** Tap Done when you're done.

## >>>Go Further

### iMOVIE

If you want to further edit a video you've shot, you can use the iMovie app, which is included with your iPad. This is a powerful yet easy-to-use app that lets you create *projects* that include multiple video clips, photos, music, and more.

When you create a new project, you select which elements you want to include, then add them to the project's timeline. You can select various project themes that determine the final look and feel, add fades between elements (and at the start and finish), apply filters, and more. If you're so inclined, check it out!

# Sharing Photos and Videos

When you take a photo or video that you like, you might want to share it with friends and family. Fortunately, the Camera and Photos apps both make it easy to share your pics and vids via text message, email, social media, and more.

## Share via Text Message

You can share photos and videos with your contacts via the Messages app.

1. From within the Camera or Photos app, open the item you want to share and then tap the Share icon.

2. Tap Message to display the New Message pane.

3. Enter the name of the person you want to share with into the To field. (You can enter multiple people if you want.)

**4** The photo or video is added to the conversation. Tap within the item to add a text message.

**5** Tap the Send icon to send the message.

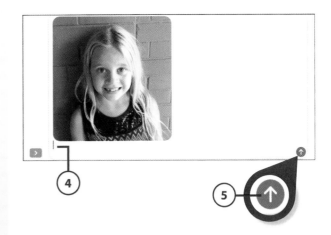

## Share via Email

You can also send a photo or video to any of your contacts via email, using your iPad's Mail app.

**1** From within the Camera or Photos app, open the item you want to share and then tap the Share icon.

**2** Tap Mail to display the New Message pane.

③ Tap within the To field and enter the names or email addresses of the intended recipients.

④ Tap within the Subject field and enter a subject for this email.

⑤ Tap within the main text area and enter any accompanying message.

⑥ Tap Send to send the email.

## Share via Facebook

If you're on Facebook or other social media, you can also post a photo or video to that social network. This example uses Facebook, but the steps are similar if you're posting to Twitter or other networks.

① From within the Camera or Photos app, open the item you want to share and then tap the Share icon.

② Tap Facebook to display the Facebook pane.

( 3 ) Tap within the Say Something field and enter the text of your post.

( 4 ) Tag any friends or locations in this photo or video, if you want.

( 5 ) Tap the right arrow to select your privacy options—who you want to see this post.

( 6 ) Tap Post to post this photo or video as a new status update.

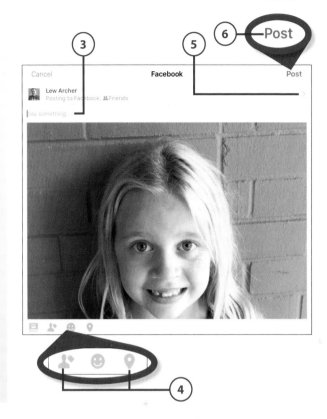

>>>*Go Further*
## OTHER SHARING OPTIONS

Your iPad offers several other ways to share your photos and videos.

If you've enabled iCloud photo sharing, and created shared folders for your friends and family members, you can upload your photos and videos to a shared folder. Just open the photo or video, tap the Share button, and then tap iCloud Photo Sharing. You can add a comment to accompany this item and select which shared album you want to post to.

When it comes to videos, many people like to post their videos to YouTube, the world's largest video sharing community. (Chapter 17, "Watching TV Shows, Movies, and Other Videos," covers watching YouTube videos.) If you have a YouTube account, it's easy to post your videos directly from your iPad. Just open the video, tap the Share button, and then tap YouTube. You're prompted to supply a title and other information for the video, and then you can begin uploading. When the uploading is complete, anyone on YouTube can view it.

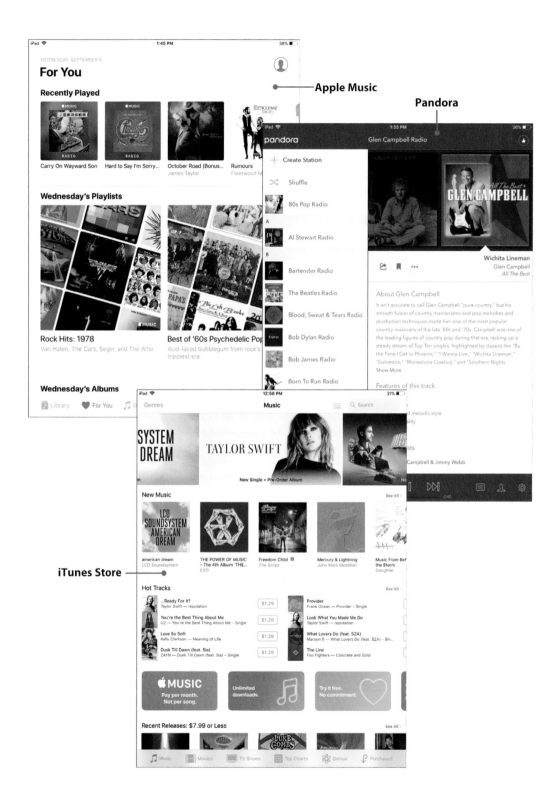

**Apple Music**

**Pandora**

**iTunes Store**

In this chapter, you learn how to listen to music on your iPad.

→ Listening to Streaming Music

→ Buying and Playing Music from the iTunes Store

# Listening to Music

If you like to listen to music, you're in luck. Your iPad is a versatile music playback system that lets you listen to the music you love wherever you happen to be. You can purchase and download music directly to your iPad, or stream just about any song in the world over your iPad if you have an Internet connection.

## Listening to Streaming Music

The way we listen to music has changed over the years. When I was growing up, I could listen to music over AM or FM radio, or buy LPs and singles to play on my record player. Later generations listened to audio-cassettes on their portable Walkman devices or purchased albums on digital compact discs. Still later generations learned how to download music from the Internet, either legally (through the iTunes Store) or illegally (via the infamous Napster).

That's all old news, however, as digital downloads are being supplanted by the concept of streaming music services. These services, such as Amazon Prime Music, Apple Music, Pandora, and Spotify, stream huge music libraries (tens of millions of tracks) over the Internet direct to any connected device—including your iPad. All you need is an Internet connection, and just about any song you want is available for your listening pleasure. There's nothing to buy, and nothing to download to your device.

### Free—or Not

Most streaming music services offer some type of free listening level, typically supported by commercials. If you want to get rid of the commercials (and gain more control over what you listen to), paid subscriptions are available.

## Listen to Apple Music

Not surprisingly, Apple offers its own streaming music service, which it would like you to use. Unlike most other services, Apple Music doesn't have a free level; you pay $9.99/month for an individual membership, after a free three-month trial. (Other pricing is also available, including a $14.99/month family membership.)

You access Apple Music from the Music app on your iPad. To sign up for the service, tap the For You tab. When prompted, opt to get your three months free, choose which plan you want (Individual, Student, or Family), and proceed from there.

When you first log on, you're prompted to choose your favorite music, which you do by selecting the genres and artists you like best. Apple Music then fills up the For You tab with music it thinks you might like.

1. From the iPad Home screen, tap the Music icon to launch the Music app.

**2** Tap For You to view recommended playlists, albums, and artists.

**3** Tap Browse to browse through new music.

**4** Tap Radio to listen to Apple Music's preprogrammed radio stations.

**5** Tap Search to search for specific music.

**6** After you tap Search, tap to select Apple Music. (If you select Your Library, you search only through the music you have stored on your iPad, not Apple Music's much larger online library.)

**7** Tap within the Search box and enter the name of the artist or track you're looking for.

**8** As you type, Apple Music displays a list of matching artists, albums, and songs. Tap to select the one you want.

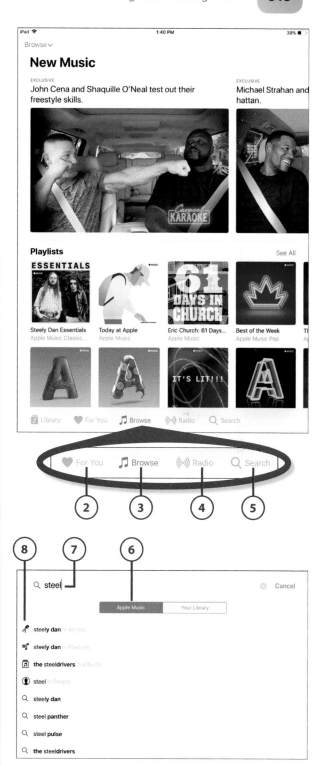

**9** Tap to listen to a given track, station, album, or playlist.

**10** Playback now begins and playback controls are displayed in the bottom-right corner of the screen. Tap Pause to pause playback; tap Play to resume playback.

**11** Tap Next to play the next track.

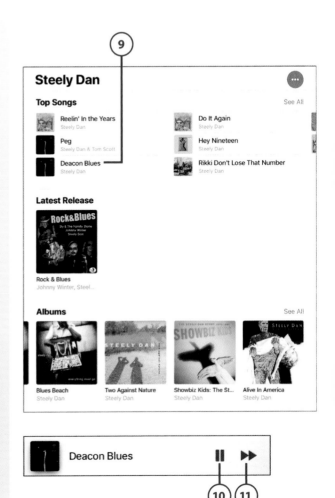

## Listen to Pandora

The most popular streaming service today is Pandora. With Pandora, you specify a song or artist or genre you like, and the service builds a custom playback "channel" based on your selection. For example, if you really like James Taylor, you can create a James Taylor Radio channel. Although you can't specify which specific songs for Pandora to play, you do get a lot of music similar to those songs or artists you like. (And Pandora fine-tunes your stations over time, based on which tracks you like or don't like.)

You listen to Pandora via the Pandora app, available for free from Apple's App Store. Basic Pandora service (with ads) is free; upgrade to Pandora Plus service ($4.99/month) to get rid of the ads. There's also a Pandora Premium plan ($9.99/month) that offers on-demand listening. (Basic Pandora doesn't let you specify which songs to listen to; it's more like traditional over-the-air radio.)

When you first launch the app, you're prompted to either sign up or log in, so do one or the other.

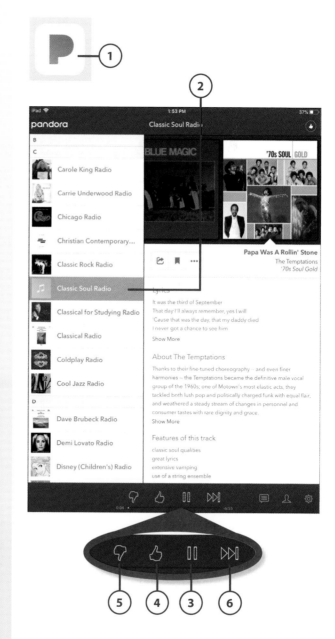

(1) From the iPad Home screen, tap the Pandora icon to launch the Pandora app.

(2) All your existing radio stations are listed on the left. Tap a station to listen.

(3) Tap the Pause button to pause playback. The button turns into a Play button; tap Play to resume playback.

(4) Tap the Thumbs Up icon if you like a track; the radio station will be fine-tuned to play more tracks like this.

(5) Tap the Thumbs Down icon if you don't like a track; it will now be skipped and the radio station fine-tuned to not play music like this.

(6) Tap the Next button if the track is okay but you just don't want to listen to it now. The track will be skipped but it won't affect how Pandora fine-tunes your station.

7 Tap + Create Station to create a new station.

8 Use the onscreen keyboard to type in the name of a song, artist, or genre.

9 Pandora lists matching artists, tracks, and genres. Tap a selection to create that station, add it to your station list, and begin playback.

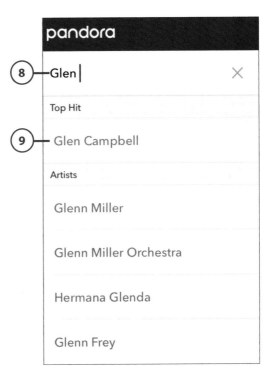

## >>>*Go Further*

### AMAZON, SPOTIFY, AND YOUTUBE

Apple Music and Pandora have a lot of competition from other streaming music services. If you like to listen to music on your iPad, there are plenty of options you can choose!

**Spotify**, for example, is the largest on-demand streaming service. It works like Apple Music, in that you "dial up" the specific artists and songs you want to listen to. There is a free version that throws a lot of stuff you may not want into the mix. Spotify Premium, at $9.99, is the on-demand plan that lets you listen to what you want, when you want. Download the Spotify app from the App Store to get started.

Then there's online retailer **Amazon.com**, which offers two different streaming music services. (That's in addition to all the digital music it has for purchase and download, of course.) Amazon Prime Music offers two million on-demand tracks for members of the Amazon Prime service. (Amazon Prime offers free two-day shipping on qualifying purchases; a one-year subscription costs $99 and includes free access to the Prime Music service.) If you want more selection, pay $9.99/month for Amazon Music Unlimited, which offers tens of millions of on-demand tracks. Get the Amazon Music app for free from the App Store.

Then there's **YouTube**. Although it's not technically a streaming music service (it's a video sharing site), a lot of people use YouTube to listen to their favorite music—and it's all free. Most major artists and record labels have official music videos on YouTube, and many artists and individuals have created and uploaded so-called "lyric videos" (music with lyrics superimposed onscreen) for other songs. In short, there's a lot of music available on YouTube, and it's all available for free. Use the YouTube app from the App Store.

# Buying and Playing Music from the iTunes Store

While streaming music may be all the rage, many of us still prefer to own the music we like, so we can take and listen to it anywhere—even if there's no Internet connection handy. The way to do this on your iPad is to purchase digital music from Apple's iTunes Store, and then download your purchases to your iPad for playback.

## Purchase Music from the iTunes Store

Apple offers tens of millions of individual tracks for purchase in the iTunes Store. Most tracks are priced from $0.99 to $1.29, which means it's affordable to build your own personal music library.

1. From the iPad Home screen, tap the iTunes Store icon to open the iTunes Store.

2. Tap the Music tab to view music available for purchase.

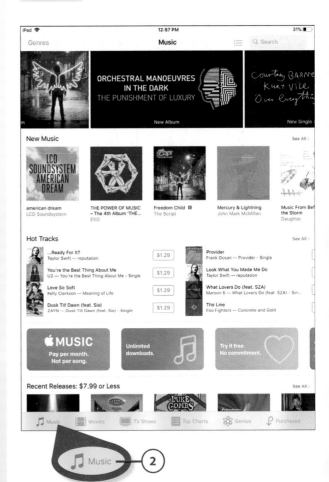

(3) Tap Genres to browse music by genre; tap to select the genre you want.

(4) Tap within the Search box and enter the name of a song, album, or artist.

(5) iTunes displays a list of matching artists or music. Tap the one you want.

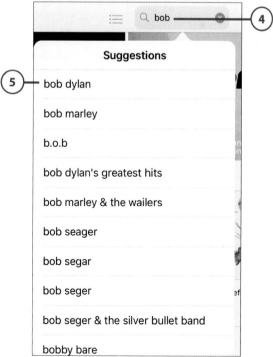

**6** Tap an album to purchase the album or view its individual tracks.

**7** Tap the price button to purchase an album or track.

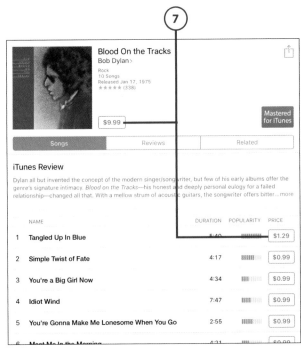

**8** Tap the Purchase button and follow the instructions to enter your Apple ID and complete the transaction.

## Play Your Tunes

When you purchase a track from the iTunes Store, that track is automatically downloaded to and stored on your iPad. You play this music with the iPad's Music app.

**1** From the iPad Home screen, tap the Music icon to open the Music app.

**2** Tap the Library tab (at the bottom of the screen) to view all the music stored on your iPad.

**3** Tap Library (at the top of the screen) to select how you view your music—Recently Added, Playlists, Artists, Albums, Songs, or Downloaded Music.

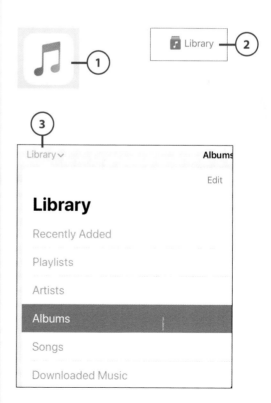

**4** If you select Artists or Albums, tap through to view individual tracks.

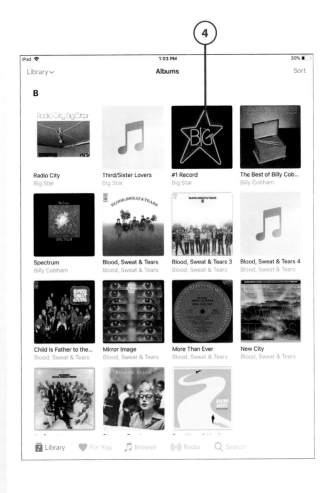

(5) Tap Play to play all the tracks in order.

(6) Tap Shuffle to play all the tracks in random order.

(7) Tap a track to play that track.

(8) Playback controls appear in the lower-right corner of the screen. Tap Pause to pause playback; tap Play to resume playback.

(9) Tap Next to skip to the next track.

## My Digital Entertainment for Seniors

If you want to learn more about digital music available on your iPad and elsewhere online, check out Que's companion book, *My Digital Entertainment for Seniors*, available at www. informit.com/title/9780789756602 or wherever books are sold. There's a lot more to listen to online if you know where to find it!

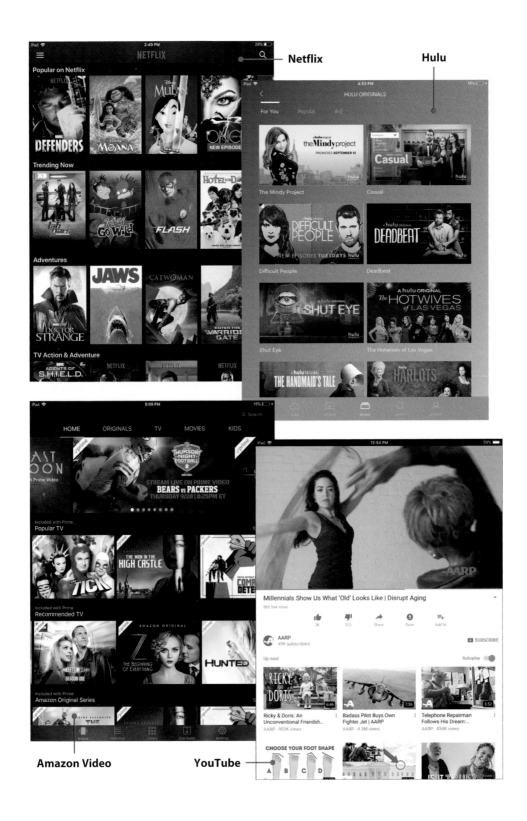

**Netflix**

**Hulu**

**Amazon Video**

**YouTube**

In this chapter, you learn how to use your iPad to watch movies, TV shows, and other videos.

→ Watching Netflix

→ Watching Hulu

→ Watching Amazon Video

→ Watching YouTube

→ Buying and Renting Videos in the iTunes Store

# Watching TV Shows, Movies, and Other Videos

Your iPad is a great device for watching your favorite movies, TV shows, and other videos wherever you happen to be. Whether you're relaxing on your couch, sitting in a coffeehouse, or traveling cross country, just pull out your iPad and dial up what you want to watch—on Netflix, Hulu, Amazon Prime, and other video services.

(If you want to learn more about movies and TV shows available on your iPad and elsewhere online, check out Que's companion book, *My Digital Entertainment for Seniors*, available wherever books are sold. There's a lot more to watch online if you know where to find it!)

# Watching Netflix

Most of the video you watch on your iPad is *streaming video*. This is video that streams in real time, over the Internet, from a streaming video service. Of course, you can also purchase and download movies and TV shows to your iPad for future viewing (which is covered later in this chapter). But most people these days watch their video entertainment via streaming video. There's nothing to download; just press "play" and you're ready to watch.

One of the most popular streaming video services today is Netflix. (You've probably heard of it.) Netflix offers a variety of movies, past and current TV shows, and original programming.

Netflix offers three subscription plans: Basic ($7.99/month), which doesn't offer high definition (HD) viewing; Standard ($10.99/month), which *does* offer HD, plus the ability to view on two different devices at the same time; and Premium ($13.99/month), which lets you watch on four different screens simultaneously. For most users, the Standard plan is the one to get.

## Use the Netflix App

You watch Netflix programming via the Netflix app, which you can download for free from Apple's App Store. The first time you launch the app you're prompted to either sign into an existing account, if you have one, or sign up for a new account. Do so.

1. From the iPad's Home screen, tap the Netflix icon to launch the Netflix app.

2. Netflix lets you create multiple viewer profiles. If you've created more than one profile, they're displayed on the Who's Watching? screen. Tap the profile you want to use.

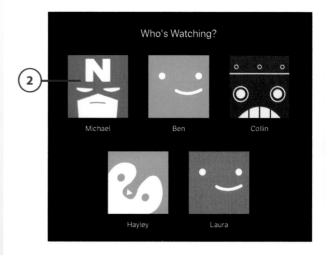

**3** On the Netflix home screen, scroll down to see various sections: Popular on Netflix, Trending Now, New Releases, and so forth.

**4** Tap the Menu icon to view programming by category: TV Shows, Action & Adventure, Comedies, Dramas, and so forth.

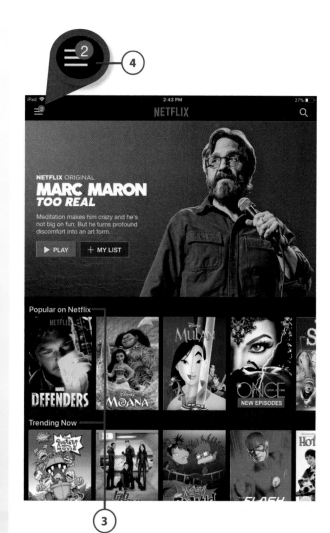

**⑤** Tap to select a category to view programming in that category.

**⑥** Tap the Search (magnifying glass) icon to display the Search page and search for specific programming.

**7** Tap the program or movie you want to watch.

**8** If you selected a television show, you see a detail panel for that show. Tap the Seasons down arrow to display all episodes from a given season.

**9** Tap a thumbnail to start watching that episode.

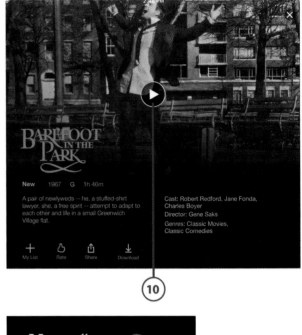

(10) If you selected a movie, you see the detail panel with information about that movie. Tap the Play icon to begin watching.

(11) Tap the screen to display the controls at the bottom of the screen. Tap the Pause button to pause playback; the button changes to a Play button. Tap Play to resume playback.

(12) Drag the slider (sometimes called a "scrubber") to move to another point in the program.

(13) Tap the Back (10) icon to skip back 10 seconds.

# Watching Hulu

Hulu is a streaming video service known for offering recent episodes of network and cable programming. You can watch just about any TV program within a few days of its original airing. (Hulu also offers a selection of movies and original programming.) You pay $7.99/month to subscribe to Hulu's basic plan (with limited commercials) or $11.99/month for the No Commercials plan.

Hulu also offers a more robust solution for cable cord cutters. The Hulu with Live TV Plan (starting at $39.99/month) lets you watch live TV from more than 50 local and cable channels, in addition to the normal on-demand streaming of movies and TV shows. You even get the option to record your favorite shows via Hulu's cloud-based DVR service.

You can sign up for any of these plans from Hulu's website (www.hulu.com) or from the Hulu app.

## Use the Hulu App

You watch Hulu from the Hulu app, which you can download for free from Apple's App Store. The first time you launch the Hulu app you're prompted to either sign into an existing account, if you have one, or create a new account. Do whichever you need to do.

1. From the iPad's Home screen, tap the Hulu icon to launch the Hulu app.

2. Tap the Home icon to view Hulu's Home screen.

3. Scroll from right to left (or tap the categories at the top of the screen) to view selections from Hulu's Lineup; Keep Watching shows you've previously watched; view available TV programs; view available Movies; and discover other recommended programming.

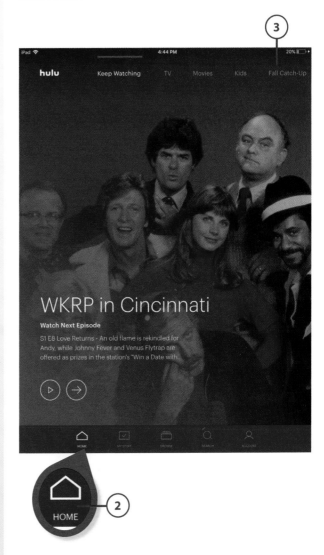

(4) Tap the My Stuff icon to view items you've tagged for Hulu to keep track of.

(5) Scroll from right to left to view selections by category (TV Shows, Movies, Expiring, or Networks).

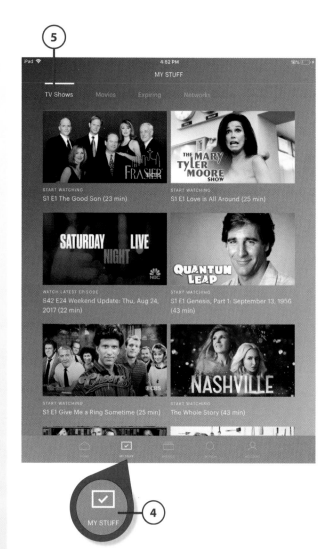

6  Tap the Browse button to
   browse programming by
   category.

7  Tap a category to view programming within that category.

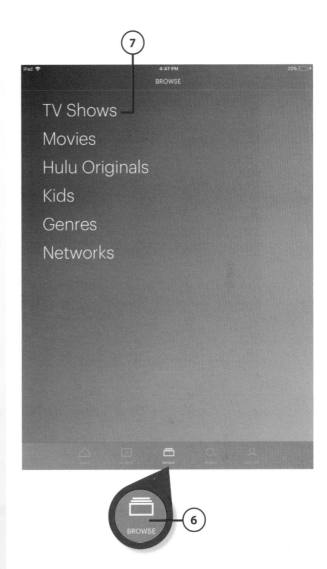

**8** Tap the Search button to search for specific programming.

**9** Enter your query in to the Search box at the top of the page.

**10** Tap a thumbnail to watch that particular program or movie.

(11) If you selected a TV program, tap Episodes and then tap the down arrow next to Seasons to select a specific season. You can then view episodes within that season.

(12) Tap to watch a given episode.

(13) If you selected a movie, tap Watch Movie to begin watching.

(14) Tap the screen to display the playback controls. Tap the Pause button to pause playback; tap Play to resume playback.

(15) Drag the slider/scrubber to move to a different point in the program.

(16) Tap the Back (10) icon to skip back 10 seconds, or the Forward (10) icon to skip forward 10 seconds.

### Widescreen Video

Because movies and TV shows are shot wider than they are tall (especially with true widescreen programming), the best way to watch movies on your iPad is to hold your device horizontally, in landscape mode.

# Watching Amazon Video

You may know Amazon as a popular online retailer. But Amazon is also in the streaming video business, with its Amazon Video service. Like Netflix and Hulu, Amazon Video offers a variety of movies, TV programs, and original programming.

You watch Amazon Video from the Amazon Video app, which you can download for free from Apple's App Store. You can purchase or rent individual programs, episodes, and movies, or subscribe to Prime Video ($8.99/month, or free if you have an Amazon Prime membership) and get many—but not all—programs for free. (Not all shows and movies are available for free with Prime; you still have to purchase some of them separately.)

## Amazon Prime

Amazon Prime Video is both separate from and a part of Amazon Prime, the service that gives you free shipping on most Amazon orders. It's separate in that you can subscribe separately; there's an $8.99/month Prime Video subscription that covers only video streaming, not physical shipping. However, if you go with a full Amazon Prime subscription ($10.99/month or $99.99/year), you not only get free shipping on your Amazon purchases, you also get a full Prime Video membership. Depending on how much shopping you do at Amazon, that might be the best deal.

# Use the Amazon Video App

The first time you launch the Amazon Video app you're prompted to sign in with your Amazon account. Do so if you have one; if you don't yet have an Amazon account, you need to go to Amazon's website and create one.

1. From the iPad's Home screen, tap the Amazon Prime icon to launch the Amazon Prime app.

2. Tap the Home tab to view Amazon Video's Home screen.

3. Tap the Originals tab to show only original Amazon programming.

4. Tap the TV tab to view only TV shows.

5. Tap the Movies tab to view only movies.

6. Tap the Kids tab to view children's programming.

(7) Tap the Search box to search for specific shows or movies.

(8) Scroll down the page to view suggestions by type.

(9) Tap to select the item you want to watch.

10. If you selected a TV show, tap to select a season.

11. Tap the Play icon for the episode you want to watch.

12. If you selected a movie, tap Watch Now to watch now.

13. Tap to display the playback controls. Tap Pause to pause playback; tap Play to resume playback.

14. Tap the Back icon to skip back 10 seconds.

15. Tap the Forward icon to skip forward 10 seconds.

16. Drag the slider/scrubber to move to another point in the program.

# Watching YouTube

Online video isn't all movies and TV shows. YouTube is a video sharing community where regular people, like you and me, can upload and share their home movies and other videos. There's also a lot of more professional content on YouTube, including lots of music videos and educational videos.

Unlike Netflix, Hulu, and Amazon Video, YouTube is completely free. You do get subjected to a fair number of commercials, however, so be prepared for that.

If you want to take advantage of all of YouTube's features, including your own personal playlists and favorites, you need to sign in with your personal account—either a YouTube-specific account or a Google account, both free.

## Use the YouTube App

You can watch YouTube from within the Safari web browser or, even better, from the YouTube app. You can download the app, for free, from Apple's App Store. The first time you launch the app you're prompted to sign in to your account or continue as a guest. Make your choice to continue.

( 1 ) From the iPad's Home screen, tap the YouTube icon to launch the YouTube app.

( 2 ) Tap the Home tab to view YouTube's Home screen.

( 3 ) Tap the Trending tab to view trending (popular) videos.

( 4 ) Tap the Subscriptions tab to view videos from channels you've subscribed to.

( 5 ) Tap the Search (magnifying glass) icon to search for specific videos.

( 6 ) Tap a thumbnail or title to view that video.

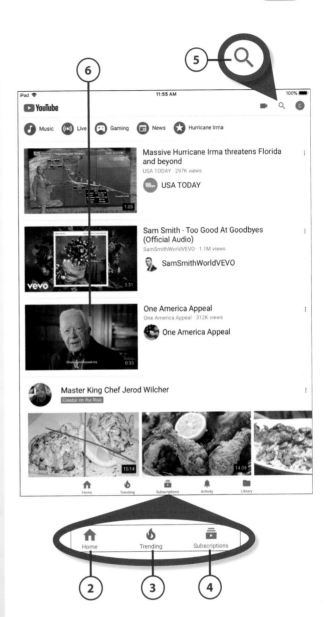

(7) The video starts playing automatically. Tap the screen to display the playback controls and then tap Pause to pause playback. Tap Play to resume playback.

## YouTube Ads

Some YouTube videos roll an advertisement before the video itself. In some instances, you can tap Skip Ad to skip the ad after the first few seconds. In other instances, you have to watch the entire ad before the video begins.

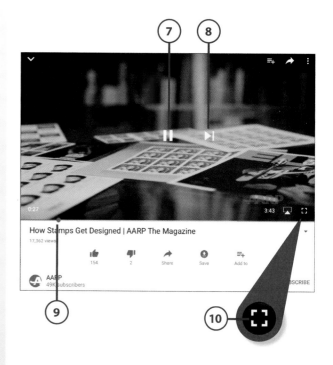

(8) Tap the Next icon to advance to the next recommended video.

(9) Drag the slider/scrubber to move to a different point in the video.

(10) Tap the Fullscreen icon to display the video full screen, and then turn your iPad so that it's horizontal. (Tap the icon again to return to the normal YouTube page.)

# Buying and Renting Videos in the iTunes Store

You can also buy and rent movies and TV shows from Apple's iTunes Store. These items are stored in your iCloud account, so you can buy a movie on one Apple device (like your iPad) and watch it on another (like your iPhone). You can even opt to download the items you purchase to your iPad, so you can watch when you don't have an Internet connection.

## Rent Versus Purchase

Items you purchase from the iTunes Store are yours to watch however many times you want. Items you rent (which costs less, naturally) are available to watch for 30 days after purchase. Once you start watching, you have 24 hours to finish.

# Rent or Purchase a Video

You can purchase and rent videos directly from the iTunes Store app or from your iPad's TV app. This example uses the TV app.

1. From the iPad's Home screen, tap the TV icon to launch the TV app.

2. Tap Store to open the iTunes Store.

3. Tap a network or channel icon to view programming from that network.

4. To shop for movies, scroll down to the bottom of the screen and tap Movies.

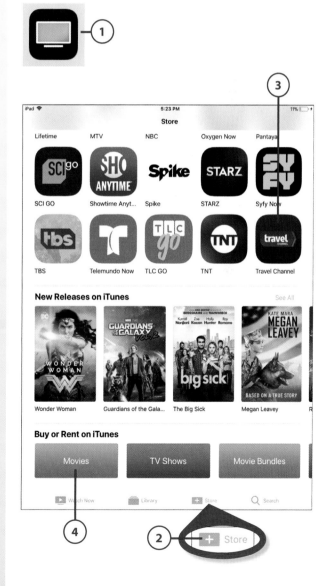

**5** Tap the movie you want to watch.

**6** Tap the Buy button to purchase the movie.

**7** Tap the Rent button to rent the movie for a 30-day period.

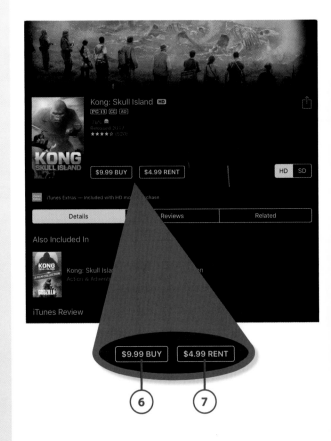

**8** Back on the main Store page, tap TV Shows to shop for television programs.

**9** Tap the program you want to watch.

**10** Tap the top price button to purchase all the episodes in the selected season.

**11** Tap an individual price button to purchase the selected episode.

## Season Pass

For some current television programs, you can purchase a season pass that enables you to watch each new episode as it's available. For more information, look for the Season Pass section in the program's description.

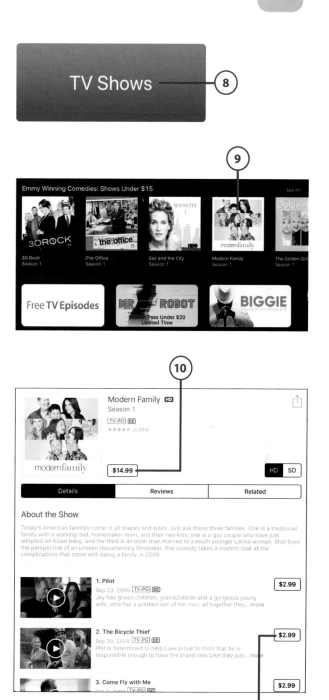

## Watch a Video

Once you've rented or purchased a video, you can watch it from the TV app.

1. From the iPad's Home screen, tap the TV icon to launch the TV app.

2. Tap Library (at the bottom of the screen) to view all items you've purchased or rented.

3. Tap Library (at the top of the screen) to display Recently Added, TV Shows, Movies, or Downloaded items.

4. Tap the show or movie you want to watch.

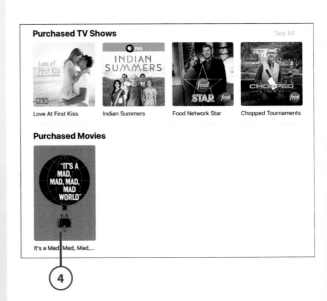

**5** If you selected a movie, tap the Play button to begin playback.

**6** If you selected a television show, available episodes are displayed. Tap the episode you want to watch.

**7** The selection begins to play. Tap the screen to display the playback controls and then tap Pause to pause playback. Tap Play to resume playback.

**8** Press and hold the Fast Forward button to fast-forward.

**9** Press and hold the Fast Back-ward button to go backward.

**10** Use the slider/scrubber at the top of the screen to move to a different point in the video.

**11** Tap Done when you're done watching.

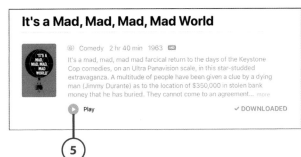

### It's a Mad, Mad, Mad, Mad World

Ⓖ Comedy  2 hr 40 min  1963  HD

It's a mad, mad, mad mad farcical return to the days of the Keystone Cop comedies, on an Ultra Panavision scale, in this star-studded extravaganza. A multitude of people have been given a clue by a dying man (Jimmy Durante) as to the location of $350,000 in stolen bank money that he has buried. They cannot come to an agreement... more

▶ Play                                    ✓ DOWNLOADED

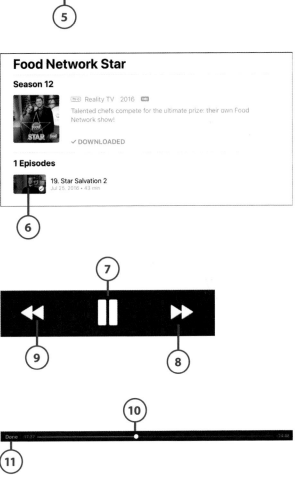

### Food Network Star

Season 12

TV-G  Reality TV  2016  HD

Talented chefs compete for the ultimate prize: their own Food Network show!

✓ DOWNLOADED

1 Episodes

19. Star Salvation 2
Jul 25, 2016 · 43 min

Done  17:27  -24:48

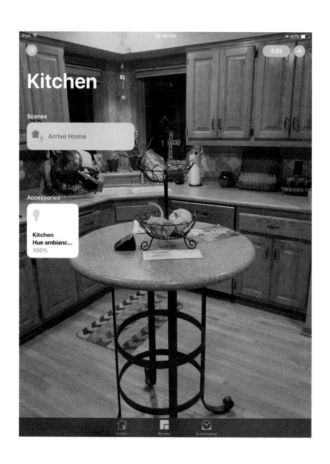

In this chapter, you learn how to use Apple HomeKit and the Home app on your iPad to control smart devices in your home.

→ Understanding Apple HomeKit
→ Adding Devices and Rooms
→ Controlling Your Smart Devices
→ Automating Multiple Devices

18

# Controlling Your Smart Home

One of the big trends today is setting up so-called "smart" devices to control various functions in your home. We're talking smart lighting that turns on and off according to a preset schedule, smart thermostats that learn your behavior and adjust the temperature accordingly, and smart locks and doorbells that let you see who's at the door and unlock the door if you wish, all from a corresponding app on your iPad or smartphone.

Most smart devices come with their own mobile apps. This is fine—unless you have multiple smart devices, in which case you have to deal with multiple apps. You can get around this multiple-app mayhem by using Apple's Home app on your iPad. The Home app works with Apple's HomeKit protocol to control multiple smart devices from multiple manufacturers.

If you'd like more information about using smart home devices and apps, check out Que's companion book, *My Smart Home for Seniors*, available wherever books are sold.

# Understanding Apple HomeKit

Apple HomeKit is a system for controlling smart devices from a variety of suppliers with a single app—or with Apple's Siri voice-controlled personal assistant. If a smart device is compatible with HomeKit (not all are), it's a simple matter to link the device to the Home app on your iPad (or iPhone) and control it along with other devices with a tap of your finger.

It's actually kind of a big deal to have centralized control of multiple smart devices with a single app. For one thing, using one app is a lot more convenient than using multiple apps. Beyond convenience, however, HomeKit also lets you centralize control of multiple devices in a single room, as well as create *scenes* that control multiple connected devices with a single tap. HomeKit makes possible a lot of combined automation that makes your smart devices work smarter together.

## How HomeKit Works

HomeKit isn't a smart home system per se; it doesn't operate from a central hub, as do SmartThings, Wink, and similar systems. Instead, HomeKit is more like the standalone smart controllers offered by Amazon (Echo) and Google (Home), but it works through a smartphone/tablet app instead of a piece of hardware.

So how does HomeKit work? It all revolves around Apple's Home app, which comes installed on your new iPad. (And can be downloaded from the App Store for use on many older models.)

If a smart device is compatible with the HomeKit standard, it's typically discovered by Apple's Home app when you first power on the device. (If it's not automatically discovered, you can add it manually to the app.) After a device is linked to the Home app, you specify what room it's in. You can then control the device from the Home app, or via any scenes or automations you create. (Your iPad must be connected to your home Wi-Fi network to do this; Home can't control your smart devices remotely.)

## What's Compatible with HomeKit

To work with HomeKit, smart devices need to be certified by Apple. This means that it's more likely that newer products will be compatible with HomeKit, as it's easier to get them certified while they're being developed, and less likely that existing products will go back and get certified.

So what's compatible? The list changes daily, but includes big names such as August, Ecobee, Honeywell, iHome, Insteon, and Philips. Missing from the list, unfortunately, are several major smart systems, including Nest, SmartThings by Samsung, WeMo by Belkin, and Wink. That said, Apple continues to work with other companies to gain compatibility with their smart devices. You can check a current compatibility list at www.apple.com/ios/home/accessories/.

# Adding Devices and Rooms

Before you can use the Home app to control devices from your iPad, you have to add those devices to the app. You can also assign devices to specific rooms in your home.

## Add a New Device

Apple calls smart devices, whether light bulbs or thermostats, "accessories." Compatible accessories are relatively easy to add to the Home app. Just make sure the accessory is powered on and connected to your home's Wi-Fi network—and that your iPad is connected to the same network.

1 Tap the Home icon to launch the Home app.

**( 2 )** The first time you open the Home app, you see the Welcome screen; tap Get Started to proceed. Each subsequent time you launch the app, you see the Home screen; tap the + button to proceed.

**( 3 )** Tap Add Accessory.

**( 4 )** Your new device should appear in the Add Accessory panel. Tap it.

**( 5 )** Look for the HomeKit code on the new device or in the device's documentation. Position the camera of your iPad to capture this code.

**( 6 )** If for some reason step 5 doesn't work, tap Enter Code Manually to enter the code with your phone or tablet's onscreen keyboard.

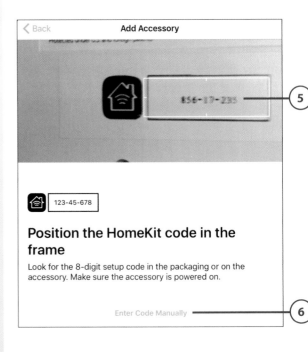

**7** Change the name of this accessory by tapping the current name and then entering a new one. (Siri identifies this device by the name you give it here.)

**8** By default, the new accessory is added to your default room. To add the accessory to a different room, tap Location and select another room.

**9** Include this accessory in your favorites on the Home app's home screen by tapping "on" the Include in Favorites switch.

**10** Tap Next.

**11** If the accessory requires additional setup, tap View and follow the onscreen instructions.

**12** Tap Done to complete the installation.

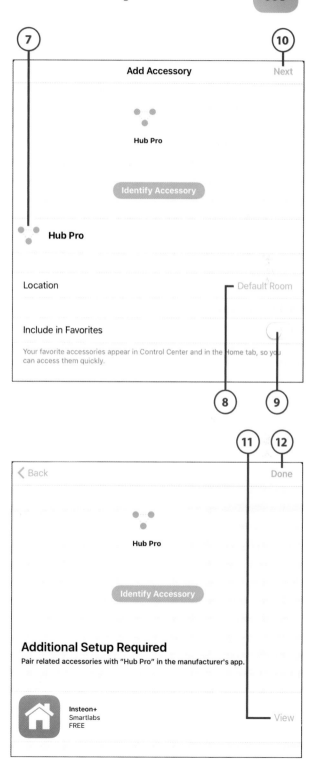

## Add a New Room

When you install a new accessory you assign this device to a given room in your home. You can create additional rooms corresponding to your actual physical rooms.

(1) Tap the Rooms icon to display the Room screen.

(2) Tap the Menu button in the upper-left corner of the screen.

(3) Tap Room Settings.

(4) Tap Add Room.

(5) Enter a name for this room into the Room Name field.

(6) Change the room's background wallpaper by tapping Choose from Existing and then making a selection.

(7) Alternatively, you can take a photo of the room to use for the wallpaper. Tap Take Photo and proceed from there.

(8) Tap Save. The room is now created and added to your room list.

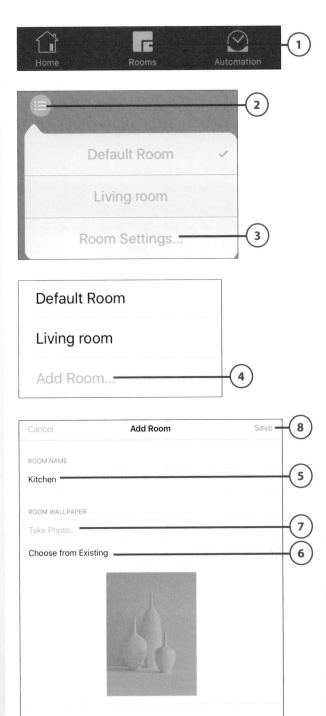

# Assign an Accessory to a Room

By default, any new accessory/device you install is assigned to the Home app's default room (which is rather unimaginatively labeled "Default Room"). You can, however, assign an accessory to a different room, or move an accessory from one room to another.

## One Room per Accessory

Just as it is in the physical world, in the Home app each accessory can be assigned to one room only. You can't assign accessories to multiple rooms.

(1) Tap the Rooms icon to display the Room screen.

(2) Swipe left or right until you get to the room that contains the accessory you want. Alternatively, tap the Menu button at the top left and select the room from those listed.

(3) Touch and hold the accessory you want to move.

(4) Tap Details.

(5) Tap Location.

(6) Tap to select the room you want to move this accessory to.

(7) Tap Done to return to the previous screen.

(8) Tap Done.

9. The accessory is moved to the room you selected.

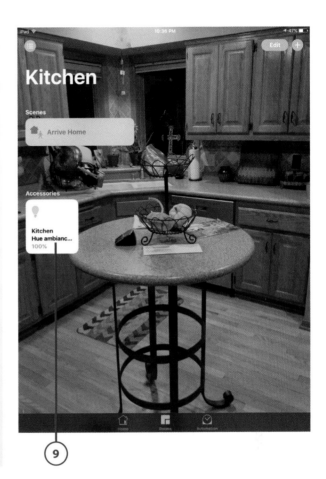

## Create a Scene

The Home app doesn't limit you to controlling one device at a time. You can control multiple accessories at the same time by creating what Apple calls *scenes*.

For example, you can create a scene called "Good Morning" that turns on the smart lights in your bedroom and turns up your smart thermostat, or one called "Arrive Home" that turns on your living room lights and unlocks the front door. You activate a scene with a single tap from the home or room screen, or via Siri command.

**1** On either the Home or Rooms screen, tap the +.

**2** Tap Add Scene.

**3** Tap one of the suggested scenes (Arrive Home, Good Morning, Good Night, or Leave Home) or tap Custom to create a different scene.

**4** If you chose one of the default scenes for a given room, you see the devices for that room. To include additional devices or to remove one of the current ones, tap Add or Remove Accessories.

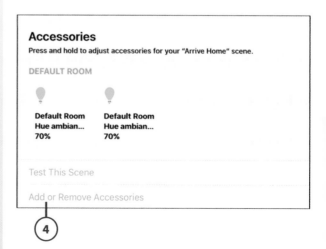

(5) Tap those accessories you want to add, or tap to remove those accessories you don't want to include.

(6) Tap Done.

(7) Back in the New Scene pane, tap and hold an accessory to adjust its settings.

(8) Tap Test This Scene to see if the scene works as you want.

(9) Make sure the Show in Favorites switch is "on" to display this scene on the home screen.

(10) Tap Done to add this scene.

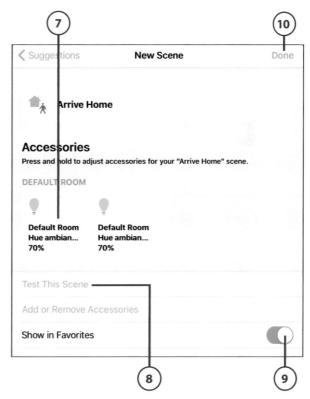

# Controlling Your Smart Devices

Once you've installed a device/accessory in the Home app, you can then use your iPad to control that device in various ways.

## Control a Device or Scene

Turning a device on or off, or activating a scene, is as easy as tapping your phone or tablet's screen. For many devices, additional controls are also available.

1. On either the Home or Rooms screen, tap an accessory or scene to turn it on or off. The tile for the accessory or scene dims when the device is turned off; the tile has a white background when the device is turned on.

2. Tap and hold the tile for an accessory to access additional controls.

3. For example, with smart lights, you can tap and drag the divider bar to increase or decrease the light's brightness.

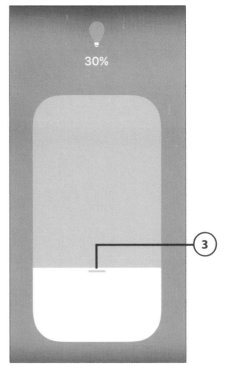

## Controlling Devices and Scenes with Siri

You're probably used to asking your iPad's Siri personal assistant to do all manner of things, from looking up information to reading the latest news and weather reports. Well, you can also use Siri within the Home app to control your connected smart devices, using voice commands.

To use Siri to control any devices and scenes you've added to the Home app, all you have to do is say "Siri," then speak the desired command. It's that easy.

Obviously, which commands you speak depend on which devices you have installed, and what you want them to do. For example, if you want to turn off the lights in your bedroom, say

> *Siri, turn off the lights in the bedroom.*

Pretty simple. If you want to reduce the brightness for a given light or room, say

> *Siri, set brightness for the living room lights to 50 percent.*

To set your smart thermostat, say

> *Siri, set the temperature to 70 degrees.*

You can even ask questions of Siri regarding your smart devices, like this one:

> *Siri, did I lock the front door?*

If you have scenes created (refer to the "Create a Scene" task earlier in this chapter), you can turn on a scene by saying

> *Siri, set my relaxing scene.*

It's all very common sense. All you have to do is speak to Siri via your iPad, and she works within the Home app to do the rest.

# Automating Multiple Devices

Until now you've seen how to use the Home app to directly control individual accessories or groups of accessories in a given room, by tapping a tile for a device or scene. You can also use the Home app to automate operations across multiple accessories based on a specified trigger. You can trigger these *automations* when your location changes (when you leave the house, for example), at a specified time of day, or when another accessory does something.

# Set Up Your iPad as a Home Hub

Normal Home commands flow directly from your iPad to the device or devices specified. Automations, however, are triggered by other events—a given time, a location change, or a control from another device. For automations to work, then, you need some sort of central control that's active even if your phone is with you across town.

To create and use automations, then, you need to set up what Apple calls a Home Hub. You can do this with your iPad.

### Apple TV

If you have an Apple TV box connected to a television in your home, you can also use this as your Home Hub.

If you choose to use your iPad as a Home Hub, it needs to stay in your home, connected to your home Wi-Fi network, to work. (It can't control your home devices when it's not home!) And, of course, you need to set it up in advance.

( 1 ) From the Dock or a Home screen, tap Settings to open the Settings app.

( 2 ) In the left column, tap Accounts & Passwords.

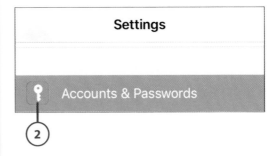

Settings

🔑 Accounts & Passwords

(**3**) In the right column, tap iCloud.

(**4**) Make sure that Home and Keychain are both turned on.

(**5**) In the left column, tap to select Home.

(**6**) Tap "on" the Use This iPad as a Home Hub switch.

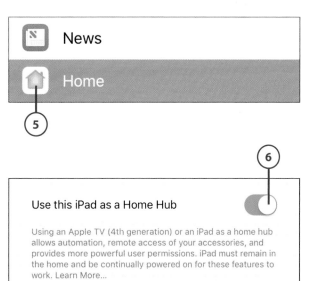

## Create a Location Automation

A location automation is triggered when your iPhone comes near or leaves a specified location. That location can be your home (to trigger actions for when you leave or arrive home), your office or club, or any place on the map.

1. From within the Home app, tap the Automation icon to display the Automation screen. Any previously created automations are displayed here.

2. Tap Create New Automation.

3. In the New Automation pane, tap My Location Changes.

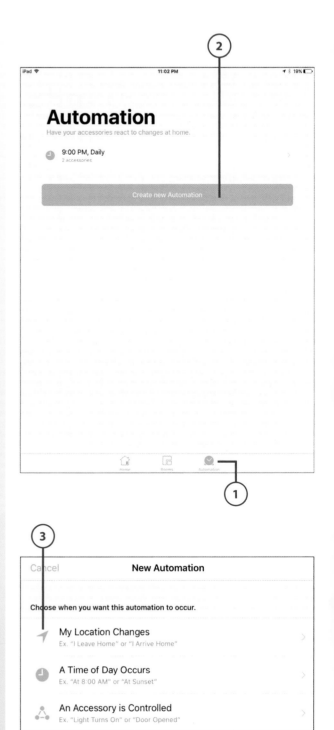

(4) Your home and other nearby locations are listed. Tap to select one of these, or enter a name or address into the search box to search for and select a different location.

(5) Tap When I Arrive to trigger the automation when you arrive at the selected location, or tap When I Leave to trigger the automation when you leave the location.

(6) Your selected location displays as a red pin on the map at the bottom of the pane. Drag the blue dot to enlarge or shrink the area around the selected location; this will be the range that triggers the action.

(7) Tap Next.

(8) Select those scenes and accessories you want to trigger when you arrive at or leave the selected location.

(9) Tap Next.

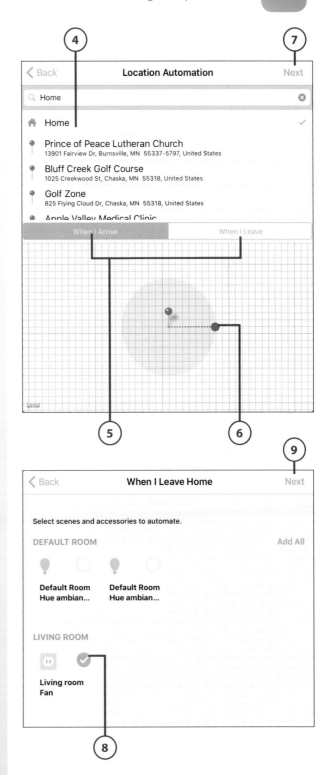

**10** Review the automation you've created and then tap Done.

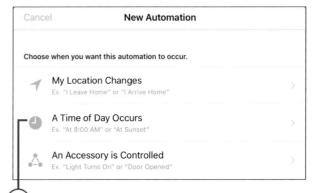

## Create a Time Automation

A time automation is triggered at a specific time on a specific day or days. This is kind of like an alarm that triggers the designated accessories or scenes.

**1** From the Automation screen, tap Create New Automation.

**2** In the New Automation pane, tap A Time of Day Occurs.

**3** Use the Time of Day controls to select the hour, minute, and AM/PM you want this automation to run. (Alternatively, you can opt to run the automation at sunrise or sunset.)

**4** Tap those days of the week you want this automation to run. You can select one, some, or all days.

**5** Tap Next.

**6** Select those scenes and accessories you want to trigger at the designated time.

**7** Tap Next.

8 Review the automation you've created and then tap Done.

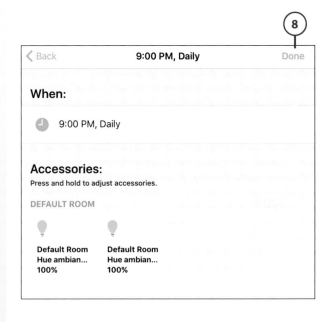

## Create a Controlled Automation

Finally, you can create a controlled automation. This is an automation that is triggered when a designated device is activated. For example, the automation may be triggered when the front door opens.

1 From the Automation page, tap Create New Automation.

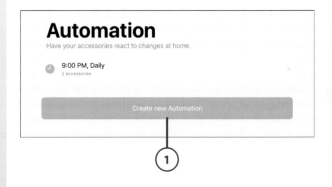

**2** In the New Automation pane, tap An Accessory Is Controlled.

**3** On the Accessory Automation pane, tap the device that will start this automation.

**4** Tap Next.

**5** Tap the action that will start this automation.

**6** Tap Next.

**7** Tap the scenes or accessories you want to activate when the automation is triggered.

**8** Tap Next.

**9** Review your new automation and then tap Done.

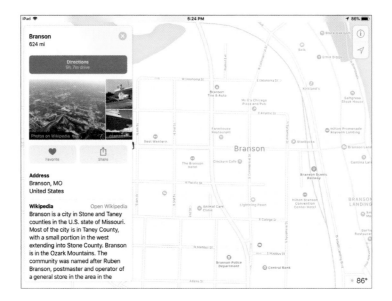

In this chapter, you learn how to use your iPad when you're traveling.

→ Traveling with the Maps App
→ Exploring Other Travel-Related Apps

19

# Traveling with Maps and Other Travel Apps

Your iPad is a handy device when you're at home or out and about. It's even more handy when you're traveling—you can use the Maps app to generate maps and driving directions, and there are all sorts of other fun and useful travel-related apps you can use.

## Traveling with the Maps App

Apple's Maps app can show you how to get just about anywhere from wherever you may happen to be. It displays maps of any location, as well as driving directions for how to get there.

### Other Driving Apps

Apple's Maps app isn't the only driving/map app available. There is also the popular Google Maps app; it offers a few more features and is sometimes more accurate than Apple's Maps app. Waze Navigation & Live Traffic is also popular, as it offers crowd-sourced live traffic info to find the fastest route to where you're going. Other popular mapping apps include inRoute Route Planner, MAPS.ME, and Sygic GPS Navigation & Maps.

# Display a Map

The Maps app is, as the name implies, a maps app. Enter any location—street address, intersection, major landmark—and it will generate a map of that location.

**1**   From the iPad's Home screen, tap Maps to open the Maps app.

**2**   Tap within the search panel and enter the location you want mapped. You can enter a street address (accompanied by city and state, if you like), intersection (10th and Main, for example), landmark (such as Brooklyn Bridge or Wrigley Field), or business.

**3**   As you type, the Maps app displays suggested matches. Tap the one you want to map.

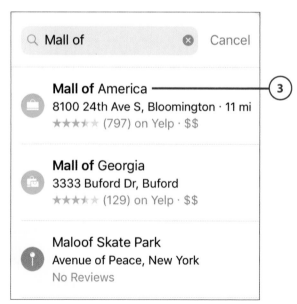

**4** The app now maps the location you entered, which is pinpointed in the middle of the map. (If you mapped a public location, there's also an information panel on the left.) Use your fingers to drag the map left, right, up, or down, or expand/pinch your fingers to zoom into and out of the map.

**5** Tap the Home (arrow) icon to return to (and map) your current location.

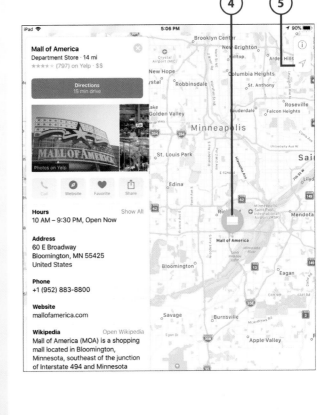

# Generate Driving Directions

One of the most useful aspects of the Maps app is to generate driving directions to a given location. It's good to know how to get to where you're going before you leave home!

**1** From within the Maps app, tap within the search panel and enter the address or description of the destination location.

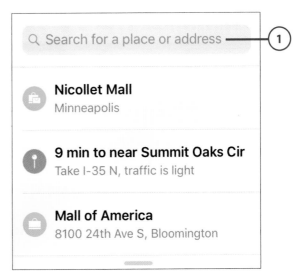

**(2)** This location is now mapped, and a descriptive panel appears on the left side of the screen. Tap the Directions button.

**(3)** Suggested routes are displayed. Tap the route you want to take; this route is now mapped onscreen in dark blue. (Alternate routes are in light blue.)

**(4)** Tap the Go button for your selected route to display turn-by-turn instructions.

## Walking and Mass Transit

Maps can generate directions if you're walking or taking mass transit. Just tap the Walk or Transit icons at the bottom of the directions panel to change your mode of transport.

5 Swipe right to left in the instructions pane to advance to the next step. Swipe from left to right to return to the previous step.

6 Tap End to return to the previous screen.

## Getting Home

The Where Do You Want to Go? panel also tells you how many minutes it will take to get home, with the best route highlighted. (Assuming you've entered your home address into the Contacts app, of course.) Tap this item to display driving directions to your home.

## >>>Go Further

## DIRECTIONS WHILE DRIVING

If you have an iPad with cellular connectivity, you can use the Maps app in your car to generate turn-by-turn directions while you drive. Because most iPads have only Wi-Fi connectivity, this isn't an option for most users. Instead, use the iPad to preview your route while you're still inside and connected to Wi-Fi. (You can always use the Maps app with your iPhone to guide you while you're driving.)

# Exploring Other Travel-Related Apps

The Maps app isn't the only iPad app useful to travelers. Let's take a look at other travel-related apps you might want to consider. (For more information about using travel-related apps, check out Que's companion book, *My Digital Travel for Seniors*, available wherever books are sold.

## Discover Travel Apps

Here are just a few of the many travel-related iPad apps in Apple's App Store. You can search for specific apps by name, or search for *travel* to see all available apps.

1. Find and book hotel rooms, airline flights, rental cars, and more with the Airbnb, Expedia, Hotels.com, Hotel Tonight, Priceline, Travelocity, and similar apps.

Expedia app

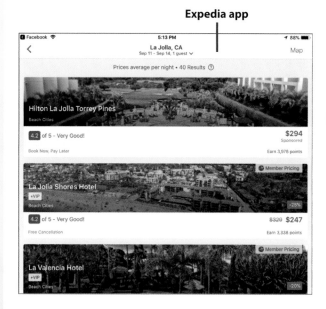

(2) Use the TripAdvisor app to learn more about what's available at a given destination—and book your travel plans, too.

**TripAdvisor app**

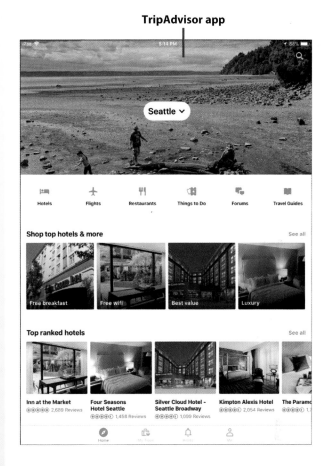

③ Use a hotel chain's app to book lodging directly.

④ Use airline apps to book flights directly.

**Marriott app**

**Delta app**

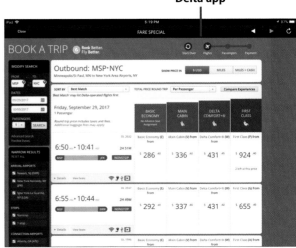

(5) Use the Yelp app to find
and read reviews for local
restaurants—then use the
OpenTable app to make a
reservation online!

**Yelp app**

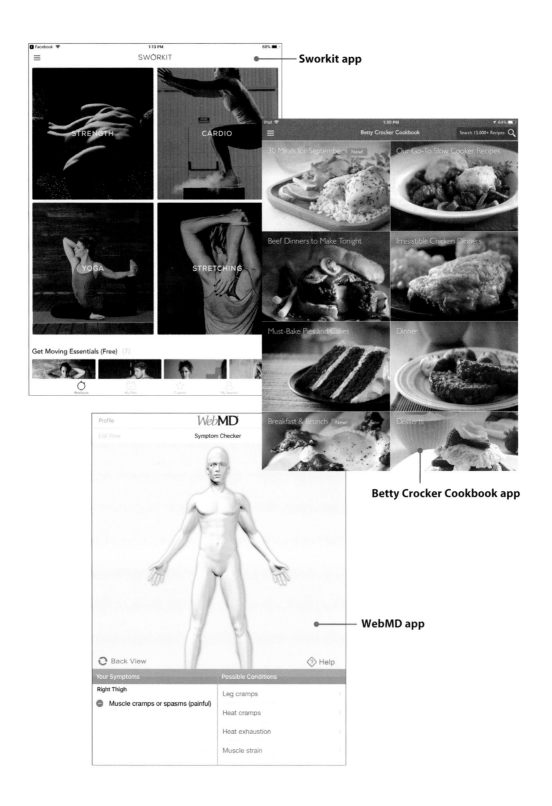

**Sworkit app**

**Betty Crocker Cookbook app**

**WebMD app**

In this chapter, you discover a variety of health and fitness apps for your iPad.

→ Exploring Health and Fitness Apps
→ Exploring Food and Nutrition Apps
→ Exploring Medical Apps

20

# Keeping Fit and Healthy

Many people use their tablets to help them manage their daily health and fitness needs. You can find workout and yoga apps, food and nutrition apps, even apps to help you find important medical information. These apps add more value to your iPad and can help you keep healthier!

And if you want to learn more about health options available on your iPad and elsewhere online, check out Que's companion book, *My Health Technology for Seniors*, available wherever books are sold. There's a lot of good health-related information available online, if you know where to find it!

## Exploring Health and Fitness Apps

When it comes to staying fit, nothing beats the combination of a healthy diet and a regular exercise routine. We'll cover diet-related apps in the next section, but for now let's focus on the fitness end of things.

# Discover Exercise and Yoga Apps

It's important to make sure you get enough exercise each day. You can use the following apps to track your daily exercise—and guide your workouts.

1. Streaks Workout ($2.99) offers personalized exercise routines you can use at home or at the gym. It offers a variety of workouts of different lengths and levels.

2. Sworkit (free) offers a variety of personalized video workouts, from 5 to 60 minutes long.

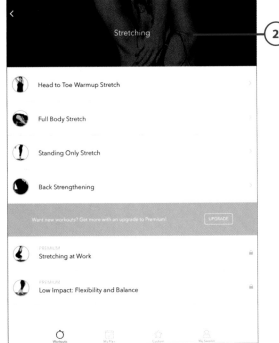

**3** Daily Yoga (free with in-app purchases) gets you started with a variety of entry-level exercises.

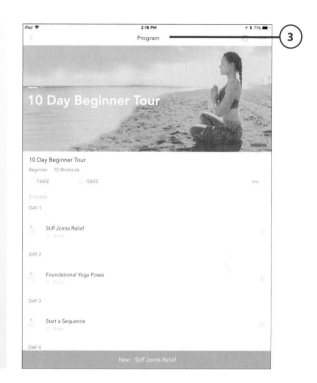

## Finding Health and Fitness Apps

You can find all the health and fitness apps discussed in this chapter—and more!—in Apple's App Store. Just launch the App Store app and search for a particular app by name or type.

*It's Not All Good*

### In-App Purchases

Many purportedly "free" apps offer in-app purchases for additional features or content. Just because you get an app for free doesn't mean it won't always cost you nothing!

# Exploring Food and Nutrition Apps

When it comes to staying healthy, exercise is just part of the equation. You also need to watch what you eat—which you can do with these dieting and food apps.

# Discover Dieting Apps

Use these apps to keep track of what you eat—and eat healthier!

1. My Diet Coach (free) helps you set diet goals, tracks your calorie intake, and motivates you with tips and photos.

2. MyFitnessPal's Calorie Counter & Diet Tracker (free) is an easy-to-use calorie counter with a huge database of more than 5 million different foods.

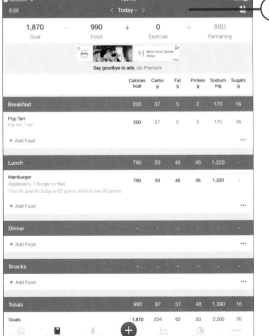

**3** When you want to eat healthy, MyPlate Calorie Tracker (free) tracks everything you eat with a database of more than 2 million food items.

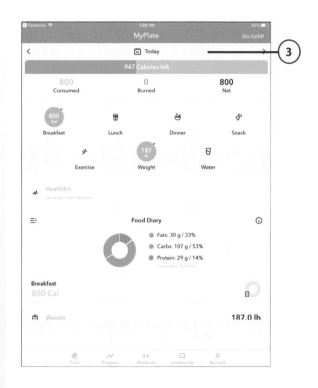

# Discover Cooking and Recipe Apps

Whether you're trying to eat healthy or just want to spice up your dinner routine, check out these cooking and recipe apps, for all types of cuisine.

**1** Use the Allrecipes Dinner Spinner (free) to access popular recipes from the 30 million members of the Allrecipes community—and watch more than 1,000 step-by-step cooking videos, too!

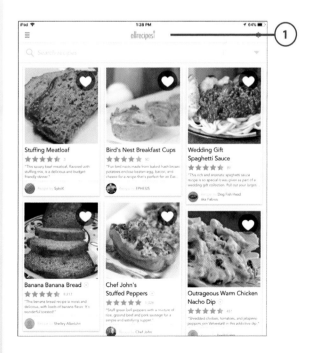

**2** The Betty Crocker Cookbook app (free) offers more than 15,000 recipes inspired by the best-selling Betty Crocker cookbooks.

**3** Yummly Recipes and Shopping List (free) offers more than 1 million unique recipes and lets you create your own menu plans and shopping lists.

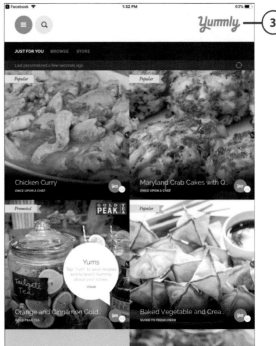

# Exploring Medical Apps

There's a ton of medical services and information available on the Internet. The following apps let you access that information—and better track your own medical needs.

## Discover Medical-Related Apps

The following apps let you access large online databases about medical conditions, symptoms, and medications. (You still should contact your own personal physician if you think there's something wrong, of course!)

1.  The Drugs.com Medication Guide app (free) lets you look up prescription drug information, identify any random pills you might have lying around the house, check drug interactions, and manage your own personal prescription records. Also popular: Formulary Search (free) and PocketPharmacist (free).

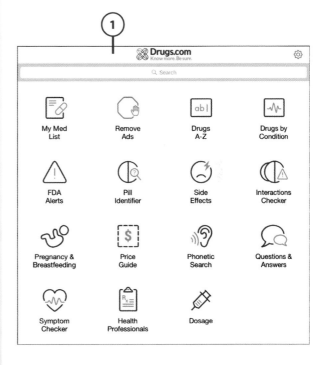

(2) Medical Dictionary (free) is a medical dictionary app with more than 180,000 medical terms, 50,000 audio pronunciations, and 12,000 images.

(3) The WebMD app (free) is a one-stop shop for everything medical, including a huge database of medical conditions, a symptom checker, medication reminders, drug information, first-aid essentials, and local health provider listings.

## *It's Not All Good*

### Don't Self-Diagnose

As tempting as it is to plug your symptoms into one of these medical-related apps and see what pops out, these apps should never replace the experience, knowledge, and advice you get from your own personal physician. Although these apps can be informative, they're not always accurate or complete. It's always best to consult with your own doctors—and use these apps to supplement, not replace, that information.

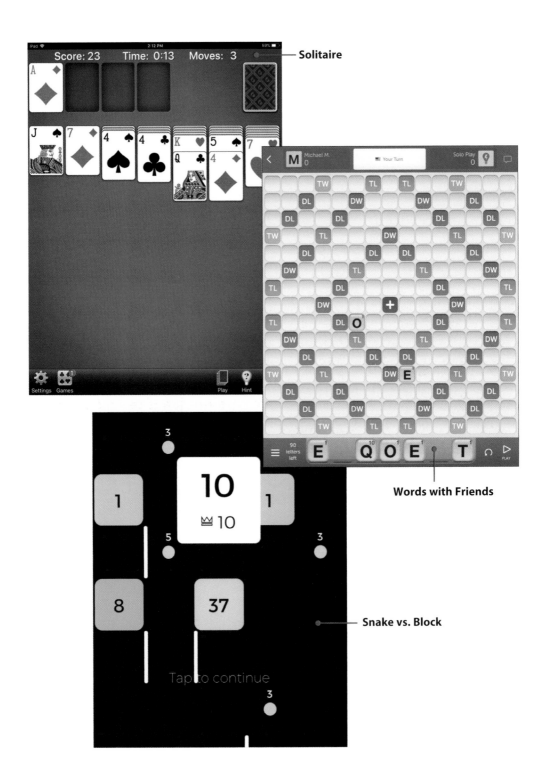

**Solitaire**

**Words with Friends**

**Snake vs. Block**

In this chapter, you learn how to find and play games on your iPad.

→ Finding Games to Play
→ Discovering Popular Games

# Playing Games

Yes, you use your iPad to send and receive emails and text messages, listen to music, watch videos, and read and post to Facebook and other social networks. You may even take a few photos or videos, or even do some real productive work.

But let's be honest. You also spend a fair amount of time on your iPad playing games. And if you don't, your kids or grandkids do. No need to hide it; the iPad is a great game-playing device, and there are lots of fun games you can play on it. If you'd like more information about entertaining games, check out Que's companion book, *My Digital Entertainment for Seniors*, available wherever books are sold.

## Finding Games to Play

A game is just a certain type of app. Just as you find regular apps for your iPad in Apple's App Store, that's also where you find the games you want to play on your iPad.

# Download Games from the App Store

The App Store has a separate section just for games. It's easy to browse through the game categories or search for specific games to download.

① From your iPad's Home screen, tap the App Store icon to open the App Store.

② Tap the Search icon to search for a specific game. *Or…*

③ Tap the Games icon to view all games.

④ Scroll down the page to see recommended games by type.

⑤ To view games by category, scroll to the Top Categories section and tap See All.

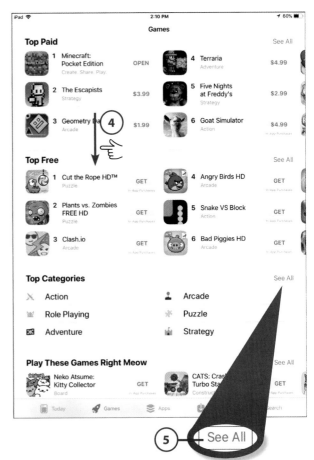

**6** Tap the type of game you want to browse: Action, Adventure, Arcade, and so forth.

**7** Tap the game you want to play.

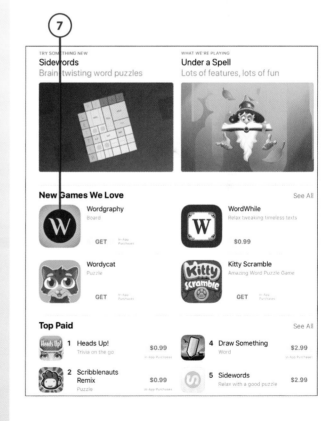

8. Some games are free. To download a free game, tap Get.

9. Many games cost money to play. To purchase a game, tap the price button.

(10) Tap the Purchase button, and when prompted, enter your Apple ID and password to pay for and complete the purchase.

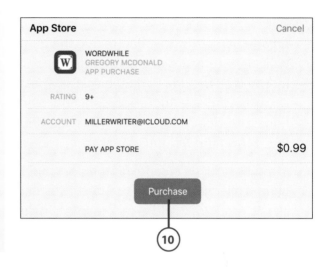

# Discovering Popular Games

What types of games can you find in the App Store? Apple organizes games by category, as you'll soon discover.

## Action Games

Action games are those that emphasize physical challenges and require good hand-eye coordination. Popular action games for the iPad include Angry Birds, Clash of Clans, Five Nights at Freddy's, Plants vs. Zombies, and Snake vs. Block.

## Adventure Games

When you play an adventure game, you assume a starring role in some sort of episodic story. Popular adventure games include Criminal Case, LEGO City, Pearl's Peril, and ROBLOX.

All that said, the most popular adventure game for the iPad or any device is Minecraft. This is a world-building game, where you use your block-like character to explore new environments, mine for resources, and build complex structures. While Minecraft might not be your thing, your grade school-aged children and grandchildren are probably already hooked.

# Arcade Games

Arcade games for the iPad mimic the gameplay of classic coin-operated games, typically with state-of-the-art animation and operation. Popular arcade games for the iPad include Bad Piggies, Bowmasters, Candy Crush Saga (and its endless variants), Cut the Rope, and Sonic the Hedgehog. You can also find some real, honest-to-goodness classic arcade games in the App Store, including Breakout, PAC-MAN (and Ms. PAC-MAN, too), and various variations of electronic pinball.

If you like classic arcade games, you should also check out a couple of vintage game collections. Atari's Greatest Hits includes paid access to more than 100 classic Atari 2600 and arcade games, including Asteroids, Centipede, and Missile Command. And the 80s Arcade Games pack offers authentic reproductions of Centipede, Defender, Donkey Kong, Joust, and more.

# Board Games

Board games for the iPad are just like traditional board games, except you play them on your iPad screen, either by yourself (against the computer) or with others (over the Internet). Popular board games include The Game of Life, Mahjong, Monopoly, SCRABBLE, and YAHTZEE.

# Card Games

There are many games for the iPad that mimic traditional physical card games. These include Canasta, Gin Rummy, Skip-Bo, and Solitaire.

# Casino Games

Just about any game you can play in a casino is available in an iPad-friendly version. Popular casino games include Card Shark Collection, Gold Fish Slots Casino, Jackpot Party Casino Slots, Official Caesar's Casino Slots, and Zynga Poker—Texas Holdem.

# Family Games

If you want to occupy your kids or grandkids, check out these fun family games, including Elmo Loves ABCs, Gymnastics Superstar, My Talking Hank, My Town: Pets, and Pokemon TCG Online.

# Indie Games

These are games from independent game developers (instead of the big game companies). Check here for some of the newer and more innovative games of all types.

# Music Games

Many games revolve around music creation and quizzes. In particular, check out Five Little Monkeys Jumping on the Bed, Incredibox, My Singing Monsters, Note Rush, Piano Tiles 2, and Rolling Sky.

# Puzzle Games

These games require you to slide your tiles around until you solve or form a puzzle. Popular puzzle games for the iPad include Jigsaw Puzzle Collection, Merge Town, One More Brick, Roll the Ball, and Scribblenauts.

# Racing Games

Strap yourself in to race all sorts of virtual vehicles in Bike Race Pro, Car Driving School Simulator, CSR Racing 2, Hot Wheels: Race Off, Need for Speed: Most Wanted, and Real Racing 3.

# Role-Playing Games

These are even more involved adventure games, many of them with lots of shooting and violence. Popular games of this type include Darkest Dungeon, Dragon City, Final Fantasy XV, Monster Legends, and Teeny Titans—Teen Titans Go!.

## Simulation Games

When you want to simulate some fun real-world activity or persona, check out games like AdVenture Capitalist, Goat Simulator, and Terraria.

## Sports Games

Just about every popular sport is represented in the App Store, including Bowling King, FIFA Mobile Soccer, MADDEN NFL Football, NBA JAM, True Skate, and WWE 2K.

## Strategy Games

Strategy games require more thinking than action. The most popular include The Escapists, Plague Inc., Prison Architect, and Star Wars: Galaxy of Heroes.

## Trivia Games

Who was the first actor to play James Bond? What is the longest river on Earth? What was the top boy band in the 1990s? Answer these and other questions in games such as 100 PICS Quiz, Guess the Emoji, Jeopardy, Tricky Test, and Trivia Crack.

## Word Games

For many people, this is saving the best category for last. Word games let you put your word-building skills to the test, playing either solo or against other players. The most popular word games for the iPad include SCRABBLE, Sidewords, Word Cookies, Word Connect, Words with Friends, and WordWhizzle.

### *It's Not All Good*

**In-Game Purchases**

Many games strongly suggest that you pay money to get additional levels or resources. These in-game purchases can quickly add up, so think twice before tapping the "buy now" button in any given game.

**Document in Pages app**

**Spreadsheet in Numbers app**

**Presentation in Keynote app**

In this chapter, you learn how to use your iPad
for business with key productivity apps.

→ Using Your iPad's Built-In Productivity Apps
→ Discovering More Productivity Apps

# 22

# Getting Productive

It might not look like it, but your iPad is as powerful as many notebook computers. That means you can use your iPad for just about any office tasks from word processing to spreadsheets to presentations. You can also use your iPad to take notes and create illustrations. All you need are the right apps—and the right accessories, like a physical keyboard. (Learn more about iPad accessories in Chapter 24, "Accessorizing Your iPad.")

## Using Your iPad's Built-In Productivity Apps

Your iPad comes with three apps that can help you be more productive in the office and beyond. These apps are Pages, for word processing; Numbers, for spreadsheets; and Keynote, for presentations. These free apps, which are comparable to and file-compatible with similar Microsoft Office apps, serve the day-to-day productivity needs of many users.

## iPad Pro for Productivity

Although the standard iPad is the best solution for most home users, productivity apps work even better if you have an iPad Pro. The Pro's larger screen, more powerful processor, and Smart Keyboard make office work as easy and intuitive as it is on a traditional notebook computer. If you want to take your work on the road (even if it's just to your local coffee shop), this is the combination for success.

## Pages

The Pages app is a word processor, much like Microsoft Word, but optimized for use on the iPad. You can use Pages with your iPad's onscreen keyboard or, even better, use a wireless keyboard for faster and more accurate typing.

(1) From the iPad's Home screen, tap the Pages icon to launch the Pages app.

(2) You now see tiles for documents you've previously created. Tap one of these tiles to reopen an existing document, or tap the Create Document tile (or the + at the top right) to create a new document.

**3** Tap to select a template for your new document.

**4** Most documents include place-holder text as defined by the template you selected. Tap any block of placeholder text to replace that text with your own text, using the onscreen keyboard.

**5** Tap the paintbrush icon in the toolbar to format the selected text.

**6** Tap the Paragraph Style control to change the paragraph style.

**7** Tap Font to change the font family.

**8** Tap B to boldface text.

**9** Tap I to italicize text.

**10** Tap the – and + buttons to decrease or increase the size of the selected text.

**11** Tap the + icon to insert a table, chart, shape, or picture.

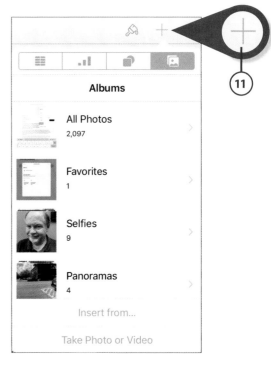

**(12)** Tap the More icon to collaborate with others, send a copy of this document, print this document, and more.

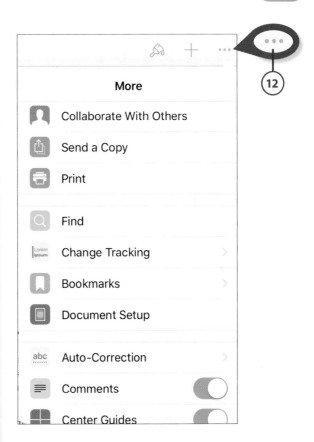

## Stored in the Cloud

By default, all Pages, Numbers, and Keynote documents are stored in the cloud—in Apple's iCloud, to be specific. This means you don't have to manually save your work; all changes are saved automatically, as you make them. It also means that your documents won't fill up the limited storage on your iPad, and they will be available to any device connected to the Internet, via your iCloud account.

# Numbers

You use the Numbers app to… well, to work with numbers. You can create spreadsheets in which you can enter and manipulate numerical data. It's great for creating budgets, expense reports, financial plans, and the like. You can perform all sorts of complex calculations and then display your results in attractive charts and graphs.

**(1)** From the iPad's Home screen, tap the Numbers icon to launch the Numbers app.

**2** You now see tiles for spreadsheets you've previously created. Tap one of these tiles to reopen an existing spreadsheet, or tap the Create Spreadsheet tile (or the + at the top right ) to create a new spreadsheet.

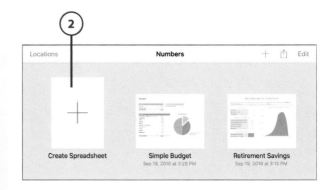

**3** Tap to select the template you want to use for your new spreadsheet.

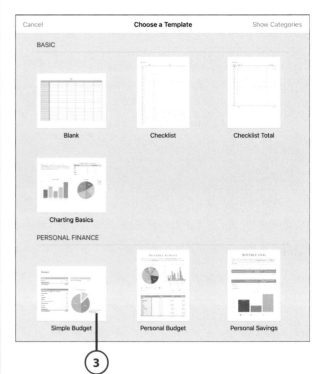

**4** The new spreadsheet includes placeholder text and numbers entered into cells. Tap any cell to replace its placeholder contents with your own text and numbers, using the onscreen keyboard. (To select more than one cell, use your finger to drag any of the selection corners to include additional cells.)

## Rows, Columns, and Cells

A spreadsheet consists of multiple *rows* (arranged down the left edge of the screen) and *columns* (arranged along the top of the screen). The intersection of any given row and column is called a *cell*; all the contents of a spreadsheet are contained in individual cells.

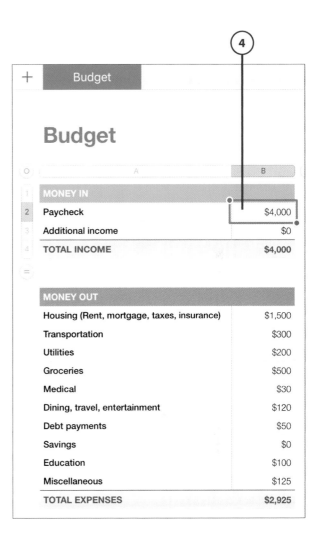

| | A | B |
|---|---|---|
| 1 | **MONEY IN** | |
| 2 | Paycheck | $4,000 |
| 3 | Additional income | $0 |
| 4 | TOTAL INCOME | $4,000 |
| | **MONEY OUT** | |
| | Housing (Rent, mortgage, taxes, insurance) | $1,500 |
| | Transportation | $300 |
| | Utilities | $200 |
| | Groceries | $500 |
| | Medical | $30 |
| | Dining, travel, entertainment | $120 |
| | Debt payments | $50 |
| | Savings | $0 |
| | Education | $100 |
| | Miscellaneous | $125 |
| | TOTAL EXPENSES | $2,925 |

⑤ Tap the paintbrush icon to format the selected cell(s).

⑥ Tap the Table tab to format the selected cells as a table.

⑦ Tap the Cell tab to format the contents of the selected cell(s). You can apply text formatting (bold, italic, underline, strike-through); change text options (size, color, and font); apply cell fill color; add various types of borders; and opt to wrap long text in a cell, or not.

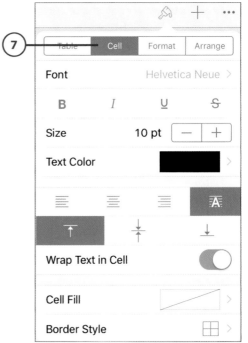

**8** Tap the Format tab to format the numerical data in the selection. You can choose a general Number format, Currency format, Percentage, and so forth.

**9** Tap the Arrange tab to move the selected element forward or backward on the page.

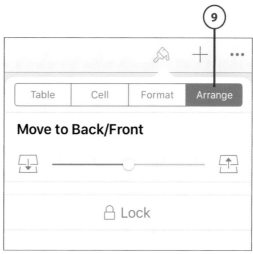

**(10)** Tap the + icon to insert a table, chart, shape, or picture.

**(11)** Double-tap a cell to enter a formula or function to perform a numerical calculation.

## Formulas and Functions

You perform a calculation in a spreadsheet by entering a formula that may include the contents of specified cells. You can include built-in formulas, called functions, within your larger formulas. (Unfortunately, the whole concept of formulas and functions is much more involved than we can discuss in this chapter; tap More, scroll down, and select Numbers Help to view coaching tips onscreen.)

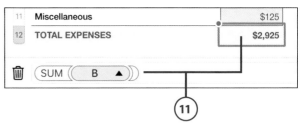

# Keynote

When you need to put on a presentation to any size group, Keynote can't be beat. The Keynote app lets you create highly visual presentations that you can present on your iPad or through a larger monitor or projector. (You first have to connect your iPad to said monitor, of course.)

① From the iPad's Home screen, tap the Keynote icon to launch the Keynote app.

② You now see tiles for presentations you've previously created. Tap one of these tiles to reopen an existing presentation, or tap the Create Presentation tile (or the + at the top right) to create a new presentation.

③ Tap to select the template you want to use for your new presentation.

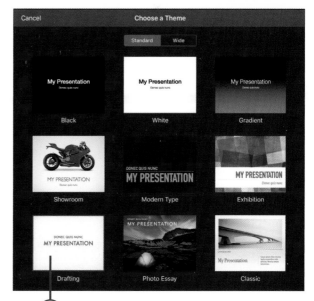

**4** The new presentation includes a preselected visual theme, along with a single opening slide. The slides in your presentation are displayed in the slide sorter on the left side of the screen. Tap any slide to view it in the larger editing area.

**5** Each new slide includes place-holder text and graphics. Double-tap any placeholder to replace its contents with your own.

**6** Select a block of text and then tap the paintbrush icon to for-mat the text's Style (background and text colors), format selected Text (font family and size, bold and italic formatting, and text alignment), and Arrange ele-ments on the screen.

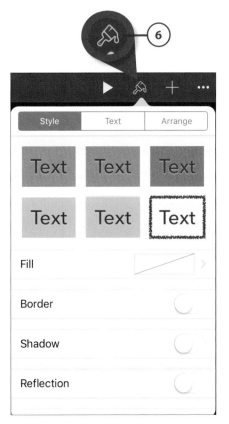

7. Tap the + icon to insert a table, chart, shape, or picture.

8. Tap the New Slide (+) icon in the lower-left corner to add a new slide to the presentation.

9. Tap to select the type of slide you want to add. (Repeat the preceding steps to add your own slide content and add additional slides to the presentation.)

**10** To add a transition between slides, press and hold a slide in the slide sorter and select Transition.

**11** Select the Effects tab and then tap Effects to see available transitions.

**12** Select the Options tab to set transition duration and how the transition is triggered.

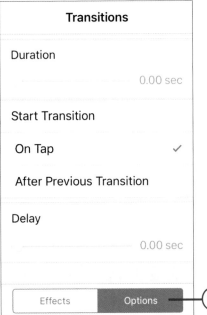

(13) Tap the Play button in the toolbar to play your presentation. Tap or swipe the screen to advance to the next slide.

## >>>Go Further
### KEYNOTE REMOTE

The Keynote app lets you use your iPad as a remote control to present slideshows on other Apple devices, including Macs and iPhones. To use the Keynote Remote, open your presentation, tap More, and then tap Allow Remote Control. Follow the onscreen instructions to pair your iPad to another Apple device via Wi-Fi or Bluetooth.

# Discovering More Productivity Apps

As good (and as free) as Apple's productivity apps are, they're not the only such apps available for your iPad. Google, Microsoft, and other software publishers offer similar productivity apps for iPad users, all available from Apple's App Store.

## Evernote

Evernote is a popular app that lets you take and share notes, create to-do lists, and save content you find online, and then organize your notes in various ways. You can also sync your Evernote content across multiple devices, including iPhones, Macs, Windows PCs, and even Android phones and tablets. The Evernote app is free.

---

### Other Note-Taking Apps

Other popular note-taking apps include GoodNotes 4 ($9.99), Notability ($7.99), and Notepad+ ($14.99—also available in a free version).

---

# Google Docs, Sheets, and Slides

Taken together, Apple's Pages, Numbers, and Keynote apps comprise what some call an *office suite*—a collection of apps that let you perform most office productivity functions. Apple's apps are kind of an ad hoc or unofficial suite, compared to the more formal app suites from other companies.

Case in point is Google's office suite, dubbed Google Docs. The apps in the Google Docs suite include Docs (word processing), Sheets (spreadsheet), and Slides (presentations). These apps are a little more traditional in their operation than the iPad- (and Mac-) focused nature of Apple's productivity apps. But, unlike Apple's apps, they're cross-platform compatible; you can use the Google Docs apps on your iOS device, your Android device, your Windows computer, and your Google Chromebook, if you have one.

All three Google Docs apps are free, and work great on the iPad.

# Microsoft Excel, PowerPoint, and Word

Speaking of office suites, the big daddy of all office suites is Microsoft Office. Long available only on Windows PCs, Microsoft now has Office apps available for all platforms, including Apple's iOS. The apps available—all free, by the way—include Word (word processing), Excel (spreadsheet), and PowerPoint (presentations).

Functionality of Microsoft's iOS apps isn't quite as robust as that of their PC counterparts, but files are fully compatible. If you're used to using Office apps in your office, then using those same apps on your iPad makes a lot of sense.

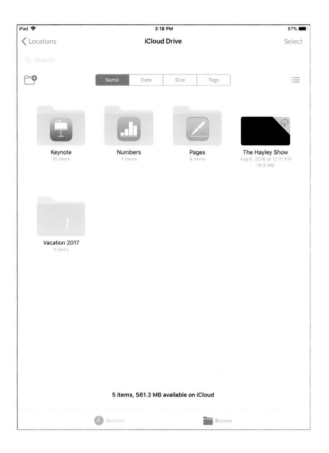

→ Managing Your iPad Storage
→ Managing iCloud Files with the Files App
→ Using AirDrop and AirPlay to Share Content with
  Other Devices
→ Backing Up Your iPad to iCloud

# Managing Files on Your iPad and in the Cloud

How do you get your photos and other files from your iPad to your computer—or vice versa? How do you manage those files stored on your iPad? How can you share your files with others? This chapter shows you how to do all these things. (Hint: It's all about the "cloud.")

## Managing Your iPad Storage

First off, let's find out how much storage you're using on your iPad. You have limited storage, after all; if you fill it, you won't have enough space to install new apps or shoot new pictures or videos.

# Examine Available Storage

You can see how much storage space you've used—and still have available—from your iPad's Settings screen.

1. From the Dock or Home screen, tap the Settings icon to open the Settings screen.

2. Tap General in the left column.

3. Tap iPad Storage in the right column.

4. The iPad bar graph shows the amount of storage spaced used by type of file (Media, Apps, Photos, and so on). The light gray area shows the amount of remaining storage space available.

| General | |
| AA | Display & Brightness |

iPad Storage

Background App Refresh

iPad          42.7 GB of 64 GB Used

Media   Apps   Photos   Mail   Books   Other

## Manage Available Storage Space

Which apps are using the most storage space? If you're running short on space, which apps are the best to delete?

Fortunately, Apple makes it easy to look at storage on an app-by-app basis—and, just as easily, delete those apps and files that you're not using.

**(1)** From the Settings screen, tap General and then tap iPad Storage.

**(2)** At the bottom of the iPad Storage screen, you see a list of all the apps installed on your iPad, with the largest apps (those using the most storage space) first. Tap an app to view more details.

**(1)**

| | |
|---|---|
| iPad Storage | > |
| Background App Refresh | > |

**(2)**

| | | |
|---|---|---|
| TV<br>Last Used: Sep 8, 2017 | 13.62 GB | > |
| Music<br>Never Used | 6.42 GB | > |
| Photos<br>Never Used | 2.84 GB | > |
| GarageBand<br>Never Used | 1.44 GB | > |
| iMovie<br>Never Used | 654.5 MB | > |
| Keynote<br>Last Used: Sep 13, 2017 | 602.4 MB | > |
| Barbie Magical<br>Never Used | 481 MB | > |
| Pages<br>Last Used: Sep 12, 2017 | 396.4 MB | > |

(**3**) The TV and Music apps list the corresponding media files used by each app—individual songs (and songs by artist) for the Music app and TV shows and movies for the TV app. Tap an item to view more details.

(**4**) Delete a media item by tapping Edit in the top-right corner.

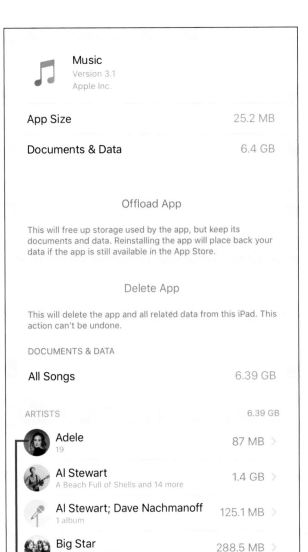

**Music**
Version 3.1
Apple Inc.

| | |
|---|---|
| App Size | 25.2 MB |
| Documents & Data | 6.4 GB |

Offload App

This will free up storage used by the app, but keep its documents and data. Reinstalling the app will place back your data if the app is still available in the App Store.

Delete App

This will delete the app and all related data from this iPad. This action can't be undone.

DOCUMENTS & DATA

| | |
|---|---|
| All Songs | 6.39 GB |

| ARTISTS | 6.39 GB |
|---|---|
| Adele<br>19 | 87 MB > |
| Al Stewart<br>A Beach Full of Shells and 14 more | 1.4 GB > |
| Al Stewart; Dave Nachmanoff<br>1 album | 125.1 MB > |
| Big Star<br>Radio City and 2 more | 288.5 MB > |

(**3**)

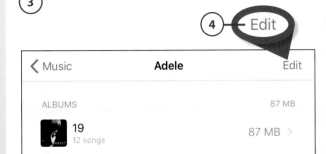

(**4**) — Edit

| ‹ Music | **Adele** | Edit |
|---|---|---|

| ALBUMS | 87 MB |
|---|---|
| 19<br>12 songs | 87 MB > |

( 5 ) Tap the red – icon.

( 6 ) Tap Delete.

( 7 ) Tap Done.

( 8 ) Other apps display the amount of space used by that app and its data. Tap Delete App to delete the app and its corresponding data.

( 9 ) Tap Delete App in the confirmation box.

## >>>Go Further
### WHAT TO DELETE

When you're looking to free up storage space on your iPad, it makes sense to look at the largest apps first—which is why Apple sorts them that way. You get the most bang for your buck by deleting a single large app than by deleting several smaller ones. So look at the apps in order of largest to smallest, and find those you no longer use or want. The first ones you come across are the ones you should delete.

# Managing iCloud Files with the Files App

It used to be that the only way to transfer media files to and from your iPad was by connecting your device to a computer. Today, however, you use Apple's iCloud service to store and transfer your files.

iCloud is a cloud-based storage service, which means it stores your files on Apple's servers, over the Internet. All files are synced wirelessly when you're connected to a Wi-Fi network, so you don't have to physically connect your iPad to your computer.

## >>>Go Further
### UNDERSTANDING iCLOUD AND CLOUD STORAGE

When it comes to storing data, there are two types of storage: local and cloud. Local storage means that your data is stored locally, on your device. (In your case, your iPad.) Cloud storage stores your data on computer servers in the "cloud"—that is, on the Internet. The advantage of local storage is that you always have your data at hand, even if you don't have an Internet connection. The advantage of cloud storage is that you can access your data from any device connected to the Internet, from wherever you might happen to be. All you need is an Internet connection and the username and password for your cloud storage account.

Apple's cloud storage service is called iCloud, and it's integrated into iOS and your iPad. This is a good thing, as you have a lot more storage space available in the cloud than you do on your iPad itself. You can also access the photos and videos you shoot with your iPad from any other device—your iPhone, for example, or your desktop or laptop computer.

One nice thing about how iCloud works is that once you enable it, you really don't have to do much else. Any new photo or file you create on your iPad is automatically uploaded to iCloud; you don't have to manually transfer any files. This also syncs your data between multiple devices; if you have a shared calendar, when you add an event on your iPad's Calendar app, that new event appears on all other devices linked to your iCloud account.

Access isn't limited to Apple devices, either. You can log onto iCloud.com from any computer or mobile device, using any web browser. It's all connected.

You were prompted to create an iCloud account when you first powered up your new iPad. You can also create a new account at a later date by going to iCloud.com and selecting the Don't Have an Apple ID? Option.

You get 5GB of free storage with your iCloud account. That's a lot, and it might be all you need. If it's not enough storage space, however, you can upgrade your account to get more storage. In the U.S., you pay $0.99/month for 50GB of storage (that's ten times the default storage space), $2.99/month for 200GB, or $9.99/month for a whopping 2TB (that's two terabytes, or 2,000 gigabytes!).

# Configure iCloud on Your iPad

You probably set up iCloud when you first powered up your iPad. You can change any iCloud settings at any time from your iPad's Settings screen.

1. From your iPad's Settings screen, tap Accounts & Passwords in the left column.

**2** In the right column, go to the Accounts section and tap iCloud.

**3** Tap your username to change contact information, password, payment information, and other account info.

**4** Tap Set Up Family Sharing to share photos, music, movies, schedules, and more with other family members.

**5** The Storage section tells you how much iCloud storage space you have free. Tap Storage to manage your storage or buy more storage space.

**6** Tap iCloud Drive to enable/disable storage for specific apps.

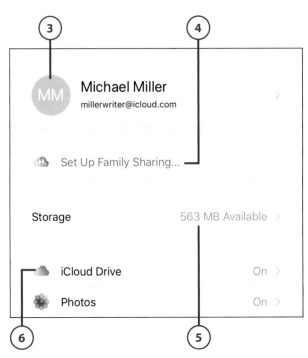

**7** Tap "on" the iCloud Drive switch to enable apps to store their documents and data in iCloud.

**8** Tap "on" the switch for each individual app for which you want to enable storage.

**9** Tap the back arrow to return to the previous screen.

**10** Tap Photos to enable/disable photo sharing via iCloud.

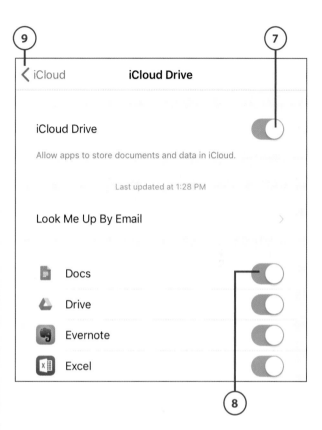

**9**

**7**

‹ iCloud          **iCloud Drive**

iCloud Drive

Allow apps to store documents and data in iCloud.

Last updated at 1:28 PM

Look Me Up By Email                          ›

Docs

Drive

Evernote

Excel

**8**

iCloud Drive                          On ›

Photos                                On ›

**10**

(11) Tap "on" the iCloud Photo Library switch to automatically upload and store your photo library in iCloud.

(12) Tap Optimize iPad Storage to store all your photos online and automatically delete them from your iPad. *Or…*

(13) Tap Download and Keep Originals to keep your original photos on your iPad (and copies in iCloud).

(14) Tap "on" Upload to My Photo Stream to automatically share your photos and videos with other iCloud-connected devices.

(15) Tap "on" iCloud Photo Sharing to create photo albums to share with other users.

(16) Tap "on" Upload Burst Photos to upload to iCloud all the photos you shoot in a burst. (By default, this is switched off and only key photos in a burst are uploaded, to save storage space.)

(17) Tap the back arrow to return to the previous screen.

**18** Tap "on" the switch for any app or service that you want to sync via iCloud. (Probably all of them.)

**19** Tap Keychain to enable iCloud Keychain, which stores passwords and credit card information across other iCloud-connected devices.

**20** Tap iCloud Backup to enable iCloud Backup, which automatically backs up important data from your iPad to iCloud.

**21** Tap Find My iPad to enable the Find My iPad service, which helps you find or disable your iPad if it's lost.

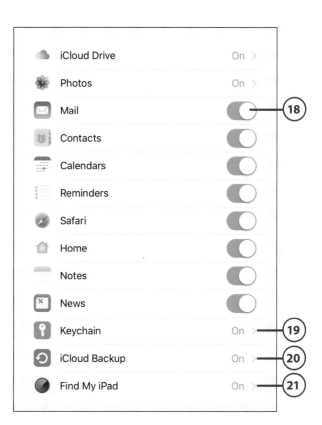

| | | |
|---|---|---|
| ☁ iCloud Drive | On > | |
| ✳ Photos | On > | |
| ✉ Mail | ⬤ | — **18** |
| 👥 Contacts | ⬤ | |
| Calendars | ⬤ | |
| Reminders | ⬤ | |
| 🧭 Safari | ⬤ | |
| 🏠 Home | ⬤ | |
| Notes | ⬤ | |
| News | ⬤ | |
| 🔑 Keychain | On > | — **19** |
| ↻ iCloud Backup | On > | — **20** |
| ● Find My iPad | On > | — **21** |

## Find My iPad

Learn more about Find My iPad in Chapter 6, "Keeping Your iPad Safe and Secure."

# View and Open Files with the Files App

You use the Files app (new with iOS 11) to view and manage those files you've stored in iCloud.

**1** From your iPad's Home screen, tap the Files icon to open the Files app.

( 2 ) Files are stored in folders. You can sort folders by name, date, size, or tags. Tap Select, and then select a sort criteria at the top of the screen.

( 3 ) By default, each app has a folder for its own files. Tap a folder to view its contents.

( 4 ) Tap a file to open that item.

( 5 ) Tap Select to copy, move, or delete a file.

**6** Tap to select one or more items. A blue check mark indicates selected items.

**7** Tap Move to move the selected item(s) to another folder.

**8** Tap Duplicate to copy the selected item(s) to another folder.

**9** Tap Delete to delete the selected item(s) item from iCloud.

**10** Tap Done when you're done moving or deleting files.

## >>>Go Further

### ACCESS iCLOUD FROM YOUR COMPUTER

You can view all items stored in your iCloud account from any connected device, including your desktop or laptop computer. Just open your web browser, go to iCloud.com, and then enter your Apple ID and password.

Once you've signed in, you see icons for all the iCloud-related services—Mail, Contacts, Calendar, Photos, and such. If you want to view your uploaded photos, click Photos. If you want to view other uploaded files, click iCloud Drive. From there you can navigate through the folders to view individual files.

## Create a New Folder

You don't have to settle for the default folders created by your iPad apps. You can create your own custom folders and move appropriate files there.

1. From within the Files app, tap the New Folder icon.

2. Type a name for this folder.

3. Tap Done.

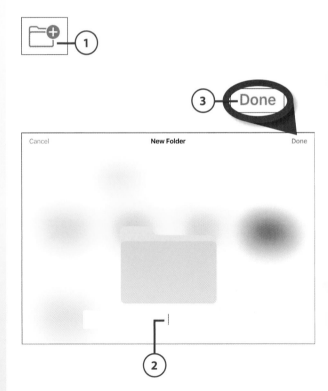

## Add Other Cloud Storage Services to the Files App

The Files app manages files stored in iCloud by default. You can also use the Files app to manage files stored in other cloud-based storage services, including Google Drive and Microsoft's OneDrive. All you have to do is enable those drives (what the Files app calls *locations*) within the app.

1. From within the Files app, tap Locations. This opens the Browse panel on the left side of the screen.

2. Tap Edit.

3. Tap the service(s) you want to enable.

4. Tap Done.

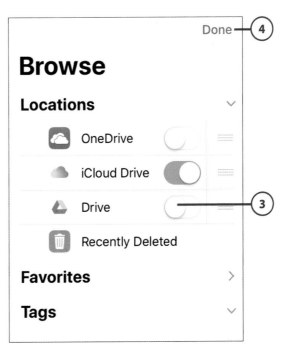

**5** To view files in another location, open the Browse panel and tap the name of the cloud service.

**6** If prompted, select or enter the name of your account and the password.

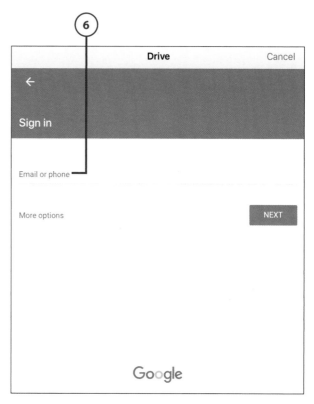

**7** You now see the contents of the selected drive. Tap to open a file.

Drive                                              Cancel

✕    My Drive                                    🔍  ⊞

Files                                              ↑ NAME

      20170214_205100.mp4
      ⚙ Modified Feb 18, 2017

PDF   Getting started
      Modified Apr 18, 2016

**7**

# >>>Go Further

## SYNC FILES BETWEEN YOUR iPAD AND YOUR COMPUTER

In the past (pre-iCloud), you had to connect your iPad to a personal computer to back up and sync files. With the advent of iCloud and other cloud-based services, however, you do all your file backup and syncing in the cloud, and you don't need a personal computer for these tasks.

That said, you can still connect your iPad to your computer to manage your files, using Apple's iTunes software. Just connect a Lightning-to-USB cable between your iPad and your computer (Mac or Windows); this should automatically launch the iTunes software on your computer. (If the iTunes software doesn't launch automatically, open it manually.)

Within iTunes, click the iPad icon below the menu bar. Click Summary in the left column to view key information about your iPad and to turn on automatic backups to either your computer or your iCloud account. Click Music, Movies, TV Shows, Audiobooks, or Photos to manage which items are synced to your iPad. Click File Sharing to transfer data and documents for selected apps between your iPad and your computer.

# Using AirDrop and AirPlay to Share Content with Other Devices

One nice thing about committing to the Apple ecosystem (that is, using multiple Apple devices—iPads, iPhones, Mac computers, and the Apple TV set-top device) is that it's easy to share data and files between each device. This is particularly easy using Apple's AirDrop and AirPlay feature. AirDrop lets you easily sync files between devices, whereas AirPlay enables wireless streaming of music and videos to other devices.

## Share Files with AirDrop

Use AirDrop to share photos, videos, locations, websites, and more with other compatible devices. AirDrop uses both Wi-Fi and Bluetooth to transfer data; if the other device isn't on the same Wi-Fi network as your iPad, you can connect them via Bluetooth, instead.

To use AirDrop, you must have your iPad's Wi-Fi and Bluetooth turned on, and each device must be connected to the same network and signed into iCloud. All transfers are encrypted for security.

1. Within an iPad app, tap the Share icon.

2. Nearby users are displayed in the top row of the share panel. Tap the name of a user to share this file with that user.

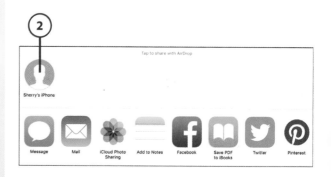

3. To receive files from another user, swipe up from the bottom of any screen on your iPad to display the Control Center, and then tap the AirDrop tile.

( 4 ) Tap Contacts Only to receive files from people in your contacts list only.

( 5 ) Tap Everyone to receive files from anyone nearby.

( 6 ) Tap Receiving Off to turn off AirDrop for receiving files.

# Stream Media with AirPlay

Use AirPlay to stream music and videos from your iPad to any compatible device in real time. You can use AirPlay to stream music from your iPad to an Apple TV box, AirPort Express device, AirPlay-enabled wireless speakers, or other AirPlay-enabled devices (such as some audio/video receivers). You can also use AirPlay to stream photos and videos to an Apple TV box.

To stream media via AirPlay, both your iPad and the target device need to be connected to the same Wi-Fi network. You may also need to enable AirPlay on the other device.

( 1 ) With music or a video playing, swipe up from the bottom of any screen to open the Control Center, and then long press the Now Playing pane.

( 2 ) From the enlarged Now Playing pane, tap the AirPlay icon.

**3** AirPlay looks for and displays nearby devices. Tap the device to which you want to stream.

**4** Use the playback controls to start and pause playback. The current media is now streamed to the selected device—and *not* played on your iPad.

**5** Tap iPad to return playback to your iPad.

## Screen Mirroring

Your iPad also offers Screen Mirroring, which lets you display your entire iPad screen (apps and all) on an Apple TV set-top device. Open the Control Center, tap the Screen Mirroring tile, and then select your Apple TV device from the list. (If a passcode appears on your TV screen, enter that code into the appropriate field on your iPad screen.) You now see your iPad screen on your TV display.

# Backing Up Your iPad to iCloud

The data that you store on your iPad—pictures, videos, music, and more—is valuable to you. You don't want to lose these items if you happen to lose or damage your iPad, or if your iPad quits working.

This is why you want to back up all your data—and settings and apps—in case something bad happens. When you have a backup of your important stuff, you can then restore those items to your iPad when it's found or fixed.

You back up your iPad files online to your iCloud account. It's easy to do.

# Back Up to iCloud

When your iPad is connected to the Internet via Wi-Fi, backups happen automatically in the background. All you have to do is configure your iPad for automatic iCloud backup.

1. From your iPad's Settings screen, tap Accounts & Passwords in the left column.

2. In the right column, go to the Accounts section and tap iCloud.

3. Scroll down the list of apps and tap iCloud Backup.

4. Tap "on" the iCloud Backup switch.

5. If you want to back up your data now, tap Back Up Now.

# Featured iPad accessories.

Smart Keyboard for 10.5-inch iPad Pro
$169.00

Leather Smart Cover for 10.5-inch iPad Pro - Saddle Brown
$69.00

●●●●●●

Leather Sleeve for 10.5-inch iPad Pro - Taupe
$179.00

●●●●●

Apple Pencil for iPad Pro
$99.00

Smart Cover for 10.5-inch iPad Pro - White
$49.00

●●●●  ●●●●●●

In this chapter, you discover various accessories to personalize and power up your iPad.

→ Protecting Your iPad with Cases and Covers
→ Adding Functionality with Keyboards and Styli
→ Extending Your iPad with Bluetooth Devices

**24**

# Accessorizing Your iPad

Numerous third-party companies make a variety of accessories you can add to your iPad. We're talking everything from covers to keyboards to wireless headphones. These accessories keep your iPad safer and make it more functional and more personalized.

## Protecting Your iPad with Cases and Covers

The iPad is an exceptionally sleek and stylish bit of technological design. Unfortunately, this thin, light, mostly glass device is prone to break if you happen to drop it or give it a good twist.

This is why it's a good idea to encase your iPad inside some sort of protective cover. Of course, a rugged case tends to hide the sleek and stylish design, but that cool iPad design won't mean much if you crack the screen or just plain break the thing.

## Smart Covers

There are all manner of covers and cases available for the iPad, whether you have a regular iPad, a mini, or Pro. One particularly useful type is the *smart cover*, which automatically puts your iPad to sleep when closed and wakes it up when opened. You can find smart covers from Apple and a variety of third parties, many of which feature foldable backs to function as stands for your device.

## Other Covers and Cases

Other companies make other types of covers and cases for your iPad. These range from soft silicone coverings to harder, more rugged protective cases. Some covers are optimized for use by children, making the device easier to hold and more impervious to unintentional destruction. There are even cases designed for presentation use, with hand straps or grips so you can hold the device in one hand when you give a presentation.

### Desktop Stands

Some covers have folding backs that let you sit your iPad more vertically, but you might prefer a more single-purpose approach. Several companies offer desktop iPad stands that make it easier to read books and newspapers on your device, or to function as more of a desktop monitor—especially if you add a wireless keyboard.

# Adding Functionality with Keyboards and Styli

If you want to use your iPad for office work, you need something other than the onscreen keyboard for typing. The good news here is that there are a variety of keyboards available that will turn your iPad into something more resembling a notebook computer—as well as "smart" styli to let you draw onscreen.

## Apple's Smart Keyboard

If you're the proud owner of an iPad Pro, you need to seriously consider investing in Apple's Smart Keyboard. Functioning as a keyboard, cover, and folding stand, the Smart Keyboard connects to your iPad Pro via the device's Smart Connector. It's a wireless connection that transfers both data and power between the two devices.

Apple sells Smart Keyboards in different sizes for all of its iPad Pro models. Prices range from $149 to $169.

## Other Wireless Keyboards

You can use the Smart Keyboard only with the iPad Pro, but if you have a regular iPad or a mini, there are lots of other wireless keyboard choices available—priced substantially lower, unsurprisingly. Some of these are freestanding keyboards; others come as part of a keyboard/cover/stand. Prices range from around $25 up to $100 or more.

## Apple Pencil

The iPad Pro is a unique beast in the iPad jungle. It's designed for both heavy-duty office productivity and delicate onscreen drawing. If you plan to do drawing on your iPad, or even just take a lot of handwritten notes, the Apple Pencil is for you.

The Apple Pencil is a wireless stylus that you can use to write or draw on the iPad Pro screen. It connects to your iPad Pro via the Smart Connector, and it's sensitive enough to let you vary line weight by increasing or decreasing pressure on the screen.

Like the Smart Keyboard, the Apple Pencil isn't cheap. We're talking $99, folks. But if you do a lot of onscreen drawing or note-taking, it's worth the price.

## Other Styli

The Apple Pencil isn't the only stylus you can use with your iPad. Styli from other companies connect via Bluetooth, and can thus be used with any model iPad. You can find styli in all manner of shapes, sizes, and prices, so look for the model that fits best in your hand—and does what you need it to do.

### Active Versus Passive

Don't confuse active styli, such as the Apple Pencil, with passive styli. An active stylus connects to your iPad, typically via Bluetooth, to interact with the screen. A passive stylus is little more than a pointy stick that you tap the screen with instead of your finger.

# Extending Your iPad with Bluetooth Devices

There are lots of other wireless devices you can connect to your iPad, all using Bluetooth technology. Setting up a Bluetooth connection is as easy as opening up the Settings page, tapping Bluetooth, tapping "on" the Bluetooth switch, and then selecting the desired device from the list displayed. (When Bluetooth is enabled, your iPad is discoverable by other devices—and discovers other devices, in return.)

## Wireless Headphones and Earphones

Probably the most popular type of Bluetooth accessory for the iPad is the wireless headphone or earphone. When you want to use your iPad to listen to music or videos but don't want to disturb others nearby, just connect a Bluetooth listening device and you can crank it up as loud as you want.

Although there are many Bluetooth earphones from third-party companies, Apple would like it very much if you invested in a pair of their wireless AirPods. These are high-end Bluetooth earbuds that connect seamlessly with your iPad (or iPhone). They're pretty cool but also pretty expensive, priced at $159. If you need to have the latest and greatest Apple stuff, this is the way to go; otherwise, look for similar performance from lower-priced models elsewhere.

### Wireless Flexibility

Naturally, you can also connect wired headphones and earphones to your iPad, but Bluetooth models provide a degree of flexibility you just don't get when you're connected via a cable.

## Wireless Speakers

Speaking of sound, if you want to use your iPad to host the music for your entire living room, you don't have to settle for the two tinny little speakers built into the device. Connect one or more wireless speakers via Bluetooth and turn your iPad into the centerpiece of an honest-to-goodness home audio system.

>>>*Go Further*

### SHOPPING FOR iPAD ACCESSORIES

Where can you find all the accessories mentioned in this chapter? iPad accessories are offered from a variety of different manufacturers and sold through Best Buy, Target, Walmart, and other traditional retailers, as well as Amazon.com and other online retailers. Apple also sells a bevy of iPad accessories (both its own and third-party items) on its website, at www.apple.com/shop/ipad/ipad-accessories. Prices do vary from store to store, of course, so make sure you shop around for the best price!

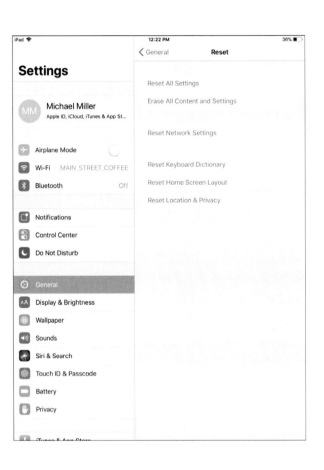

In this chapter, you learn how to troubleshoot
and fix problems you may encounter with
your iPad.

→ Troubleshooting iPad Problems
→ Updating and Resetting Your iPad

25

# Fixing Common Problems

Something wrong with your new iPad? Maybe it's just running slowly,
or having trouble connecting to the Internet. Have no fear—most iPad
problems are easy to fix, if you know what to do.

That's where this chapter comes in. Read on to learn how to troubleshoot and fix the most common problems you might encounter with
your iPad.

## Troubleshooting iPad Problems

Your iPad is a technological marvel. The amount of computing power
it packs into such a small device is nothing short of amazing. When I
was growing up in the 1960s, before the dawn of personal computers,
videogames, and even handheld calculators, we couldn't have con-
ceived of such a device or the things it could do.

That said, with all technology comes some degree of complexity—and
with complexity sometimes comes problems. You ever pick up your
iPad and not been able to turn it on? Or have the screen freeze on you?

Or have the darned thing drop an Internet connection? Then you know what I mean. The iPad is great, but it ain't always perfect.

So when your iPad is less than perfect, work through the troubleshooting tips in this section. Chances are, you'll have it up and running again in no time.

## Your iPad Is Frozen

Okay. You're using your iPad, tapping along, when all of a sudden nothing you tap seems to work. You can do all the tapping in the world, but your screen is completely frozen. What do you do?

Well, the one thing you don't want to do is panic. That's because a frozen iPad, as scary as it may seem, typically isn't a major problem. There are a few simple things to try that will likely get your iPad working again.

( 1 ) Try restarting your iPad by pressing and holding the Top button for a few seconds. When the slider appears, slide it to the right to power off. Then restart the iPad by pressing the Top button until the Apple logo appears.

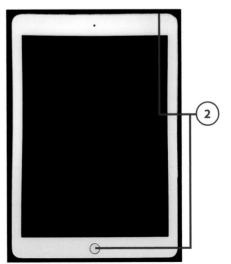

( 2 ) If your iPad won't restart, then you need to do what Apple calls a *force restart*. (Don't worry; this won't delete any of your content.) Press and hold the Top and Home buttons at the same time, for at least 10 seconds, until you see the Apple logo onscreen. When you see the logo your device has restarted and should be unfrozen.

## Your iPad Won't Turn On

What do you do if you can't even turn on your iPad? This situation may be caused by a few different problems.

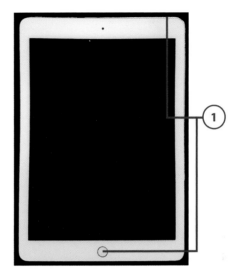

( 1 ) Your iPad may essentially be frozen in sleep mode. Try resetting the device by pressing and holding the Top and Home buttons at the same time, for at least 10 seconds. If you see the Apple logo onscreen, your iPad is good to go.

( 2 ) It's also possible that your iPad is simply out of juice. Plug it in and let it charge up for 10 minutes or so, then try starting it up again. (If you see the charging screen with a low battery graphic a few minutes after you plug it in, this was your problem.)

( 3 ) If you don't see the charging screen when you plug it in, check the connecting cable, power adapter, and the connections between the cable, connector, and wall outlet. Make sure everything is firmly connected, and that the power outlet actually has power. (That is, turn on the wall switch!)

## It's Not All Good

**Freezing During Startup**

If your iPad starts up but then freezes during the process (the Apple logo appears but doesn't go away), you can try connecting your device to your computer, launching iTunes, and then doing a force restart. When you get to the Apple logo screen, keep pressing the Top and Home buttons until you see the Recovery Mode screen. From here, choose the Update option, and iTunes will try to reinstall iOS without deleting any of the data stored on your iPad.

## Your iPad Won't Turn Off

If you think it's a pain when your iPad won't turn on, imagine what it's like when your device won't turn off. If this happens to you, try the following:

1. See if a given app is causing the problem. Swipe up from the bottom of the screen or press the Home button twice to display the App Switcher and then close each app individually (by pressing and dragging the app thumbnail off the top of the screen). When all the apps are closed, try turning off your iPad.

( **2** ) Do a force restart by holding the Top and Home buttons simultaneously for at least 10 seconds.

( **3** ) If your iPad still won't shut off, just keep it running until the battery runs out and then recharge it.

## An Individual App Freezes or Doesn't Work Right

If an individual app freezes on you, you have several options to try.

( **1** ) Swipe up from the bottom of the screen or press the Home button twice to display the App Switcher. Drag the unresponsive app up and off the screen. You can then relaunch the app and see if it works properly.

( **2** ) If the previous step didn't solve your problem, you might have to restart your iPad to close the frozen or misbehaving app. Press and hold the Top and Home buttons for about 10 seconds, until the Apple logo appears onscreen.

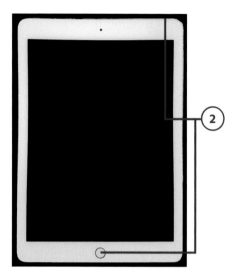

( **3** ) If the app is still giving you trouble, uninstall and then reinstall the app. From the Home screen, press and hold the icon for the app until it starts to jiggle, and then tap the X to delete the app. You can press the Home button to exit delete mode and then go to the App Store and reinstall a new version of the app.

## Your iPad Runs Slowly

When your iPad seems slower than normal, it's probably because there's one or more apps running that are slowing things down. Here are a few things to try:

1. Swipe up from the bottom of the screen or press the Home button twice to display the App Switcher and then close any app that you're not currently using. (If you have more than a half-dozen apps open, that's probably too many.)

2. Do a force restart by holding down the Top and Home buttons simultaneously for at least 10 seconds.

### Forced Restart

As you might have gathered, doing a forced restart is an amazing cure-all. You'd be surprised all the problems that this solves!

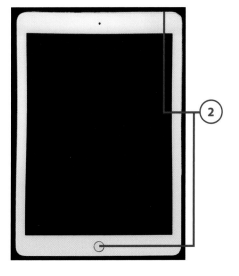

# Your iPad's Wi-Fi Connection Doesn't Work

You're sitting in your living room or in a local coffeeshop, doing your daily Internet surfing, when all of a sudden you can't access any websites or send email. Something's happened to your Wi-Fi connection—but what?

1. Turn your Wi-Fi off then back on by opening the Control Center, and tapping "off" the Wi-Fi control. Wait a few seconds, then tap the control back on.

2. Make sure that you're connected to the right network. Open the Settings page, select Wi-Fi, and then look at the list of available Wi-Fi networks. If the wrong network is selected, tap the right one to connect.

3. If that doesn't work, try restarting your iPad. Hold down the Top button and then slide the slider to the right to power off. You can restart your iPad normally and see if the Wi-Fi is now working.

(4) You can also reset your iPad's network settings. From the Settings screen, select General, tap Reset, and tap Reset Network Settings. This also restarts your iPad; you'll have to go in and choose the correct Wi-Fi network again.

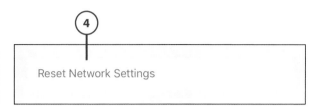

Reset Network Settings

## Your iPad Charges Slowly or Not at All

If you find your iPad taking longer than usual to charge, not charging at all, or simply not holding a charge as long as it used to, there are several things to check.

(1) Make sure the connecting cable is firmly plugged into your iPad, and to the power adapter. For that matter, make sure the power adapter is firmly plugged into a wall outlet—and that the wall outlet is turned on.

(2) Try changing charging cables. Cables do go bad, and when they do charging times suffer.

(3) If you have a spare power adapter around, try using that one instead of your old one. These gizmos go bad, too.

(4) If you've been trying to charge your iPad by connecting to your computer (via USB), plug directly into the wall outlet (via the power adapter) instead. Charging via computer is much, much slower than charging via wall outlet. In fact, some computers simply don't send enough juice to their USB ports to charge your iPad at all!

## It's Not All Good

### Old Batteries

If your iPad isn't holding a charge as long as it used to, it could be that your device's battery is getting old. iPad batteries become less efficient over time; if you've had your iPad for a year or more, it simply won't hold as much of a charge as it did when new. The only solution to this is to install a new battery, which you can't do yourself. (You'll have to go to an Apple Store or other service center for this.)

# Your iPad Doesn't Rotate

One of the things I like about the iPad is how the screen rotates when you turn the device one direction or another. What do you do if your iPad *doesn't* automatically rotate?

( 1 )  First, know that not all iPad apps rotate. (This is more of a problem with older apps than newer ones.) If you're using an app and turn your iPad and nothing happens, switch to another app or back to the Home screen and see if it rotated. If so, then the problem is a non-rotating app.

( 2 )  It's possible that you accidentally turned on something called *rotation lock*. With rotation lock enabled, your iPad screen simply won't rotate, no matter what you do. To switch this off, swipe up from the bottom of the screen to open the Control Center. If the rotation lock is enabled, the Lock Rotation icon is red against a white button background. Tap this button to turn it off. (You need to close the Control Center for the auto-rotation to start working again.)

## Your iPad Keeps Asking for Your iCloud Password

Here's another thing that's happened both to me and to my wife (on different devices). I start using my iPad, and sooner or later (mostly sooner) it nags me with a prompt to sign into my iCloud account. Even if I'm already signed into my iCloud account. It just keeps nagging me.

Is there any way to stop this constant nagging? Here's how.

(1) It may sound obvious, but try signing into your iCloud account. Sometimes doing what your device asks for is the proper approach.

(2) If the iPad keeps prompting you to sign into your iCloud account, something's stuck in the authorization process that makes your iPad think it needs the password when it really doesn't. Try restarting your iPad (by pressing and holding the Top button until you see the power-off slider) and see if this makes the annoying prompts go away.

(3) If this doesn't do it, try signing out of iCloud and then signing back into the service. You do this from the Settings screen; tap iCloud and then tap the Sign Out option. (You're prompted to enter your iCloud password to sign out.) After you sign out, return to the same Settings screen and sign back in again.

# >>>Go Further
## FORGOTTEN PASSWORD

What do you do if you simply can't remember your iCloud password? You need to reset your account with a new (and different) password, which you can do by pointing any web browser (on your iPad or computer) to iforgot.apple.com and following the onscreen instructions there.

## You Forgot Your iPad Passcode

Given how many passwords we're all required to keep in our heads for various devices, websites, and services, you're bound to forget one now and then. And if you can't remember the passcode you use to unlock your iPad, you're left with a locked device that is of no use to anybody.

That's because every iPad is programmed to lock out all users if the wrong passcode is entered ten times in a row. It's a safety measure, to keep ne'er-do-wells from trying to force their way into a stolen device. Too many wrong passcodes and the iPad is disabled.

(This actually happened to my daughter-in-law, through no fault of her own. Her six-year-old son—my rambunctious little grandson—got hold of her iPad and tried to break into it by entering random numbers on the Lock screen. Ten tries later, and her iPad was completely inaccessible.)

When this happens, the only way to get back into your iPad is to completely erase everything stored on your device, and revert to factory-fresh condition. You can then restore your data (if you've backed it up, that is) and create a new passcode.

The easiest way to erase your iPad is via iTunes. Follow these steps:

(1) Connect your iPad to your computer and launch the iTunes software.

(2) Wait for iTunes to sync your iPad to your computer and make a backup. Once the sync and backup are completed, click Restore.

(3) Your iPad now is reset to factory-fresh condition and the setup process commences on your device. When you're prompted to restore your iPad, tap Restore from iTunes Backup.

(4) Back in the iTunes software on your computer, select your device.

(5) Select the most recent data backup and follow the onscreen instructions to restore the backed-up data.

## >>>Go Further
### APPLE SUPPORT

If you work through the tips in this chapter and still have problems with your iPad, it's time to turn to Apple's official technical support. You can get support at any Apple Store location, or online at https://support.apple.com/ipad. There are also many third-party repair companies who specialize in repairing iPads and other local devices; search Google to find one in your area.

# Updating and Resetting Your iPad

It's important to keep your iPad up-to-date, which is what updating the operating system is all about. Operating system updates sometimes contain new features and almost always contain all manner of bug fixes. So if you've been having recurring issues with your iPad, chances are that they'll be fixed in the next version of the operating system.

Sometimes, however, things can get so gunked up that the only way to fix a recalcitrant iPad is to wipe it clean and reset it to the original factory condition. This should be the method of last resort, however, as it wipes out all the apps and data you've accumulated on your device.

## Update to the Latest Version of iOS

Your iPad is controlled by an operating system that Apple calls iOS. This operating system is updated from time to time, and you want to make sure that your iPad is running the latest iOS version.

In most instances, your iPad tells you (via an onscreen notification) that a new version is available, and walks you through the update procedure. You can, however, manually check for and install iOS updates.

**1** From your iPad's Settings screen, tap General in the left column.

**2** Tap Software Update.

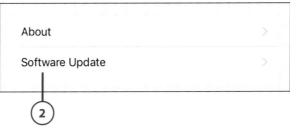

**3** If a software update is available, tap Download and Install and then follow the onscreen instructions.

**iOS 11**
Apple Inc.
1.83 GB

iOS 11 brings hundreds of new features to iPhone and iPad including an all new App Store, a more proactive and intelligent Siri, improvements to Camera and Photos, and augmented reality technologies to enable immersive experiences. iOS 11 is also the biggest release for iPad ever and adds powerful new multitasking features, a new Files app and more ways to use Apple Pencil.

Learn More >

Download and Install

**3**

## Factory Reset Your Device to "Like New" Condition

If you've tried everything to get your iPad working again and nothing has worked, you might need to take the drastic step of resetting your iPad to "like new" condition. You should only attempt this device reset when all other steps have failed; it's a big thing.

What's big about it is that resetting your iPad erases all the data and apps stored on your device. You'll lose all your music, videos, pictures, you name it, and have to reinstall everything from scratch.

That said, the "reinstall from scratch" process isn't as dire as it sounds. If you've backed up your iPad in advance (via either iTunes or iCloud), you can reinstall all your backed-up data and settings.

### Backing Up Your iPad

Learn more about backing up your iPad via either iCloud or iTunes in Chapter 23, "Managing Files on Your iPad and in the Cloud."

When the reset is done, your iPad is wiped and restarts with the original out-of-the-box setup process. You need to walk through the setup as if you just purchased the iPad, but then you can connect to iTunes or iCloud and reinstall your backed-up files.

## It's Not All Good

I will repeat this warning. *Resetting your iPad to factory-fresh condition erases all the data, apps, and settings stored on your device.* If you've previously backed up your iPad (to iCloud or iTunes), you can restore your data, apps, and settings. If you have not made a backup, your data and settings will be lost—*permanently.* (You can always restore apps you've previously downloaded from Apple's App Store.)

## Reset Your iPad

(1) From your iPad's Settings screen, tap General in the left column.

(2) Scroll to the bottom of the right column and tap Reset.

(3) Tap Erase All Content and Settings.

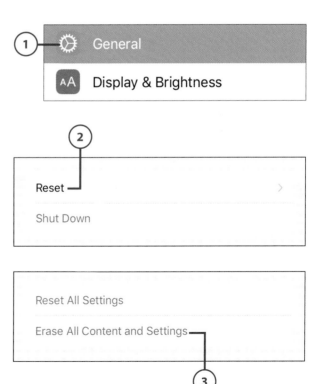

(4) Enter your passcode.

(5) When prompted, tap Erase. (Or tap Cancel to not proceed.) Your iPad—and all its data, settings, and apps—will be erased.

# Restore from an iCloud Backup

When you reset your iPad, everything is wiped clean and your device is back to its factory-fresh condition. After the reset is complete, your iPad's initial setup process starts, and it's back to the "Hello" screen (discussed in Chapter 1, "Buying and Unboxing Your iPad").

You restore your iPad during this initial setup process—so look sharp at each screen you see and follow these instructions.

1. Proceed through the onscreen setup until you reach the Apps & Data screen and then tap Restore from iCloud Backup.

2. When prompted, sign into iCloud with your Apple ID.

3. On the next screen, choose a backup. You'll likely want to choose the most recent backup.

4. The backup starts. When prompted, you need to sign into the App Store with your Apple ID to restore your apps and purchases.

5. Make sure you stay connected to the Internet during the entire process, which might take up to an hour to complete. When the files are restored, you can finish the initial setup and start using your iPad as normal.

# Restore from iTunes Backup

If you've previously backed up your iPad to your computer, via iTunes, you can restore your device from iTunes during the initial setup process.

1. Proceed through the onscreen setup until you reach the Apps & Data screen, then connect your iPad to your computer.

2. This should launch the iTunes software on your computer. Select your iPad from the available devices.

3. Back on your iPad, on the Apps & Data screen, tap to select Restore from iTunes Backup.

4. In iTunes, select Restore Backup.

5. Select the backup you want to restore from. (Probably the most recent one.)

6. Click Restore.

7. Keep your iPad connected to your computer until the restore process is complete. When it's done, you can finish your iPad's initial setup and start using it as normal.

# Glossary

**AirDrop**   The feature that enables sharing of media files between an iPad and other Apple devices.

**AirPlay**   The feature that streams music and videos from an iPad to other Apple devices.

**app**   A software application running on the iPad or other mobile devices.

**App Store**   Apple's online store that offers apps and games for iPads and iPhones.

**App Switcher**   The screen mode that displays all running apps in a swipeable carousel.

**Apple**   The company that created the iPad and iPhone.

**Apple Pay**   Apple's mobile payment system.

**Apple Pencil**   The active stylus designed for use with the iPad Pro.

**AssistiveTouch**   A feature that overlays a group of large icons onscreen for common functions.

**Bluetooth**   Wireless technology designed to connect two devices together.

**cloud storage**    File storage on Internet-based servers.

**Control Center**    The panel that swipes up from the bottom of the iPad screen and enables control of many common system settings.

**Do Not Disturb mode**    An iPad operating mode that hides notifications, alerts, and system sound effects.

**Dock**    That area at the bottom of every iPad screen that displays the same four or five app icons.

**eBook**    An electronic book; a traditional book in electronic form.

**email**    Electronic mail; messages sent electronically from one computer or device to another.

**FaceTime**    Apple's video chat service.

**FaceTime camera**    The front-facing camera on the iPad, typically used for selfies and FaceTime conversations.

**forced restart**    The process of manually forcing the iPad to restart by pressing and holding the Top and Home buttons simultaneously.

**front-facing camera**    The camera above the iPad display, typically used for selfies and video chats.

**HDR**    High dynamic range, a process that combines the results of multiple photos to create a single high-contrast photo.

**Home button**    The small round button beneath the iPad screen when held vertically.

**Home screen**    Those screens that host the icons for all the apps installed on an iPad.

**hotspot**    A location where you can get Internet access via Wi-Fi.

**iCloud**    Apple's cloud-based storage service.

**identity theft**    The fraudulent acquisition and use of an individual's personal information.

**in-app purchase**    The purchase of additional services from within an app or game.

**iOS**    The operating system used by iPad and Apple's other mobile devices.

**iPad** Apple's popular tablet computer.

**iPad Air** Apple's main iPad model, with a 9.7-inch screen.

**iPad mini** Apple's smallest and most affordable iPad, with a 7.9-inch screen.

**iPad Pro** The iPad designed for business productivity, with 9.7- and 12.9-inch models.

**iPhone** Apple's smartphone.

**iSight camera** The rear-facing camera on the Apple iPad.

**iTunes** Apple's software that enables users to manage their iPads and iPhones on their Mac or Windows computers.

**iTunes Store** Apple's online store that offers music and videos for purchase and rental.

**Keynote** Apple's presentation app for the iPad and iPhone.

**Lightning connector** The port on the bottom of the iPad that connects the iPad to the power adapter, computers, and other USB devices.

**Lock screen** The screen that appears before you unlock your iPad.

**malware** Short for malicious software—viruses, spyware, and other files that can damage a computer or mobile device.

**multitasking** The capability of using more than one app at the same time.

**Multi-Touch Display** Apple's touchscreen display.

**newsreader** An app that consolidates news items from multiple sources.

**Night Shift** The feature that enables you to adjust the color temperature of the iPad display for night-time viewing.

**Notification Center** The iPad screen that displays system notifications and app alerts.

**Numbers** Apple's spreadsheet app for the iPad and iPhone.

**operating system** A core software program that controls a device's underlying hardware and operations.

**Pages** Apple's word processing app for the iPad and iPhone.

**passcode**   On the iPad, a six-number code that must be entered to unlock the device.

**Perspective Zoom**   A type of parallax effect that displays a slight motion on the Home or Lock screens when you tilt your iPad.

**pixel**   A single dot or picture element that makes up a photo or video picture.

**post**   See *status update*.

**predictive keyboard**   A virtual keyboard that attempts to figure out what you're typing and enter that word for you.

**rear-facing camera**   The camera on the back of the iPad that faces away from you.

**reset**   Wiping your iPad of all data, settings, and apps and returning it to factory-new condition.

**Retina display**   The iPad display that offers 300 pixels or more resolution.

**Safari**   Apple's web browser app, included with iOS.

**Safari Reader**   A special reading mode, within the Safari browser, that makes some web pages easier to read by removing ads, images, videos, and other extraneous elements.

**Search screen**   That iPad screen that includes system notifications, widgets, and a search box.

**selfie**   A picture you take of yourself.

**Siri**   The voice-activated software that functions as a virtual personal assistant on your iPad and other Apple devices.

**Slide Over**   A feature that enables you to open a second app onscreen without closing the one you're currently in.

**Smart Connector**   The wireless connector unique to the iPad Pro, designed to connect the Smart Keyboard and Apple Pencil.

**smart cover**   An iPad cover that wakes the unit from sleep when open and puts it in sleep mode when closed.

**Smart Keyboard**   Apple's wireless keyboard designed for use with the iPad Pro.

**social media**   See *social network.*

**social network**   An Internet-based service that hosts a community of users and makes it easy for those users to communicate with one another.

**spam**   Also known as junk mail, any unsolicited email advertisement.

**Split View**   The mode that makes two apps active onscreen at the same time.

**status update**   A short message (with text and/or images and video) that updates friends on what a user is doing or thinking.

**streaming media**   Music and video that are transmitted in real time to a connected device. ˝

**tablet**   See *tablet computer.*

**tablet computer**   A small computer in the shape of a handheld tablet. The iPad is a tablet computer.

**text messaging**   Short electronic messages sent from one device to another.

**Top button**   The physical button at the top-right corner of the iPad (when held vertically) used to put the device to sleep and wake it up.

**touch gestures**   Taps and motions on the iPad screen that perform various common operations.

**Touch ID**   Apple's fingerprint sensing system.

**touchscreen**   A device display that can be operated by touch gestures.

**URL**   Uniform Resource Locator, the address of a web page.

**USB**   Universal Serial Port, a type of connection common to personal computers.

**video chat**   A face-to-face onscreen chat between two users.

**VoiceOver**   A feature that describes out loud any screen element or text on the iPad.

**wallpaper**   The background image on the iPad's Home and Lock screens.

**Wi-Fi**   Short for wireless fidelity, the wireless networking standard used by most computers and connected devices today.

**YouTube**   The Internet's largest video-sharing community.

# A

Index

accessing
   apps with Siri, 140-143
   iCloud from computer, 434
accessibility options, 74
   gestures
      *AssistiveTouch, 89*
      *optimizing, 87*
      *touchscreen displays, 87*
   hearing, 85
      *closed captioning, 86-87*
      *hearing aids, 85*
   vision, 78
      *inverted screen colors, 82*
      *magnified screens, 81-82*
      *modified text, 84*
      *VoiceOver, 78-80*
accessories, 444
   Apple Pencil, 445
   assigning to rooms, 355-357
   cases and covers, 443-444
   Smart Keyboard, 444
   styli, 445
   wireless headphones and
     earphones, 446
   wireless keyboards, 445
   wireless speakers, 447
Accessory Automation pane
  (Home app), 369
Account panel (App Store), 160
action games, 397
action sounds, 71
Add Accessory panel (Home app),
  352-353
addresses (web), entering, 98-99
addressing text messages, 205

Add Scene option (Home app), 358
adjusting. *See* modifying
ads
   blocking, 108
   YouTube, 342
adventure games, 397
AirDrop, 438-439
AirPlay, 439-440
alarms, 45
albums
   People, 294
   picture management, 291-295
   Places, 295
alerts, 35
   displaying as banners, 68
   event formatting, 253
Allow Notifications switch, 67
All tab (App Store), 161
Amazon Music Unlimited, 317
Amazon Prime Music, 317
Amazon Prime Video, 337
Amazon Video
   browsing selections in, 337
   launching, 337

playback controls, 339

selecting programs in, 338

subscription plans, 336-337

An Accessory Is Controlled option (Home app), 369

Android tablets, 4

answering video chats, 217-218

Apple support, 460

Apple HomeKit, 349-350. *See also* Home app

  compatibility, 351

  how it works, 350

Apple IDs, 13

Apple Music, listening to, 312-314

Apple Pencil, 9, 445

applications. *See* apps

apps. *See also* individual app names

  App Store

    *browsing, 153-157*

    *downloading apps from, 158-160, 394*

    *payments, 160*

    *purchasing apps from, 158-160*

  arranging, 57

  closing, 152

  configuring, 72

  definition of, 5, 147

  deleting, 163, 425-426

  dragging files between, 25, 168-169

  locating, 158

  managing, 59-60, 160-161

  moving, 158

  opening, 31-32

    *from Dock, 149*

    *from Home screen, 148*

    *with Slide Over, 164-166*

    *with Split View, 25, 167-168*

  paying for, 160

  searching for

    *from Home screen, 150*

    *in App Store, 153-157*

side apps, 164

switching between, 26, 151

troubleshooting, 453

updating, 162

viewing, 160-161

App Store

  browsing, 153-157

  downloading apps from, 158-160, 394

  payments, 160

  purchasing apps from, 158-160

Apps tab (App Store), 156

App Switcher, 25, 36, 151-152

arcade games, 398

arranging apps, 57

assigning accessories to rooms, 355-357

AssisitiveTouch, 89

attaching pictures to email, 183-185

audio

  audio calls, 219

  audio messages, 206

  configuring, 71

  mono audio, 86

  notifications, 67

  wireless speakers, 447

audiobooks, listening to, 267

audio calls, placing, 219

audio messages, sending, 206

Auto-Enhance, 297

auto focus, 281

Automatic Setup features, 12

automatic updates, 73

automating smart devices, 361

  controlled automation, 368-370

  Home Hub setup, 362-363

  location automation, 364-366

  time automation, 366-368

available storage

  checking, 422

  managing, 423-425

# B

backups
    restoring from, 465
    creating on iCloud, 431, 440-441
back of iPad, 19
Badge App Icon switch, 67
banners, displaying alerts as, 68
Barnes & Noble Nook, 271
basic operations, 34
    alarms, 45
    alerts, 35
    brightness controls, 38
    Control Center, 36
    Do Not Disturb mode, 41
    rotating, 40
    stopwatches, 47-48
    text
        copying/pasting, 44
        entering, 42-43
    timers, 46
    volume controls, 39
batteries
    managing, 48, 50-51
    troubleshooting, 457
blocking ads, 108
Bluetooth, 446
board games, 398
bookmarking, 103-105
books. See eBooks
bottom of iPad, 18
Braille displays, 81
brightness
    configuring, 69-70
    modifying, 38
    Night Shift mode, 38
    pictures, 298
Browse option
    Amazon Video, 337

Apple Music, 313
App Store, 153-157
Hulu, 331-333
Music app, 313
burst shots, 281, 430
buying
    apps, 158-160
    eBooks, 262-263
    games, 394
    iPad models, 10-11

# C

calculations, 412
Calendar app, 243
    adding events, 248-249
    alerts, 253
    inviting people, 254
    managing with Siri, 141-142
    recurring events, 249-250, 253
calls
    audio calls, 219
    video calls
        answering, 217-218
        starting, 214-216
        with Skype, 220
Camera app. See also photos
    configuring, 281-282
    pictures
        panoramic pictures, 283-284
        selfies, 282-283
        taking, 209, 279-281
        viewing, 286, 290
    starting, 278
cameras. See also Camera app
    FaceTime HD, 17
    iSight, 19
    managing with Siri, 142
card games, 398

cases, 24, 443-444
casino games, 398
cellular connectivity, 7
changing. *See* modifying
charging
  batteries, 457
  iPad, 12
chats (video
  answering, 217-218
  starting, 214-216
  with Skype, 220
checking available storage, 422
choosing iPad model, 5-6
  buying tips, 10-11
  iPad, 8
  iPad mini 4-7
  iPad Pro, 9-10
  older models, 9
Clock
  alarms, 45
  stopwatches, 47-48
  timers, 46
closed captioning, 86-87
closing
  apps, 31-32, 152
  Control Center, 37
  iPads, 452
cloud storage, 426
  Cloud storage services, adding, 435-437
  iCloud, 426-427
    *accessing from computer, 434*
    *backing up to, 431, 440-441*
    *copying files on, 433*
    *costs, 427*
    *creating folders on, 434*
    *deleting files on, 433*
    *moving files on, 433*
    *opening files from, 431-433*
    *passwords, 459*

    *Photo Library, 291*
    *restoring from, 465*
    *setting up, 363, 427-431*
    *upload photos to, 285*
    *viewing files on, 431-433*
color blindness, 83
colors
  color blindness, 83
  Night Shift mode, 38
  pictures, 298
  screens, inverting, 82
commands (Siri), controlling smart homes
  with, 361
Compose icon (Messages app), 204
configuring. *See* setup
connecting
  Bluetooth, 446
  home wireless networks, 92-93
  to Internet, 12
  Lightning connectors, 18, 49
  networks, 96
  public wireless hotspots, 94-95
  troubleshooting, 97
  Wi-Fi, 92, 456
connectors
  Smart Connector, 17
  USB connectors, 11
consolidating Contact app, 196
Contact app
  consolidating, 196
  deleting, 195
  editing, 194
  email, 201
  managing, 192
  modifying, 199-200
  searching, 198
  viewing, 198
Control Center, 36
  closing, 37

customizing, 63, 66-68
displaying, 25, 36
Night Shift mode, 38
controlled automation, 368-370
controlling
scenes
    with Home app, 360
    with Siri, 361
smart devices
    with Home app, 360
    with Siri, 361
controls
adding to Control Center, 64
displaying additional options for, 37
removing from Control Center, 64
turning on/off, 36
control system functions (Siri), 140
converting measurements, 145
cooking apps, 387
copying
iCloud files, 433
text, 44
costs
Amazon Music Unlimited, 317
Amazon Prime Music, 317
Amazon Video, 336-337
Apple Music, 312
cellular connectivity, 7
Hulu, 330
iCloud, 427
iPad flagship model, 8
iPad mini 4, 7
iPad Pro, 10
Netflix, 326
Pandora, 315
Spotify, 317
covers, 443-444
Cover Sheet
displaying, 25

viewing notifications on, 29-30, 67
Create New Automation option
(Home app), 364-368
cropping pictures, 296
Customize Controls option, 63
customizing. *See also* setup
Control Center, 63, 66-68
Home screen, 54
    *arranging apps, 57*
    *managing apps, 59-60*
    *moving icons, 58*
    *wallpaper, 54-56*
inboxes, 177
news, 272
Search screens, 61
wallpaper, 54

## D

default email accounts, selecting, 174
Delete App option, 425
deleting
apps, 163, 425-426
Contact app, 195
iCloud files, 433
controls from Control Center, 64
media items, 424
messages, 185
reminders, 259
desktop stands, 444
devices, setting up, 64
apps, 72
brightness, 69-70
notifications, 66
system sounds, 71
viewing Settings pages, 65
dieting apps, 386-387
directions, getting (with Siri), 145.
*See also* Maps app

displaying. *See* viewing
displays
Braille, 81
configuring, 69-70
modifying, 87
Multi-Touch Displays, 16
moving to, 58
opening apps from, 149
Retina display, 7
Docs app, 418
documents
selecting words in, 26
zooming in/out, 26
Do Not Disturb mode, 41
downloading
apps, 158-160
games, 394
dragging/dropping files between apps, 24-25, 168-169
driving directions, getting (with Siri), 145. *See also* Maps app

### E

earphones, 446
eBooks
buying, 262-263
reading, 261, 266
*on iBooks, 264*
*on Kindle, 267-271*
searching, 262-263
editing
Contact app, 194
pictures, 285
*Auto-Enhance, 297*
*brightness/colors, 298*
*cropping/straightening, 296*
*filters, 297*
*marking up, 300*

*viewing, 286, 290*
videos, 302, 305-306
email
configuring, 171
*accounts, 172-174*
*signatures, 176-177*
*message notifications, 174*
Contact app, 201
pictures
*attaching, 183-185*
*sharing, 307*
sending/receiving, 177-189
emojis, adding to text messages, 42, 205
enabling. *See* setup
entering
events, 258
text, 42-43
web addresses, 98-99
erasing data, 122
events
adding, 248-249
alerts, 253
entering, 258
recurring, 249-250, 253
Siri, 141-142
viewing, 244
Evernote app, 417
examining available storage, 422
Excel app, 418
exercise apps, 384
expanding (gesture), 25
exposure, 281

### F

Facebook, 224
navigating, 225-226
posting, 227-229
sharing pictures on, 308-309

FaceTime app, 214
  answering, 217
  audio calls, placing, 219
  HD cameras, 17
  video chats
    *answering, 217-218*
    *starting, 214-216*
factory resets, 462-464
Family Sharing, 428
file management
  AirDrop, 438-439
  AirPlay, 439-440
  available storage
    *checking, 422*
    *managing, 423-425*
  file sharing
    *AirDrop, 438-439*
    *AirPlay, 439-440*
    *dragging between apps, 25*
  iCloud, 426-427
    *accessing from computer, 434*
    *backing up to, 431, 440-441*
    *copying files on, 433*
    *costs, 427*
    *creating folders on, 434*
    *deleting files on, 433*
    *moving files on, 433*
    *opening files from, 431-433*
    *passwords, 459*
    *Photo Library, 291*
    *restoring from, 465*
    *setting up, 363, 427-431*
    *upload photos to, 285*
    *viewing files on, 431-433*
  other Cloud storage services, 435-437
  syncing files between iPad and
    computer, 437
Files app
  Cloud storage service, adding, 435-437

iCloud, 426-427
  *accessing from computer, 434*
  *backing up to, 431, 440-441*
  *copying files on, 433*
  *costs, 427*
  *creating folders on, 434*
  *deleting files on, 433*
  *moving files on, 433*
  *opening files from, 431-433*
  *passwords, 459*
  *Photo Library, 291*
  *restoring from, 465*
  *setting up, 363, 427-431*
  *upload photos to, 285*
  *viewing files on, 431-433*
filters, 297
finding apps
  from Home screen, 150
  in App Store, 153-157
Find My iPad service, 431
fingerprint recognition. *See* Touch ID
fitness apps, 383-384
folders
  creating, 434
  managing, 59-60
food and nutrition apps, 385
  cooking/recipes, 387
  dieting apps, 386
force restarts, 23, 450, 455
forgotten passcodes, 459-460
formatting
  events
    *alerts, 253*
    *recurring, 249-250, 253*
  signatures, 176-177
formulas, 412
For You tab (Music app), 312-313
fraud, 129-131
free games, 394
front of iPad, 16

frozen screens, 450
functions, 412

# G

games
    action, 397
    adventure, 397
    arcade, 398
    board, 398
    card, 398
    casino, 398
    music, 399
    playing, 393
    puzzle, 399
    racing, 399
    role-playing, 399
    searching, 393-394
    simulation, 400
    sports, 400
    strategy, 400
    trivia, 400
    word, 400
Games tab (App Store), 155
General Settings, 73
    iPad Storage, 422-423
    Software Update, 10
Genres (iTunes Store), 319
gestures
    AssistiveTouch, 89
    hidden, 25
    multi-touch, 24
    optimizing, 87
    touchscreen displays, 87
    VoiceOver, 80
getting directions (with Siri), 145
Google
    searching, 112
    Siri, 144

Google Docs app, 418
group messages, sending, 205

# H

HDR (high dynamic range), 280
headphones, 446
headset jacks, 17
health and fitness apps, 383-384
hearing impaired use, 85
    applying closed captioning, 86-87
    using hearing aids, 85
help, 460
high dynamic range (HDR), 280
history of iPad, 4
history, displaying notifications in, 67
Home app
    managing with Siri, 143
    rooms
        adding, 354
        assigning accessories to, 355-357
    scenes
        controlling, 360-361
        creating, 357-359
    smart devices
        adding, 351-353
        automating, 361-370
        controlling, 360-361
Home button, 13, 148
Home Hub, 362-363
HomeKit, 349-350. See also Home app
    compatibility, 351
    how it works, 350
Home screen, 26-27
    finding apps from, 150
    icons, 58
    managing apps on, 59-60
    moving apps on, 57

opening apps from, 148
personalizing, 54
returning to, 25
wallpaper, 54-56
home wireless network, connecting to, 12, 92-93
hotel Wi-Fi, connecting to, 94
hotspots, connecting to, 94-95
Hulu
    browsing selections in, 331-333
    launching, 331
    playback controls, 336
    searching, 334
    selecting programs in, 334
    subscription plans, 330

I

iBooks app
    audiobooks, 267
    navigating, 262-263
    reading, 264-266
iCloud, 426-427
    accessing from computer, 434
    backing up to, 431, 440-441
    copying files on, 433
    costs, 427
    creating folders on, 434
    deleting files on, 433
    moving files on, 433
    opening files from, 431-433
    passwords, 459
    Photo Library, 291
    restoring from, 465
    setting up, 363, 427-431
    upload photos to, 285
    viewing files on, 431-433
icons, moving, 58

identity theft, 127-128
IDs, Apple IDs, 13
images. *See also* Camera app; photos
    attaching to email, 183-185
    editing, 285
    managing with Siri, 142
    viewing, 286, 290
iMessage service, 204
iMovie app, 306
importing contacts, 194
inboxes, selecting, 177
Internet connections, 12
inverting screen colors, 82
inviting people to events, 254
iOS, 10
    updating, 461
    upgrading, 10
iPad models, 5-6
    buying tips, 10-11
    cellular connectivity, 7
    charging, 12
    initial setup, 12-13
    iPad, 8
    iPad mini 4, 6-7
    iPad Pro, 9-10
    older models, 9
    powering up, 12-13
    Retina display, 7
    turning on/off, 13
    unboxing, 11
iPad Storage settings, 422-423
iPhone, 5
iSight cameras, 19
iTunes, 342
    playing music from, 321-323, 347
    purchasing music from, 318-321
    renting/purchasing video from, 343-345
    restoring from, 465
    watching video from, 346-347

## J-K

junk email, 188-189

keyboards, 444
    onscreen keyboard, splitting, 26
    predictive, 43
    Smart Keyboard, 9, 444
    text
        *copying/pasting, 44*
        *entering, 42-43*
    wireless, 445
Keychain, 431
Keynote app, 413-417
Kids tab (Amazon Video), 337
Kindle app, 267-271

## L

language information, entering, 12
launching. *See* opening
Library tab (Music app), 321
Lightning connectors, 11, 18, 49
LinkedIn, 237-240
links (web), 100
listening to audiobooks, 267
listening to music, 311
    iTunes Store
        *playing music from, 321-323*
        *purchasing music from, 318-321*
    streaming music, 311-312
        *Amazon Music Unlimited, 317*
        *Amazon Prime Music, 317*
        *Apple Music, 312-314*
        *paid subscriptions, 312*
        *Pandora, 314-316*
        *Spotify, 317*
        *YouTube, 317*
locating apps, 158

location automation, 364-366
Location Services, 12
locking iPads, 21
Lock screen, 118
    erasing data, 122
    passcodes, 118-119
    personalizing, 54
    Touch ID, 120-122
logging in
    Apple IDs, 13
    Touch ID, 12
long press, 37

## M

magnifying screens, 81-82
Mail app
    configuring, 171
        *accounts, 172-174*
        *signatures, 176-177*
        *message notifications, 174*
    sending/receiving, 177-189
    Siri with, 140-141
malware, 129
managing
    apps, 57-60, 160-161
    batteries, 48-51
    Contact app, 192
    messages, 186-189
    pictures, 291-296
    reminders, 256
        *adding, 257-258*
        *deleting, 259*
    system settings, 73-74
Maps app, 373-376
marking up pictures, 300
mass transit maps, 376
media, deleting, 424
medical apps, 389-391
meetings, 141-142

messages
  audio messages, 206
  Contact app, 201
  deleting, 185
  iMessage service, 204
  managing, 186-189
  notifications, 174
  photos, sending, 207-210
  replying to, 180-181
  sending/receiving, 177-180
  text messages, 203
    emojis in, 205
    group messages, 205
    receiving, 204-205
    sending, 204-205
  video messages, 211-213
Messages app, 203
  audio messages, 206
  photos, 207-210
  text messages
    emojis in, 205
    group messages, 205
    receiving, 204-205
    sending, 204-205
  video messages, 211-213
microphones, 19
Microsoft Office app, 418
models of iPads, 5-6
  buying tips, 10-11
  cellular connectivity, 7
  charging, 12
  initial setup, 12-13
  iPad, 8
  iPad mini 4-7
  iPad Pro, 9-10
  older models, 9
  powering up, 12-13
  Retina display, 7
  turning on/off, 13
  unboxing, 11

modes
  Do Not Disturb, 41
  Picture in Picture, 169
modifying
  brightness, 38
  Contact app, 199-200
  Home screen, 26-27
    finding apps from, 150
    icons, 58
    managing apps on, 59-60
    moving apps on, 57
    opening apps from, 148
    personalizing, 54
    returning to, 25
    wallpaper, 54-56
  networks, 96
  pictures, 285
    Auto-Enhance, 297
    brightness/colors, 298
    cropping/straightening, 296
    filters, 297
    marking up, 300
    viewing, 286, 290
  search engines, 114
  text, 84
  volume, 39
monitoring battery usage, 50-51
mono audio, 86
movies. See videos
Movies tab (Amazon Video), 337
moving. See also rotating iPad
  apps, 57, 158
  iCloud files, 433
  icons, 58
multiple apps
  dragging and dropping between,
    168-169
  opening
    with Slide Over, 164-166
    with Split View, 25, 167-168

multiple pages, viewing, 101-102
multitasking, 164
    dragging and dropping between
        apps, 168-169
    Picture in Picture mode, 169
    Slide Over feature, 164-166
    Split View feature, 25, 167-168
Multi-Touch Displays, 16
multi-touch gestures, 24
Music app. *See* music, listening to
music, listening to, 311
    Apple Music, 312-314
    games, 399
    iTunes Store
        *playing music from, 321-323*
        *purchasing music from, 318-321*
    with Siri, 142-143
    streaming music, 311-312, 439-440
        *Amazon Music Unlimited, 317*
        *Amazon Prime Music, 317*
        *Apple Music, 312-314*
        *paid subscriptions, 312*
        *Pandora, 314-316*
        *Spotify, 317*
        *YouTube, 317*
Music tab (iTunes Store), 318
My Digital Entertainment for Seniors, 323
My Location Changes option
    (Home app), 364

### N

navigating
    Calendar app, 243
        *adding events, 248-249*
        *alerts for events, 253*
        *inviting people, 254*
        *recurring events, 249-250, 253*
        *viewing events, 244*

Camera app
    *panoramic pictures, 283-284*
    *taking selfies, 282-283*
Facebook, 225-226
iPads, 15, 24
    *back of, 19*
    *bottom of, 18*
    *front of, 16*
    *Home screens, 26-27*
    *multi-touch gestures, 24*
    *opening/closing apps, 31-32*
    *powering on and off, 20-23*
    *Search screens, 28*
    *sides of, 17*
    *status bars, 33-34*
    *top of, 17*
LinkedIn, 238
Maps app, 373-376
News app, 271
    *personalizing, 272*
    *reading, 274-275*
Reminders app, 255
    *adding reminders, 257-258*
    *deleting reminders, 259*
    *viewing reminders, 256*
Safari, 97
    *bookmarking, 103-105*
    *configuring, 107-108*
    *entering web addresses, 98-99*
    *privacy, 106*
    *reading articles, 110*
    *revisiting past pages, 105*
    *starting, 98*
    *using web links, 100*
    *viewing multiple pages, 101-102*
    *zooming, 109*
Siri, 136
    *calendar events, 141-142*
    *cameras, 142*
    *configuring, 136*

*controlling apps, 140*
*control system functions, 140*
*Home app, 143*
*Mail app, 140-141*
*Music app, 142-143*
*searching, 144-145*
*starting apps, 140*
*summoning, 139*
Netflix
  launching, 326
  Menu, 327
  playback controls, 329-330
  searching, 328
  selecting programs in, 329
  subscription plans, 326
  viewer profiles, 326
networks
  cellular connectivity, 7
  changing, 96
  home wireless connections, 12, 92-93
  previous network connections, 96
  public wireless hotspots, 94-95
  social networks, 224
    *Facebook, 224-229*
    *LinkedIn, 237-240*
    *Pinterest, 230-232*
    *privacy, 240*
    *Twitter, 234-237*
  troubleshooting, 97
  Wi-Fi connections, 92
New Automation pane (Home app),
  364-366, 369
News app, 271
  personalizing, 272
  reading, 274-275
New Scene pane (Home app), 358-359
News Feeds, 224
Next button
  Apple Music, 314

Music app, 323
Pandora, 315
Night Shift mode, 38
Nook, 271
notifications
  configuring, 66
  Contact app, 198
  email messages, 174
  setting up, 66-67
  viewing on Cover Sheet, 29-30, 67
Numbers app, 407-410
nutrition apps, 385
  cooking/recipes, 387
  dieting, 386

## O

older iPad models, 9
online ads, blocking, 108
online safety, 127
  fraud, 129-131
  identity theft, 127-128
  privacy, 129
  shopping, 132-133
On/Off button, 13
onscreen keyboard
  splitting, 26
  text
    *copying/pasting, 44*
    *entering, 42-43*
onscreen on/off switches, 46
opening
  Amazon Video app, 337
  apps, 31-32
    *from Dock, 149*
    *from Home screen, 148*
    *with Siri, 140*
    *with Slide Over, 164-166*
    *with Split View, 25, 167-168*

Camera app, 278
Hulu app, 331
iCloud files, 431-433
iPads, 20-23, 451
Netflix app, 326
Safari, 98
Siri, 139
video chats, 214-216
YouTube app, 340
operating system. *See* iOS
Optimize iPad Storage option, 430
optimizing gestures, 87
   AssistiveTouch, 89
   touchscreen displays, 87
Originals tab (Amazon Video), 337

# P

packaging, 11
Pages app, 404
Pandora, 314-316
panoramic pictures, 283-284
passcodes
   configuring, 118-119
   remembering, 123
   troubleshooting, 459-460
passwords (iCloud), 459
pasting text, 44
Pause button (Pandora), 315
paying for apps, 160
People album, 294
performance, troubleshooting, 455
personal assistant. *See* Siri
personalizing. *See also* setup
   Control Center, 63, 66-68
   Home screen, 54
      *arranging apps, 57*
      *managing apps, 59-60*

      *moving icons, 58*
      *wallpaper, 54-56*
   inboxes, 177
   news, 272
   Search screens, 61
   wallpaper, 54
Perspective Zoom, 56
phishing, 128
Photos app. *See* photos
photos. *See also* Camera app
   albums, 291-295
   attaching to email, 183-185
   beaming to other devices, 285
   burst shots, 281, 430
   configuring, 285
   dragging between apps, 168-169
   editing, 285
      *Auto-Enhance, 297*
      *brightness/colors, 298*
      *cropping/straightening, 296*
      *filters, 297*
      *marking up, 300*
      *viewing, 286, 290*
   iCloud Photo Library, 291
   iCloud Photo Sharing, 430
   managing, 142, 291-295
   panoramic pictures, 283-284
   selfies, 282-283
   sending, 207-210
   sharing, 306-309
   storage space, 285
   taking, 209, 279-282
   uploading to iCloud account, 285
   viewing, 286, 290
Picture in Picture mode, 169
pinching, 25
Pinterest, 230-232
Places album, 295
Play button (Music app), 323

playing
 games, 393
  *action games, 397*
  *adventure games, 397*
  *arcade games, 398*
  *board games, 398*
  *card games, 398*
  *casino games, 398*
  *music games, 399*
  *puzzle games, 399*
  *racing games, 399*
  *role-playing games, 399*
  *searching, 393-394*
  *simulation games, 400*
  *sports games, 400*
  *strategy games, 400*
  *trivia games, 400*
  *word games, 400*
 music, 311-312
  *AirPlay, 439-440*
  *Amazon Music Unlimited, 317*
  *Amazon Prime Music, 317*
  *Apple Music, 312-314*
  *iTunes Store, 318-323*
  *paid subscriptions, 312*
  *Pandora, 314-316*
  *Spotify, 317*
  *YouTube, 317*
 videos, 325
  *AirPlay, 439-440*
  *Amazon Video, 336-339*
  *Hulu, 330-336*
  *iTunes Store, 342-347*
  *Netflix, 326-330*
  *widescreen video, 336*
  *YouTube, 340-342*
posting
 to Facebook, 227-229
 to LinkedIn, 239-240

power, 20
 managing, 48-51
 power adapters, 11
 powering off iPad, 23
powering up iPad, 12-13
PowerPoint app, 418
predictive keyboards, 43. *See also* keyboards
presentations
 Keynote app, 413-417
 PowerPoint app, 418
 Slides app, 418
pressing, 24
pressing and holding, 37
previews, displaying, 68
previous generation iPad models, 9
previous networks, connecting to, 96
privacy
 maintaining, 129
 private networks, 93
 social networks, 240
 web pages, 106
productivity apps, 403
 Evernote, 417
 Google Docs, 418
 Keynote, 413-417
 Microsoft Office, 418
 Numbers, 407, 410
 Pages, 404
profiles, Netflix, 326
programs. *See* apps
public networks. *See also* networks
public wireless hotspots, connecting, 94-95
Purchase button
 App Store, 159
 iTunes Store, 321
Purchased panel (App Store), 161
purchasing
 apps, 158-160
 music, 318-321
 video, 343-345
puzzle games, 399

# R

racing games, 399

Radio option (Music app), 313

reading

eBooks, 261-271

*buying, 262-263*

*on iBooks, 264*

*on Kindle, 267-271*

*searching, 262-263*

email, 178-180

Facebook, 227-229

News app, 271-275

Safari Reader, 110

Twitter, 235

VoiceOver, 78-80

receiving

email, 177-185

messages

*with Siri, 140-141*

*text messages, 204-205*

recharging batteries, 48

recipe apps, 387

Record button

FaceTime app, 212

Messages app, 206

recording

audio messages, 206

video messages, 211-213

recurring events, formatting, 249-250, 253

region information, entering, 12

Reminders app, 255

adding reminders, 257-258

controlling with Siri, 141-142

deleting reminders, 259

viewing reminders, 256

removing. *See* deleting

renting video from iTunes Store, 343-345

repinning items on Pinterest, 230-232

replying to email, 180-181

resetting iPads, 462-464

resolution, 7

responding

on Facebook, 227-229

to alerts, 35

restarting iPad, 23, 450

restoring

from iCloud, 465

from iTunes, 465

Retina display, 7

returning to Home screen, 25

revisiting past pages, 105

role-playing games, 399

rooms

adding to Home app, 354

assigning accessories to, 355-357

Room screen (Home app), 354-355

rotating iPad, 40, 458

# S

Safari, 97

articles, reading, 110

bookmarking, 103-105

configuring, 107-108

multiple pages, viewing, 101-102

past pages, revisiting, 105

privacy, 106

starting, 98

web addresses, entering, 98-99

web links, 100

zooming, 109

safety (online), 127

fraud, 129-131

identity theft, 127-128

privacy, 129

shopping, 132-133

scams, 131. *See also* fraud

scenes (Home app)
  controlling with Home app, 360
  controlling with Siri, 361
  creating, 357-359
Screen Mirroring, 440
screens
  back of, 19
  bottom of, 18
  colors
    *inverting, 82*
    *modifying text, 84*
  front of, 16
  Home, 26-27
    *finding apps from, 150*
    *icons, 58*
    *managing apps on, 59-60*
    *moving apps on, 57*
    *opening apps from, 148*
    *personalizing, 54*
    *returning to, 25*
    *wallpaper, 54-56*
  Lock, 118
    *erasing data, 122*
    *setting passcodes, 118-119*
    *Touch ID, 120-122*
  magnifying, 81-82
  navigating, 15
  Night Shift mode, 38
  Search, 28, 61
  sides of, 17
  size of, 5
  top of, 17
  VoiceOver, 78-80
screenshots, 283
searching
  App Store, 153-157
  Apple Music, 313
  Amazon Video, 338
  businesses (with Siri), 145

  Contact app, 198
  eBooks, 262-263
  for apps
    *from Home screen, 150*
    *in App Store, 153-157*
  games, 393-394
  Hulu, 334
  iTunes Store, 319
  Music app, 313
  Netflix, 328
  Search panel, 150
  Search screens, 28, 61
  Siri, 144-145
  Web, 112-114
  YouTube, 341
Search panel, 150
Search screens. *See* Today screen
security
  Lock screen, 118
    *erasing data, 122*
    *setting passcodes, 118-119*
    *Touch ID, 120-122*
  online
    *fraud, 129-131*
    *identity theft, 127-128*
    *privacy, 129*
    *shopping, 132-133*
  theft, 123-126
selecting iPad model. *See* choosing iPad
  model
selfies, 282-283
Send button (Messages app), 204
sending
  email, 177-189
  invitations to events, 254
  messages
    *audio messages, 206*
    *with Siri, 140-141*
    *group messages, 205*

*text messages, 204-205*
*video messages, 211-213*
photos, 207-210
Settings. *See also* setup
    Control Center, 63, 66-68
    General
        *iPad Storage, 422-423*
        *Software Update, 10*
    iCloud, 363, 427-431
    viewing, 65
setup
    alarms, 45
    Camera app, 281-282
    Control Center, 63, 66-68
    Find My iPad, 431
    Home Hub, 362-363
    iCloud, 427-431
    iPads, 64
        *apps, 72*
        *brightness, 69-70*
        *initial setup, 12-13*
        *notifications, 66*
        *system sounds, 71*
        *viewing Settings pages, 65*
    Lock screen, 118
        *erasing data, 122*
        *setting passcodes, 118-119*
        *Touch ID, 120-122*
    Mail app, 171
        *accounts, 172-174*
        *signatures, 176-177*
        *message notifications, 174*
        *sending/receiving mail, 177-189*
    Night Shift mode, 38
    passcodes, 118-119
    Photos app, 285
    Safari, 107-108
    Search screens, 61
    Siri, 136

stopwatches, 47-48
timers, 46
tracking, 124-126
Share button, 309
sharing files
    AirDrop, 438-439
    AirPlay, 439-440
    pictures, 306-309
Sheets app, 418
shopping online, 132-133
Show as Banners switch, 68
Show in Favorites switch, 359
Show in History switch, 67
Show on Lock Screen switch, 67
Show Previews option, 68
Shuffle button (Music app), 323
shutting down iPad, 452
side apps, 164
side of iPad, 17
signatures, 176-177
simulation games, 400
Siri, 136
    configuring, 136
    controlling apps with, 140
        *calendar events, 141-142, 258*
        *cameras, 142*
        *control system functions, 140*
        *Home, 143*
        *Mail, 140-141*
        *Music, 142-143*
        *starting, 140*
    controlling smart homes with, 361
    searching, 144-145
    summoning, 139
size
    of iPad, 4
    of screen, 5
Skip Ad option (YouTube), 342
Skype app, 220

Slide Over feature, 164-166
Slides app, 418
slow motion videos, 304
slow performance, troubleshooting, 455
Smart Connector, 17
smart covers, 24, 444
smart devices
    adding to Home app, 351-353
    automating, 361
        *controlled automation, 368-370*
        *Home Hub setup, 362-363*
        *location automation, 364-366*
        *time automation, 366-368*
    controlling with Home app, 360
    controlling with Siri, 361
smart homes
    Apple HomeKit, 350
    automating, 361
        *controlled automation, 368-370*
        *Home Hub setup, 362-363*
        *location automation, 364-366*
        *time automation, 366-368*
    rooms
        *adding to Home app, 354*
        *assigning accessories to, 355-357*
    scenes
        *controlling with Home app, 360*
        *controlling with Siri, 361*
        *creating, 357-359*
    smart devices
        *adding to Home app, 351-353*
        *controlling with Home app, 360*
        *controlling with Siri, 361*
Smart Keyboard, 9, 444
smartphones, 5
smiley faces, adding to text messages, 205
social networks
    Facebook, 224
        *navigating, 225-226*
        *posting, 227-229*

    LinkedIn, 237-240
    Pinterest, 230-232
    privacy, 240
    Twitter, 234-237
software. *See* apps
Software Update, 10
solving equations with Siri, 145
songs. *See* music
sound. *See* audio
spam, 188-189
spreadsheets (Numbers app), 407, 410
speakers, 18, 447
splitting
    onscreen keyboard, 26
    Split View, 25, 167-168
Split View feature, 25, 167-168
sports games, 400
Spotify, 317
spreadsheets, 418
stands, desktop, 444
starting. *See* opening
status bars, 33-34
status updates. *See* posting
stopwatch, 47-48
storage
    available storage
        *checking, 422*
        *managing, 423-425*
    iCloud, 426-427
        *accessing from computer, 434*
        *backing up to, 431, 440-441*
        *copying files on, 433*
        *costs, 427*
        *creating folders on, 434*
        *deleting files on, 433*
        *moving files on, 433*
        *opening files from, 431-433*
        *passwords, 459*
        *Photo Library, 291*

*restoring from, 465*
*setting up, 363, 427-431*
*upload photos to, 285*
*viewing files on, 431-433*
local storage, 426
other Cloud storage services, 435-437
syncing files between iPad and
  computer, 437
straightening pictures, 296
strategy games, 400
streaming music, 311-312
  AirPlay, 439-440
  Amazon Music Unlimited, 317
  Amazon Prime Music, 317
  Apple Music, 312-314
  paid subscriptions, 312
  Pandora, 314-316
  Spotify, 317
  YouTube, 317
streaming video
  AirPlay, 439-440
  Amazon Video
    *browsing selections in, 337*
    *launching, 337*
    *playback controls, 339*
    *selecting programs in, 338*
    *subscription plans, 336-337*
  definition of, 326
  Hulu
    *browsing selections in, 331-333*
    *launching, 331*
    *playback controls, 336*
    *searching, 334*
    *selecting programs in, 334*
    *subscription plans, 330*
  iTunes Store, 342
    *playback controls, 347*
    *renting/purchasing video from, 343-345*
    *watching video from, 346-347*

Netflix
  *launching, 326*
  *Menu, 327*
  *playback controls, 329-330*
  *searching, 328*
  *selecting programs in, 329*
  *subscription plans, 326*
  *viewer profiles, 326*
  widescreen video, 336
  YouTube, 340
    *ads, 342*
    *launching, 340*
    *playback controls, 342*
    *searching, 341*
styli, 9, 444-445
subscription plans
  Amazon Video, 336-337
  Hulu, 330
  Netflix, 326
  YouTube, 341
summoning Siri, 139
support (Apple), 460
swiping, 25
switching between apps, 26, 151
syncing files between iPad and
  computer, 437
system settings, 73-74. *See also* setup
system sounds, 71. *See also* audio

# T

tablet computers, 4-5
taking
  photos, 209, 279-284
  videos, 302-303
tapping, 24
Test This Scene option (Home app), 359

text
  copying/pasting, 44
  dragging between apps, 168-169
  entering, 42-43
  modifying, 84
text messages, 203. *See also* messages
  audio messages, 206
  emojis in, 205
  group messages, 205
  photos, 207-210
  receiving, 204-205
  sending, 204-205
  video messages, 211-213
theft
  identity theft, 127-128
  reducing risk of, 123-126
Thumbs Up/Down icons (Pandora), 315
time automation, 366-368
time-lapse videos, 304
Time of Day controls (Home app), 367
A Time of Day Occurs option
  (Home app), 366
timers, 46
Today screen, 28, 61
Today tab (App Store), 153
Top Categories tab (App Store), 156
top of iPad, 17
touch
  multi-touch gestures, 24
  Touch ID, 12, 120-122
  touchscreen displays, 87
Touch ID, 12, 120-122
touchscreen displays, 87
tracking, enabling, 124-126
traveling apps, 373-378, 381
Trending tab (YouTube), 341
trimming videos, 305-306
trivia games, 400

troubleshooting, 449-450
  Apple support, 460
  apps, 453
  battery charges, 457
  connections, 97
  forgotten passcodes, 459-460
  frozen screen, 450
  iCloud passwords, 459
  restarting, 450
  rotating, 458
  slow performance, 455
  Wi-Fi, 456
  won't turn off, 452
  won't turn on, 451
turning on/off
  controls, 36
  iPad, 13, 20-23, 451
  Safari, 98
TV shows. *See* videos
TV tab (Amazon Video), 337
Twitter, 234-237

## U

unboxing iPad, 11
unlocking iPads, 21, 118-119
Updates tab (App Store), 162
updating, 73
  apps, 162
  iPads, 461
upgrading to iOS 11, 10
USB
  charging, 49
  connectors, 11

# V

versions, updating, 461
video chats, 214
   answering, 217-218
   starting, 214-216
   with Skype, 220
video messages, sending, 211-213
videos
   closed captioning, 86-87
   editing, 302, 305-306
   sharing, 306-309
   Slo-Mo, 304
   taking, 302-303
   watching, 325
      *AirPlay, 439-440*
      *Amazon Video, 336-339*
      *Hulu, 330-336*
      *iTunes Store, 342-347*
      *Netflix, 326-330*
      *widescreen video, 336*
      *YouTube, 340-342*
viewing
   alerts, 35
   apps, 31-32, 160-161
   Contact app, 198
   Control Center/App Switcher, 25, 36
   Cover Sheet, 25
   Dock, 25
   events, 244
   iCloud files, 431-433
   maps, 374-376
   multiple pages, 101-102
   notifications, 29-30, 67
   pictures, 286, 290
   Pinterest, 230-232
   previews, 68
   reminders, 256
   Search screens, 28
   Settings pages, 65

Today screen, 28
videos, 325
   *AirPlay, 439-440*
   *Amazon Video, 336-339*
   *Hulu, 330-336*
   *iTunes Store, 342-347*
   *Netflix, 326-330*
   *widescreen video, 336*
   *YouTube, 340-342*
views, Split View, 25, 167-168
virtual personal assistants. *See* Siri
visual accessibility, 78
   screens
      *inverting colors, 82*
      *magnifying, 81-82*
      *modifying text, 84*
   VoiceOver, 78-80
voice commands. *See also* Siri
VoiceOver, 78-80
volume, 18, 39

# W

walking maps, 376
wallpaper, 54-56
watching videos, 325
   Amazon Video
      *browsing selections in, 337*
      *launching, 337*
      *playback controls, 339*
      *selecting programs in, 338*
      *subscription plans, 336-337*
   Hulu
      *browsing selections in, 331-333*
      *launching, 331*
      *playback controls, 336*
      *searching, 334*
      *selecting programs in, 334*
      *subscription plans, 330*

iTunes Store, 342
   *playback controls, 347*
   *renting/purchasing video from, 343-345*
   *watching video from, 346-347*
   Netflix
   *launching, 326*
   *Menu, 327*
   *playback controls, 329-330*
   *searching, 328*
   *selecting programs in, 329*
   *subscription plans, 326*
   *viewer profiles, 326*
   widescreen video, 336
   YouTube, 340
   *ads, 342*
   *launching, 340*
   *playback controls, 342*
   *searching, 341*
Watch Movie button (Hulu), 335
web browser, 97
   articles, reading, 110
   bookmarking, 103-105
   configuring, 107-108
   multiple pages, viewing, 101-102
   past pages, revisiting, 105
   privacy, 106
   starting, 98
   web addresses, entering, 98-99
   web links, 100
   zooming, 109
web pages
   Google, 112
   search engines, 114
   searching, 112
   selecting words in, 26
   zooming in/out, 26, 109
weight of iPad, 4
Welcome screen (Home app), 352
Where Do You Want to Go? panel, 377

widescreen videos, 303, 336
Wi-Fi
   Bluetooth, 446
   cellular connectivity, 7
   connecting, 92
   hotspots, 12
   in hotels, 94
   troubleshooting, 97, 456
wireless earphones, 446
wireless headphones, 446
wireless keyboards, 445
wireless speakers, 447
Word app, 418
word games, 400
word processing
   Docs app, 418
   Pages app, 404
   Word app, 418
words, selecting, 26
writing
   email messages, 180-181
   tweets (Twitter), 237

# Y-Z

yoga apps, 384
YouTube, 317, 340
   ads, 342
   launching, 340
   playback controls, 342
   searching, 341

zooming in/out, 26
   Perspective Zoom, 56
   Safari, 109
   screens, 81-82

# Register Your Product at informit.com/register

Access additional benefits and **save 35%** on your next purchase

- Automatically receive a coupon for 35% off your next purchase, valid for 30 days. Look for your code in your InformIT cart or the Manage Codes section of your account page.

- Download available product updates.

- Access bonus material if available.*

- Check the box to hear from us and receive exclusive offers on new editions and related products.

*Registration benefits vary by product. Benefits will be listed on your account page under Registered Products.*

## InformIT.com—The Trusted Technology Learning Source

InformIT is the online home of information technology brands at Pearson, the world's foremost education company. At InformIT.com, you can:

- Shop our books, eBooks, software, and video training
- Take advantage of our special offers and promotions (informit.com/promotions)
- Sign up for special offers and content newsletter (informit.com/newsletters)
- Access thousands of free chapters and video lessons

## Connect with InformIT—Visit informit.com/community

**inform**IT®
the trusted technology learning source

Addison-Wesley · Adobe Press · Cisco Press · Microsoft Press · Pearson IT Certification · Prentice Hall · Que · Sams · Peachpit Press

 Pearson